Balancing Communities

Balancing Communities

Nation, State, and Protestant Christianity in Korea, 1884–1942

Paul S. Cha

University of Hawai‘i Press
Honolulu

Paperback edition 2022

Printed in the United States of America

Library of Congress Cataloging-in-Publication Data

Names: Cha, Paul S., author.
Title: Balancing communities : nation, state, and Protestant Christianity in Korea, 1884–1942 / Paul S. Cha.
Description: Honolulu : University of Hawaiʻi Press, 2022. | Includes bibliographical references and index.
Identifiers: LCCN 2021015295 | ISBN 9780824888565 (hardback) | ISBN 9780824891152 (adobe pdf) | ISBN 9780824891169 (epub) | ISBN 9780824891176 (kindle edition)
Subjects: LCSH: Protestantism—Korea—History. | Church and state—Korea. | Missionaries—Korea—History. | Korea—Church history.
Classification: LCC BR1325 C44 2022 | DDC 280/.40951909041—dc23
LC record available at https://lccn.loc.gov/2021015295

ISBN: 9780824891084 (paperback)

University of Hawaiʻi Press books are printed on acid-free paper and meet the guidelines for permanence and durability of the Council on Library Resources.

Cover photo: Samuel A. Moffett in women's wing of Central Presbyterian Church, P'yŏngyang (circa 1909). Picture used with permission from UCLA Online Archive Korean Christianity.

In loving memory of my mother, Eun Soon Cha,
and sister, Debbie Cha

Contents

Preface and Acknowledgments

The publication of this work is the product of intellectual stimulation and emotional support provided by multiple communities in my career as a scholar. I will forever be grateful to the many teachers who have guided me. John B. Duncan, my mentor, has been a model of the type of scholar I aspire to be: rigorous in approach but full of humanity and wisdom. His passion for Korea and his moral compass have been inspiring. Namhee Lee's firm sense of social awareness has shaped my understanding of and approaches to modern Korean history. Sung Deuk Oak's vast knowledge of Korean Christianity, his careful documentation, and his passionate commitment to developing a still nascent field have served as constant reminders of the vast work that still needs to be done to fill out our understanding of the roles this religion has played in shaping social, political, and cultural practices on the Korean Peninsula.

I will always remember my time at UCLA fondly because of the many bright and supportive *sŏnbae* (senior) and *hubae* (junior) colleagues I had the good fortune to meet and interact with. Mary Kim warmly opened her home to me when I first arrived on campus. Hyung-wook Kim was always ready to share coffee and the occasional cheese Danish (a taste for which I acquired as a result). Elli Kim constantly pushed me to see the bigger picture in my work, and Hanmee Kim had a knack for asking insightful and critical questions, but in the sweetest and kindest possible manner. Jennifer Jung-Kim provided sage advice and a friendly ear. Youngju Ryu, Paul Nam, Yingzi Xu, Hijoo Son, Aimee Kwon, Seung-ah Lee, Howard Kahm, Sinwoo Lee, Jeong-il Lee, Dennis Lee, Janet Lee, and Youme Kim all have a voice in this work; my many discussions with them shaped my understanding of Korea and life in general.

My fieldwork in Seoul was facilitated by Professor Kim Do-hyung, whom I first met when he spent a year at UCLA as a visiting scholar. He prepared a space for me at Yonsei University, connected me to the history graduate students at the university, and pointed me to the appropriate archives. I am grateful for his willingness to share his knowledge of Korean history with me and his concern for my well-being while I was in Seoul. Special thanks also go to Kim Yunjung and Oh Sangmee, then MA students in the history program, who helped me navigate the archives and adjust to life in South Korea. Finally, Paul Chang was an early believer in my project and provided guidance during the beginning stages of my academic career.

This project took new directions after I left UCLA. I am thankful to my former colleagues at Samford University for their support of my research. Jason Wallace opened my eyes to the importance of considering more fully American religiosity and European thought. John Mayfield, James Brown, Erin Maudlin, Fred Shepherd, LeeAnn Reynolds, and Jonathan Bass all created an open and collegial environment. Marissa Grayson provided friendship and witty conversation that have been missed since I left Samford.

Since 2015, I have called Hong Kong my home. My research and teaching at the University of Hong Kong have been intellectually stimulating. The constant enthusiasm and work ethic of Su Yun Kim, Kangsoon Lee, Loretta Kim, Janet Borland, and Nick Williams have prodded me to press ahead even on days when I wearied. Tug Goddard, a fellow UCLA and Cleveland transplant, provided a welcome face when I first arrived. John Carroll served as a senior mentor and graciously read so many versions of my introduction that I would not be surprised if he could give a presentation on my work better than I could. Special thanks also go to Kendall Johnson and Charles Schencking for offering wisdom on navigating academic life in Hong Kong.

This book benefited greatly from a book manuscript workshop held by the Ricci Institute, with funding provided by the Henry Luce Foundation. I thank Antoni Ucerler and Xiaoxin Wu for inviting me to participate. I am also grateful to James Lewis, who graciously provided in-depth comments on my work and gave sound life advice during the workshop.

Donald Baker, Frank Rausch, Timothy Lee, Jun Yoo, and Albert Park have all kindly read parts of this book at various stages of its preparation. Their words of encouragement and critical insights greatly improved this work—though of course any flaws are my own. Susan Whitlock provided a needed sounding board in the final months of preparation of the manuscript. I am also thankful for the critical feedback provided by the anonymous readers commissioned by the University of Hawai‘i Press.

I reserve special thanks for three individuals who stepped in at the final moments to ensure that this work would be published. Todd Henry and Sonja Kim both carved out space in their busy schedules to give close readings and comments that shaped the final framing of this work. Words cannot express how grateful I am for their willingness to help and their words of encouragement. In addition, Masako Ikeda of the University of Hawai'i Press stuck with me and this project even when at times I lost faith in it. I am grateful to have had this opportunity to work with her. She is truly a professional and has offered well-reasoned and actionable advice throughout this process.

Early funding was provided by a Fulbright-Hays Fellowship, a Korea Foundation Grant, and an Academy of Korean Studies Junior Scholar Fellowship. Later generous support was provided by the University Grants Committee of Hong Kong (General Research Fund grant #17675916). Chapter 2 is a revised version of my article "Establishing the Rules of Engagement: American Protestant Missionaries, the U.S. Legation, and the Chosŏn State," *International Journal of Korean History* 17, no. 1 (Spring 2012): 67–107; chapter 3 is a revised version of my article "Unequal Partners, Contested Relations: Protestant Missionaries and Korean Christians, 1884–1907," *Journal of Korean Studies* 17, no. 1 (Spring 2012): 5–37. This article was included in *Critical Readings on Christianity in Korea* (Leiden: Brill, 2014). I thank the publishers of both journals and Brill Press for their permission to include materials from these works in this book.

Finally, and most importantly, I thank my family. My parents and sisters had a strange confidence that this work would see a broader audience than the small circle to which it has been limited to this point. My in-laws always welcomed my many trips to South Korea, as I scoured libraries and collections for additional information. My two little girls—Jianne and Yena—patiently endured my long hours spent in front of a computer instead of playing another game of Life or Monopoly. As I've worked on this manuscript, I've also been charting the growth of my children with pencil markings on the wall. Looking back on these markings, I realize just how much time has passed. My wife, Sejin, has been my partner through multiple transpacific migrations, my sudden trips to the archives, and my obsessive urge to revise. She's done this all while managing her own career. I thank her for her support and acknowledge that this work would have been impossible without her. Thank you.

Abbreviations

ARBFMMEC	*Annual Report of the Board of Foreign Missions of the Methodist Episcopal Church*
BFMPCUSA	Board of Foreign Missions of the Presbyterian Church in the USA
BLA	Burke Library Archive
CR	*Chinese Recorder*
GGK	Government-General of Korea
HGU	*Ŏndŏudŭ charyojip*
HKY	*Han'guk kidokkyo ŭi yŏksa*
KHOM	*Ku Han'guk oegyo munsŏ*
KLC	Korea—Letters and Correspondences
KSTN	*Kaksa tŭngnok*
KMF	*Korea Mission Field*
PHS	Presbyterian Historical Society
RGK	Residency-General of Korea
RG	Record Group
WCC	World Council of Churches Archive

Introduction

Protestant Partners?

In December 1925, John Mott—a famed evangelist, the general secretary of the International YMCA, and a founding member of both the World Student Christian Federation and the International Missionary Council (IMC)—arrived in Korea. He had journeyed to the peninsula in his capacity as a leader of the IMC and as part of a tour of mission fields around the globe. One of his objectives was to gauge the extent to which native churches were self-governing. Missionaries in Korea, such as Charles Allen Clark, welcomed Mott's visit.[1] The first resident Protestant missionary had arrived on the peninsula only four decades previously, but by the mid-1920s, the Western Christian community already acknowledged the country as a stronghold of Protestantism in Asia. Clark and his colleagues felt confident, if not proud, of their work, believing that a major reason for the success of Protestantism was their "wise" policy of having Koreans take full control of all aspects of this religion in the country from nearly the beginning of the Protestant mission.[2] As a symbol of the supposedly equal partnership between Western and Korean Protestant churches, thirty-one missionaries and thirty-one Koreans gathered to meet Mott and discuss the past, present, and future of Protestantism. Yet conflict simmered beneath the surface, and the equal number of delegates belied the power missionaries wielded to define the boundaries of the proper practice and administration of Protestantism in Korea. Tensions boiled over when Reverend Han Sŏk-chin took the floor to speak.

Han was an elder statesman of the Korean Protestant community, having graduated as a member of the inaugural class of Korea's first Presbyterian seminary, in P'yŏngyang, in 1907, three years before Japan colonized Korea. He shocked those assembled when he launched into a criticism of the missionaries. Han asserted that the proper course of missions was for missionaries to establish churches, hand control over to native leaders, and then leave the country in short order. But in Korea, despite the presence of strong and well-established congregations, the missionaries refused to leave and continued to occupy positions of power. When Samuel A. Moffett, who had been a missionary in Korea for over three decades, rose to respond, Han looked at him and declared that if he did not quickly depart, he would only harm the Korean church.[3]

This confrontation was not the first and certainly would not be the last expression of displeasure, if not anger, over the missionaries' refusal to leave and their influence in the country during the first half of the twentieth century. Indeed, Moffett would remain in Korea working with Korean Protestant leaders until 1936. He finally returned to the United States because of his failing health and a growing controversy surrounding the colonial government's demand that students at the missionaries' private schools demonstrate their loyalty to the Japanese emperor by bowing at Shinto shrines. The colonial government continued to pressure Korean Protestant communities to free themselves from missionary control, and in 1942 the handful of missionaries from Allied nations who still remained in Korea after the bombing of Pearl Harbor were forcibly repatriated.

Han's outburst, Moffett's continued presence, and the eventual intervention of the state disrupt a standard interpretation of the history of Christianity in Korea. Scholars of Korean Christianity, Christian missions, and world Christianity have long cited South Korea as one of the success stories of the spread of this religion outside the Western Hemisphere.[4] South Korea is home to vibrant and visible Christian churches. Currently, nearly 30 percent of the South Korean population identifies as Christian, and some of the largest congregations in the world are located on the peninsula. In addition, the influence of Korean churches extends beyond the borders of the country: South Korea is among the world's leaders in the number of missionaries dispatched abroad annually.[5] Buoyed by such numbers, scholars have felt confident in tying the tremendous vitality of this religion in South Korea to the agency of Korean actors, who adapted it either to align with Korean cultural or social practices or to serve as a vehicle of political protest in the construction of a modern nation-state.[6] Stated differently, scholars have been quick to demonstrate how this religion became "indigenized" or "inculturated" in Korea, becoming a part of the Korean nation.

While narratives of native agency centered on the Korean nation are not without merit, they have simplified or underconceptualized both the presence of Western missionaries and the process by which Koreans joined Christian communities.[7] Christianity may have become a part of the Korean nation, but Koreans also became Christian—or, rather, members of a Christian community, which at least in theory transcends national boundaries. Unfortunately, both scholarly and popular interpretations of the history of Christianity, particularly Protestantism, in Korea have largely focused on the former process at the expense of the latter.[8] Indeed, in its more extreme forms, the narrative of native agency has marginalized or even written out "foreign" missionaries in the history of Korean Christianity. For instance, one interpretation that has been gaining currency in explaining why this religion succeeded in Korea holds that the first missionaries to the country were Korean.[9] Whether in regard to Catholicism or Protestantism, this story emphasizes that Koreans proactively traveled abroad, willingly accepted Christianity, returned to Korea, and creatively reinterpreted this religion as they evangelized and established clusters of believers—all before the arrival of a single Western missionary.

In part, the fixation on the nationality of the first missionaries to Korea stems from concern about the problematic relationship between the spread of this religion and Western colonialism. A common assessment of missionaries is that to the early twentieth century they traveled around the globe on the coattails of imperialism and played essential roles in destabilizing the social and political order of the countries in which they worked.[10] With Bibles in hand, they viewed indigenous practices with disdain and wreaked havoc on local sociopolitical and cultural systems. In these ways, they acted as the "cultural prong" of Western imperialism—undermining and subverting indigenous regimes and governments. At worst, missionaries were openly bigoted, racist, and too assured of the superiority of their ways. At best, they were ignorant of their complicity in the oppressive colonial machinery.[11] Even those who wish to paint them in a sympathetic light usually recognize that missionaries had questionable ties to imperial powers as they imposed their visions of this religion, which were entangled with Western cultural forms, on native populations.[12]

The issue of demonstrating the agency of Korean Christians holds special significance in South Korea because of Korea's colonial past. In particular, after Korea was liberated from colonial rule in 1945, many Korean historians attempted to prove the fallacy of a generation of Japanese scholarship that had justified the colonization of the peninsula.[13] Taken together, these works argued that Korea had historically been dependent on outside forces for innovation and lacked the ability to develop on its own. The insinuation was that Japan was not merely justified in colonizing the peninsula but had a moral imperative to do so in order to bring about modernity. After 1945, nationalism and the search for those who had collaborated with the Japanese colonial enterprise dominated popular and scholarly sentiment.[14] A common theme was demonstrating the inherent ability of Koreans to develop both independently and creatively.[15]

Though the colonial power was Japan, missionaries were vulnerable to being labeled imperialists. They took advantage of extraterritoriality, established close relations with foreign officials, and wielded influence over the growth and development of Christianity in Korea. Moreover, some scholars of Korean Christianity argued that missionaries in fact endorsed Japanese rule because it provided favorable conditions for the spread of their religion.[16] In this picture, one might conclude that Korean Christians had collaborated with a foreign power, albeit a power that was not Japan and at times opposed colonialism.[17] The argument that the first missionaries were Korean appears both to explain why Christianity found such a ready audience in Korea and to circumvent the issue of the problematic ties between Christianity and Western imperialism.

Whether they are castigated for being imperialists,[18] portrayed as benevolent figures, or simply overlooked, missionaries are pressure points in the narration of Christianity's early development in Korea.[19] A major reason is that they threaten to undermine narratives of native agency in the construction of a "Korean" form of this religion. However, the history of Christianity in Korea entailed not only Christianity's becoming a part of the Korean nation (which, importantly, was in flux and formation during the period this book examines) but also Koreans' incorporation into Christian communities. Especially during the late nineteenth and early twentieth centuries, the act of balancing overlapping and at times competing communal demands—whether religious, national, or political—played a formative role in shaping Protestantism in Korea, functioning simultaneously as a source of agitation and as a mechanism for maintaining the status quo.

To return to the Han-Moffett "conflict," this episode curiously produced neither lasting dissension nor lasting change. Indeed, reporting on the conference, not only did the *Korea Mission Field* neglect to mention Han's outburst, but it also emphasized that overall a glowing spirit of unity and cooperation undergirded the meeting. The paper claimed that at no time did the delegates devolve into petty fighting. It did admit that the relationship between missionaries and Korean Christian leaders could be improved, but it blamed any problems on the more recent generations of missionaries to the country. Whereas the first generation had purportedly cultivated "intimate personal contacts" with Korean Christians based on "strong personal affection and mutual dependence," the newly arrived missionaries had a poor understanding of Korea and its people.[20] Yet Han directed his comments at Moffett, who had arrived in the country in 1890 and was one of the longest-serving members of the Presbyterian mission in Korea at the time. In fact, Moffett had had a hand in Han's own conversion, and Han had worked closely with him, serving first as his "helper." Han's criticism of Moffett was jarring because of their "intimate personal" contact.

Moffett continued to work in Korea for a decade after Han demanded he leave—and Korean Christian leaders like Han continued to work with missionaries. How are we to understand the continued tension that marked these relationships, especially paired with the persistent insistence by both Koreans and missionaries that they worked in cooperation? To begin unraveling this enigma, it is important to realize that conversion to Christianity meant more than an acceptance of a new belief system. Conversion granted Koreans membership in a community of believers that, at least in theory, transcended national or political boundaries. In calling on Moffett to leave, Han expressed anger over Moffett's continued presence and influence in Korea on the pretext of working in partnership to advance the kingdom of heaven. Yet even though he was upset over the inequality in the relationships between missionaries and Korean Christian leaders, Han continued to work with Moffett and others; he did not turn his back on the ideal of a shared community of belief.

Commencing with the formal start of the Korean Protestant missionary movement in 1884 and ending with the Japanese colonial government's expulsion of missionaries from Korea in 1942, this book critically reassesses the history of Christianity, and in particular Protestantism, in Korea. The construction of Protestantism during its formative decades in the country required the creation and balancing of multiple communal identities, which included those bound by imagined concepts of the Korean nation and of Christian universalism. Finding a harmonious balance proved difficult, as instabilities between these overlapping communal associations often led to conflicts. Yet at the same time, these instabilities were critical in providing a reason for missionaries not only to remain in Korea but also to wield positions of influence in relations with their Korean "partners" long after the formation of vibrant congregations of Korean Christians.

World Missions, the Protestant Ecumenical Movement, and "Imagined Communities"

In his classic formulation of nationalism, Benedict Anderson defined nations as "imagined" in three respects: they are imagined as "limited," in that they possess territorial boundaries; as "sovereign," in that they are separate from religions; and as "communities," in that membership is theoretically conceived as horizontal and equal in nature.[21] On the surface, Anderson's theory of "imagined communities," defined along territorial boundaries and contrasted with religion, is a poor fit for describing Protestant communities. Yet Protestant communities are equally imagined, and many Protestant leaders have believed that Christianity and nationalism go hand in hand. For instance, Robert Speer, a secretary with the Board of Foreign Missions of the Presbyterian Church in the USA, commented in 1910 that nationalism was the "greatest fact in modern politics" and that the rise of distinct national boundaries and customs was in line with the "ideals of humanity." This was because nationalism ensured the cultivation of unique social systems and cultures. In this manner, it promoted diversity and freedom as opposed to uniformity and subjugation. Speer insisted that the goal of missions was not to "denationalize" converts or to "Westernize their minds or hearts." Instead, the goal was to unify the world "in the corporate association of the Church, one over all the earth, and yet adapted to the genius and needs of each people."[22]

In pointing to the affinity between Protestant Christianity and nationalism, Speer was not making the simplistic argument that Protestants were or could be nationalists, though many Christian leaders of the day certainly made this point.[23] Instead, his observations on the relationship between nationalism and Christianity spoke to a growing movement among Protestant missionaries and church leaders to work in a spirit of ecumenical cooperation. Speer described a vision of churches and denominations that would be defined along national lines or gathered within specific territorial boundaries; that would maintain ecclesiastical autonomy, that is, "sovereignty" over church affairs; yet that would all work together in a "cooperate association" based on a spirit of communal equality. In this sense, the Protestant ecumenical movement mirrored nationalism and the nation-state system.[24]

Importantly, the Korean Protestant mission field was the latest in East Asia to be established, with the first resident missionary having arrived in 1884, and it developed during a period when the ideal of Protestant ecumenism was rapidly ascending and capturing the attention of church leaders around the globe.[25] For instance, in 1886, the Student Volunteer Movement (SVM) began in the United States and soon spread to Europe, laying the "skeleton of a global Protestant network" that would propel forward a worldwide movement for Protestant ecumenical cooperation.[26] As the rise and spread of the SVM indicates, missions and missionaries led the drive for ecumenism; their experiences abroad broadened their appreciation for non-Western cultures and brought into relief the ways Christianity, as it was currently practiced, had been shaped by the social, cultural, and political contexts of Euro-America.[27] The call for cooperation and unity led to the famed Edinburgh World Missionary Conference (1910),[28] the formation of the IMC (1921), and the eventual establishment of the World Council of Churches (1948).

Within the Korea mission field, many of the mission societies worked in partnership in a spirit of ecumenical cooperation. Scholars of Korean Christianity often cite the various comity agreements between the mainline denominations, for example, as a defining feature of the Protestant missionary movement in the country.[29] The first agreement was established in 1892 between the Northern Presbyterians and Northern Methodists, the first two Protestant organizations to establish stations in Korea.[30] Subsequently, other denominations established agreements as they entered the field. Driving the creation of these agreements was a belief that all Protestants belonged to a common church. Missionaries argued that competing for the same souls was a waste of resources. To avoid unnecessary inter- and intradenominational competition, the various Presbyterian and Methodist boards from the United States, Canada, and Australia agreed to divide the peninsula into regions of exclusive evangelization.

Territorial comity among the Presbyterian and Methodist societies proved surprisingly stable, lasting throughout the colonial period. However, while missionaries may have viewed territorial comity as a step toward unity, it also represented division. By dividing the peninsula and maintaining their denominationalism under the banner of cooperation, missionaries acknowledged both a common membership in a heavenly kingdom and divisions based on theological, ecclesiastical, and national differences. Comity agreements established by missionaries and the language of communal partnership masked numerous competing beliefs and allegiances among the various societies working in Korea. This situation was not an aberration. The ecumenical movement around the world was full of division and hierarchies. Holding together the various clusters of Protestants seeking to establish union was the notion of working in partnership to advance a universal heavenly kingdom. Put differently, to return to the concept of "imagined communities," one of Anderson's most important observations—at least from a moral perspective—was that "regardless of the actual inequality and exploitation that may prevail in each, the nation is always conceived as a deep, horizontal comradeship."[31] The language of community and the notion that all members are equal conceal, if not perpetuate, societal inequities within nations. A similar dynamic exists in Christian communities.

The longevity of the missionaries' presence and their continued interactions with Korean Christians rested on the language of common membership in a universal kingdom of heaven. But this language of cooperation was far from benign, as it masked a myriad of inequalities between Korean and Western churches. The "horizontal imagining" of Protestant communities provided a rationale for the continued presence of missionaries in Korea, even while these missionaries publicly affirmed the autonomy and "uniqueness" of Korean Protestant congregations.[32] Stated differently, the language of ecumenism had its own coercive force. If a "true" Christian believed in a universal church and the communion of all Christians—regardless of nationality and political boundaries—then should not Korean

Christians welcome the work of Western missionaries?[33] At least in the eyes of the missionaries, the rejection of their "assistance" simply because they were foreigners could be construed as an act that was "unchristian" and even "racist."[34]

Membership in church communities not only facilitated but also demanded a constant reestablishment and reformulation of ties after disruptions. From the administration of Chejungwŏn (chapter 1)—Korea's first modern, Western-style hospital, which was established in 1885 and jointly run by the Presbyterians and the Korean government—to the colonial government's efforts to regulate missionary-run private schools (chapters 5 and 7), missionaries engaged in numerous heated debates on issues concerning the running of their respective mission societies. Yet curiously, in their letters and reports, they stressed that their personal relationships were cordial. Missionaries were expected to reconcile, forgive, and carry on with the responsibility of spreading the kingdom of heaven. A similar demand was placed on Koreans. To return to Han's outburst, while he may have remained angered by the long presence of Moffett and the other missionaries, under the terms they had established, Han needed to act in a Christian spirit of "forgiveness" and common partnership as a display of his spirituality—upon which, not incidentally, his influence in the Korean Christian community depended. In sum, the necessity of using the language of cooperation led inexorably back to the status quo of hierarchical interactions with missionaries.

Demonstrations of Membership: The Ambiguity of Belonging to Christian and Political Communities

Protestant missionaries announced repeatedly that they worked in partnership with Korean Christians and desired to hand control of all relevant institutions over to native leaders. Nevertheless, as indicated by Han's outburst against Moffett, the missionaries were slow to leave. Their continued presence raises the question of why leaders like Han did not more vehemently demand control of the church. In approaching this issue, it is important to recognize that some Korean Christian leaders did in fact attempt to break free of foreign control. However, they confronted a set of constraints rooted in the way Christianity had developed in Korea, as missionaries strove to ensure the formation of "true" communities of Christian faith.

As I discuss in chapter 3, the first generation of Protestant missionaries to Korea was concerned not only with the number of converts but also with the converts' sincerity of belief. On the one hand, they consistently reported that Koreans eagerly adopted Christianity; on the other hand, they harbored seeds of doubt about whether the motives of those seeking entry into the church were spiritual or material. Their concern stemmed from the experience of those in other mission fields: converts would display a passion for the faith, rise up in the church hierarchy, but then be discovered to have converted for "nonspiritual" gain. The corruption and scandals that ensued often damaged the reputation of Christianity in these countries. With this scenario in mind, missionaries to Korea were anxious to confirm that Koreans were "true believers." But how could missionaries monitor or assess private beliefs? To address their fears, missionaries created systems and practices aimed at evaluating the interiority of Koreans. Those who desired to gain membership in church communities had to demonstrate their faith through acts of Christian obedience. Confessing one's faith with mere words was insufficient. Korean Christians had to show that conversion was in fact a transformation through faithful adherence to a set of moral prescriptions and "Christian" practices—such as mastery of prayer, devotion to Bible study, and active evangelism.

It would be a gross oversimplification to argue that this system of demonstrating belief and the responses of Koreans meant that the latter were passive objects of missionary control. Regardless of motive, church membership brought tangible benefits, from new social power within a region to an ability to take advantage of missionary connections for social or political advancement. But to secure membership in Christian communities and gain access to these benefits, Koreans had to perform acts that were, in the missionaries' minds, visible expressions of ideal Christian values and practices. In addition, it is important to note that through their actions and deeds, Korean Christians strongly challenged the missionaries' assumptions that Koreans lacked spirituality. Missionaries may have demanded signs of true belief, but the volume and urgency with which Korean Christians responded made the suspicion that Koreans were insincere increasingly untenable. As demonstrated in chapter 4, they met in large numbers not only on Sundays but also throughout the week for church-related activities, traversed the countryside for evangelism, and openly welcomed and engaged the Western Christian world.

The formation of clusters of Koreans who obeyed a set of moral precepts for the purpose of winning membership in a religious community that claimed to transcend political boundaries troubled the Korean and (after colonization) the Japanese governments. What would happen when Christians, both Korean and Western, found themselves in situations where obedience to their faith necessitated disobedience to the state? This question sheds light on the interest of government officials in Korea in learning whether Korean Christians were loyal to the state or to their "foreign" faith.

As Kyung Moon Hwang has argued, by at least 1894, a process of state making was underway on the Korean Peninsula, as government officials sought to "rationalize" the organization of state and society and the relationship between the two. One major area of reform was matters pertaining to religion.[35] Christianity in particular drew more attention from Korean and Japanese officials than can be fully explained by mere figures. The numbers of both Korean adherents and Western missionaries were still relatively small. Why was the state so concerned with this religion, and why did government officials cultivate ties with the missionary community?

To an extent, anxiety about the missionaries' activities stemmed from their demonstrated willingness to enter the political realm to promote their work. For example, as examined in chapter 2, during the first half of the 1890s, a period when the Korean government still restricted Western residence to "open ports" and the capital, missionaries used their status as private citizens of foreign nations to test the limits of government prohibitions on Christianity and to establish bases of operations in the interior of the country. The practice of leveraging their status as citizens of a particular political state to advance their religious goals was more the rule than the exception and was a cause for concern among government officials.

Importantly, the government's concern about this foreign religion was also rooted in the ways it affected efforts at state making. As noted above, missionaries sought to do more than spread a faith; they were attempting to establish churches that would assume membership in a transnational community of believers. In practice, this meant creating a new ecclesiastical order. The formation of Korean Methodist churches, for instance, required the cultivation of a cohort of ordained pastors, the establishment of rules of membership and a church hierarchy, the outlining of bylaws, the creation of different districts (groupings of churches), the systematic collection of money (tithes) to support the administration of these institutions, and the formation of a general conference, which would bring all the churches together into one coherent system of governance. Furthermore, these churches needed to determine their relationship to the Methodist General Conferences in the United States. Thus, as the central government embarked on a process of state making, missionaries and Korean Christian leaders engaged in the construction of a network of churches that led to a reorganization of social structures at the local level. Rationalizing society was not simply a top-down, state-led process. It was also a local process that at times clashed with the state's efforts to centralize power.

Missionaries, then, oversaw the reformulation or restructuring of local societies and the creation of a network of churches connected to the international community, even if they did not explicitly lead these efforts. Understanding this situation brings into focus a major reason government officials were concerned with this minority religion. As Gauri Viswanathan has argued, religious conversion in certain contexts is an act of subversion, allowing converts to "willfully" resist the dominant sociopolitical order by living "outside the fold."[36] Did Christians seek to reject the new sociopolitical system that was being constructed by the state?[37] Political loyalty was a matter of particular concern to the Japanese colonial government after the annexation of Korea in 1910. The Government-General of Korea's demand during the 1930s that students of mission schools bow at Shinto shrines to demonstrate their fidelity to the Japanese emperor echoed the missionaries' own requirement that Korean converts demonstrate their faith. For colonial officials, verbal declarations of loyalty to the state were mere words; to confirm their loyalty, Korean students at schools run by missionaries needed to exhibit obedience to the state through the act of bowing.

Significantly, Protestant missionaries shared with government officials an interest in making sure that Christians were politically obedient and productive members of society, though for different reasons. In part, the missionaries worried that Koreans were converting for material gain. But the missionaries were also reacting to the anti-Christian edicts that had been in force in the country since the beginning of the nineteenth century. The Korean government had issued these measures in response to what it perceived to be a threat from Catholicism, which had entered the country during the late eighteenth century. Particularly alarming to Korean officials was a "silk letter" that they had discovered requesting that the pope have troops sent to the country to stop the persecution of Korean Catholics.[38] The early Protestant missionaries to Korea were aware of this history and sought to distinguish their branch of Christianity from Catholicism. The latter supposedly had questionable loyalty to political authorities.[39] In contrast, missionaries argued, Protestants were upright subjects of their respective governments. They believed that once the Korean government realized this "fact," officials would not only permit Protestantism but even promote it.

In reality, Protestant missionaries were no less prone than their Catholic counterparts to intervening in "political" issues and, in this manner, challenging government authority. The ideals of loyalty and respect for laws, however, came to figure prominently in their relationships with both Korean believers and government officials. First, as noted above, missionaries publicly declared they respected local authorities. Thus, they faced pressure to act in accordance with government regulations and laws. Second, missionaries searched for signs of true belief. One sign was being an obedient subject of the Korean state and later, after colonization, of the Japanese empire. Of course, the question of what constituted loyalty and what was an illicit transgression of the purported boundary between church and state was open to debate.

Balancing Communities begins in 1884, with the arrival in Korea of Horace N. Allen, a missionary with the Northern Presbyterian Mission, and weaves together two interlocking narratives: the story of the relationships between missionaries and the state and the story of the relationships between missionaries and Korean Christians. When the first generation of Protestant missionaries arrived in Korea, they claimed that they were careful to avoid involvement in political affairs. In reality, from nearly the start of their work, they formed close and problematic ties to the government. Specifically, as a method of evangelism, the mission societies to Korea established social institutions such as hospitals and schools to provide a firm foothold in the country during a period when anti-Christian edicts were still in place. But these institutions were also sources of dissension within the missionary ranks, in large part because they afforded officials an opportunity to regulate religion.

The administration and control of these social institutions, as well as of churches, were also sites of contestation between missionaries and Korean Christians. As noted above, from nearly the formal start of the Protestant missionary movement in Korea, the mission societies operating in the country created systems of conversion that sought to assess the sincerity of those seeking to join the church. The relationships between missionaries and Korean Christians were, in short, hierarchical. This relational pattern was on display at institutions like schools. The missionaries maintained that they would hand over administration of these properties to Koreans, but only when the local actors demonstrated that they possessed both the spiritual maturity and the ability to run them. In other words, these institutions gave missionaries another way to oversee and regulate Korean Christian behavior and, as a corollary, to define the boundaries of Korean Christian orthodoxy. Though many Korean Christians engaged their new faith with surprising vitality, missionaries dominated these structures well into the colonial period. This situation rankled many Korean Christian leaders, some of whom sought to break free of missionary control. As a result, the first half of the twentieth century witnessed a number of attempted church schisms (chapter 6).

Balancing Communities concludes with an examination of the colonial government's demand that all schoolchildren, including those attending mission-run private schools, bow at State Shinto ceremonies during the 1930s (chapter 7). This order and the ensuing controversies that beset Protestant communities in Korea laid bare the competing interests of missionaries, Korean Christians, and the state, exposing resentments that had been simmering throughout the colonial period. Certainly, the order to bow at shrines concerned "religion." But the command also represented an argument about the nature of education and private schools and raised the question of ownership. In regard to the former, were these institutions "secular" spaces that should be governed by the state? In regard to the latter, did they belong to the mission societies who founded them or to Korean Christians—those with whom missionaries had so long "partnered" and for whom these institutions were originally established? The debates and struggles over addressing these overlapping questions led to an attenuation of the missionaries' presence as secular education became an increasingly minor part of their work in Korea.

In the late 1930s, missionaries began to trickle out of the country. The trickle became a torrent in 1940, after the US State Department advised its citizens to leave Japanese-controlled territory. Finally, after the bombing of Pearl Harbor, in December 1941, the Japanese government arrested the handful of missionaries who had stubbornly remained in Korea. These missionaries were repatriated in June 1942. The stories that unfold in the following pages, however, reverberated long after the missionaries' expulsion. Most obviously, missionaries returned to the peninsula after the conclusion of World War II. In this sense, 1942 represents a break, not an ending; the relationships among Korean Christians, Western missionaries, and government officials continued. Throughout the second half of the twentieth century, missionaries and Korean Protestants would work together and play pivotal roles in both shaping religious practice and advancing sociopolitical change. At times fractious and at others harmonious, these relationships were maintained through a tense balancing of multiple overlapping communal identities and demands.

Chapter 1

Tangled Relations

Missionary Work at the Royal Hospital

For many who view the history of Christianity in Korea from a positive perspective, the Kapsin Coup (1884) shines as a fortuitous event that marked an important turning point in the story of this religion's presence in the country. Before 1884, the prospects that Korea would permit the practice of Christianity seemed bleak. One century previously, Yi Sŭng-hun, while accompanying his father on a diplomatic mission to Beijing in 1784, had sought out Catholic priests and received baptism. Yi returned to Korea with religious tracts, and a community of Catholic converts soon sprouted. However, Catholicism clashed with rituals—in particular ancestor rites—that buttressed the power of the state and the ruling elites. The central government reacted violently, giving Korean Catholicism its first martyrs in 1791. Throughout the nineteenth century, the central government conducted a series of anti-Catholic persecutions. These bloody campaigns, coupled with the repeated refusal of the Korean government to enter into diplomatic relations with Western nations—a practice that would earn the country the moniker the "Hermit Kingdom"—marked Korea as a closed country with a deep-seated hatred of all things Western, including Christianity.

But the fortunes of Christianity, and especially Protestantism, changed suddenly and unforeseeably with the Kapsin Coup.[1] In 1876, Japan applied lessons it had learned from its own subjection to the Western system of international relations and "unequal treaties" to force Korea to "open" its borders with the signing of the Treaty of Kanghwa. Thrust into the world capitalist system of trade and diplomatic relations, Korean officials confronted such pressing issues as how to engage the West, whether to adopt modern technology, and what course of reforms to pursue. Opinions varied from the belief that Korea must strive to keep foreigners and foreign culture at a distance to the conviction that Korea had to embrace Western institutions and aggressively adopt modern reforms. King Kojong negotiated a comparatively moderate course. Yet for officials who were more committed to the Confucian sociopolitical system and those who benefited the most from the status quo, even these limited measures were too radical, while for officials who sat on the fringes of power and who believed Western technology and knowledge needed to be pursued more vigorously, the pace of reforms was much too conservative.

In late 1884, a group of young and aggressive reformers from what scholars have dubbed the Enlightenment Party (Kaehwa p'a) decided to take matters into their own hands by plotting to seize control of the king and the administration of the government. After securing assurances of support from the Japanese minister stationed in the country, they timed their attack for the night of a special celebration honoring the establishment of a new postal system. On the night of December 4, they set fire to several buildings in the capital, falsely informed Kojong that Chinese troops were creating a disturbance, and quickly moved him to a "secure" location. They also attacked the banquet, hoping to eliminate a number of officials who staunchly opposed reforms. Though they succeeded in gaining control over Kojong, their success was short-lived, as Chinese forces mobilized and put an end to the coup on December 6.

During the initial attack on December 4, Min Yŏng-ik, a nephew of King Kojong, suffered serious injuries. Paul G. von Möllendorf, a Prussian serving as adviser to Kojong, quickly requested the services of Horace N. Allen, a doctor to the US legation. Allen was, in fact, a Northern Presbyterian missionary sent by the Board of Foreign Missions of the Presbyterian Church in the USA (BFMPCUSA; Home Board), who had arrived in Korea that fall. However, the anti-Christian edicts that had been in effect in the country since the early nineteenth century necessitated that he, the first resident Protestant missionary to the country, find nonreligious means to enter and work in Korea. While Allen and other American missionaries remained hopeful that the door to proselytization might one day be opened, that day appeared to be a long way off. Thus, following the tactics practiced by other missionaries when pioneering fields where Christianity was prohibited, they avoided overt evangelistic work and instead prepared for a future day when the gospel could be spread without incurring the displeasure, let alone wrath, of the Korean state; they studied the language while engaging in educational and medical work.

Though Min's injuries were severe, Allen managed to save his life. Allen thus won the favor of Kojong, who appointed him the royal physician. Taking advantage of his newfound influence, Allen petitioned Kojong to start a Western-style hospital, with doctors supplied by a "benevolent society of America."[2] Kojong agreed, and in 1885, Kwanghyewŏn, which was later renamed Chejungwŏn, opened its doors to treat the sick of Korea. The benevolent society that Allen spoke of was the BFMPCUSA.

The Presbyterian missionaries celebrated the establishment of the royal hospital as a miracle that had allowed them surreptitiously to gain a foothold for the Northern Presbyterian missionaries in a country hostile to Christianity. Gifts, however, at times come with a price. The tangling of the Presbyterian missionaries with the government soon proved less a fortuitous event than an unfortunate yoke. While perhaps unaware when Allen presented his petition that the benevolent society was a religious organization, the Korean government certainly suspected that Allen had ties to the missionary movement, and it took measures to control these foreign evangelists and ensure that they adhered to the existing anti-Christian edicts. In this manner, the Korean state mired the Northern Presbyterian Mission in dissension mere years after it commenced. More than a decade would elapse after the Kapsin Coup before the Presbyterians would be able to untangle their relationship with the state and redefine their association with Chejungwŏn.

Acrimony in the Field

The first generation of Northern Presbyterians sent to Korea was beset by strife and discord.

In explaining these early clashes within the Presbyterian community, scholars of Korean Christianity have conventionally focused on the relationships among the first three Presbyterian missionaries to the field: Horace Allen, Horace G. Underwood, and John Heron. With regards to mission policy, these three split on the question of how aggressively to pursue open evangelism: Allen sought to avoid causing any political incident by navigating a conservative course, while Heron and Underwood wanted to pursue more direct and open work in spreading the gospel. Exacerbating this difference in opinion were differences in personality. In his classic study of Allen, for example, Fred Harrington described him as a "thin-skinned" and "short-tempered" individual who "neither yielded nor forgave."[3] Not surprisingly, Harrington argued that the sources of acrimony were the personal failings of the participants involved—in particular Allen. In the half-century since Harrington's study, his focus on the personality and moral flaws of the early missionaries has been repeatedly echoed by other scholars. For example, Everett Hunt Jr. described Allen as "crotchety," and Martha Huntley suggested that Allen was fixated on wealth and position.[4] Reducing the missionaries' conflicts solely to personality flaws, however, is unsatisfying as an explanatory model and diverts attention from deeper issues that may have sparked and fanned these conflicts.

The Protestant missionary movement in the nineteenth century employed some of the brightest, most cosmopolitan, and most capable segments of American society.[5] Typically, missionaries to Korea arrived not as independent actors rashly pursuing personal evangelical fervor but as employees of a large-scale mission board. These boards carefully hired individuals for their intelligence, commitment, and capabilities. In other words, the selection of missionary candidates was neither haphazard nor based merely on applicants' passion for "God's work." A basic requirement was a postsecondary degree, and many had graduated either from a seminary or from medical school. Candidates submitted a letter of application detailing their religious beliefs, health, education, habits, financial situation, and marital status.[6] The mission boards also sent the writers of letters of recommendation questionnaires requesting frank assessments of the candidates' spirituality, personality, intelligence, poise, work ethic, sociability, temperament, and "mind for business."[7] The concern with business aptitude reveals that while mission boards in theory eschewed the seeking of profit, in fact they were businesses with interests and outposts spanning the globe. Stated differently, the skill set necessary to operate a mission was similar to that needed to run a for-profit business—the main difference being that mission boards calculated profit primarily in terms of churches built, natives converted, and the kingdom of heaven extended rather than financial gain.

Mission boards carefully examined candidates for a range of skills, and they recruited individuals who displayed the organizational and leadership aptitude necessary to work in these large-scale bureaucracies. In contrast to the stereotype of the passionate zealot, prone to emotional outbursts, the missionaries chosen by these boards were, as a group, meticulous and analytical in their work. Certainly, disputes and differences of opinion often arose among missionaries. But while stubbornness, private beliefs, and personalities may have intensified church disagreements, the missionaries curiously consistently reported that their personal relationships were amicable even as their working relationships fractured. For example, in one letter explaining the dissension in the field, Underwood reported that he was in fact on "good terms personally" with Allen but could not work with him on a professional level "in harmony."[8] Underwood was not alone in this attitude toward Allen. When Samuel A. Moffett wrote a series of reports on difficulties surrounding what policy to follow during his first year in the field, he indicated that during a period when Allen was absent from the country, the missionary community had finally achieved harmony on how to approach the anti-Christian edicts. (Allen at the time was working for the Korean government.) In response to a rumor that Allen might rejoin the missionary ranks, Moffett pleaded with his superiors to send him anywhere but Korea.[9] Yet Moffett would later insist that despite his request to send Allen elsewhere, their personal relationship was in fact cordial.[10]

Likewise, although Allen may have been a curmudgeon, any personal feelings of animosity he held toward Moffett and Underwood did not predetermine his assessment of their abilities or his working relationships with them. After Allen's appointment as head of the US legation in Korea in 1897, he frequently communicated with both Moffett and Underwood in his official role regarding missionary activities, and Allen was quick to aid his former coworkers. While he may have believed that they were rash in their judgments, and while his conflict with Underwood may have played a role in Allen's eventual exit from the Korea mission field, he still recognized that he had a responsibility to provide them consular support. In this manner, he sought to separate any personal misgivings he may have held from his professional interactions.

Many missionaries in Korea approached their chosen occupations with similar professionalism. Whatever their personal flaws, they sought to act with the decorum befitting their status. They were in Korea to perform a job, and regardless of any feelings of distaste for any one individual, most strove to adhere to the etiquette and responsibility demanded by their positions. This picture of missionaries raises an important question. If the BFMPCUSA had selected Allen, Underwood, and Heron for their temperament and aptitude to establish and run the Korean branch of the Northern Presbyterian Mission, and if each of these individuals believed that a certain level of decorum and bureaucratic procedure needed to be followed, how did they so quickly become embroiled in endless bickering? For within a few years after the start of their in-country work, what has often been described as petty infighting threatened the health of their mission.

Debating Missionary Policy

Allen arrived in Korea in September 1884. Underwood and Heron followed the next year. Only six months after Heron and Underwood arrived, Allen wrote to Francis Ellinwood, a secretary with the BFMPCUSA, that he was contemplating resignation because of poor relations in the field.[11] Though Allen would write again stating that he had decided against resigning, relations among the Presbyterian missionaries continued to be fractious. Broadly speaking, Allen, Heron, and Underwood debated three related issues. The first regarded the proper strategy to be followed in light of the Korean prohibitions on evangelism and Christianity. This question was potentially a matter of life and death. While in hindsight we might assume that as Americans, these individuals occupied a position of strength, in reality they felt vulnerable. The most recent campaign against Catholicism had started in 1866, less than two decades before Allen's arrival. Scholars currently debate the number of Catholics who were executed, with estimates ranging from a couple thousand to eight thousand. However, it is worth nothing that one missionary, writing in 1890, reported that the number executed was twenty thousand.[12] In the minds of Protestant missionaries in Seoul, they faced a government that had demonstrated a willingness to kill Christians vigorously and comprehensively.

Heightening the sense of danger was the political situation in the capital at the start of the Protestant missionary endeavor. Although Allen was able to use the Kapsin Coup as an opportunity to establish close ties with the court, the same event led to a purge of those who favored Westernization. This meant that missionaries were targets for backlash from those who strove to stymie Western-style reforms. Indeed, Underwood originally entered Korea in April 1885 along with Henry G. Appenzeller and his wife. On their arrival, a US naval officer apprised them of the political situation and advised that they return to Japan until the scene settled. Underwood chose to stay, but the Appenzellers heeded the officer's warning and left.[13] The missionaries, and Americans generally, felt endangered regardless of whether the threat was real.[14]

Deciding how to proceed in this climate was critical for the future of Christianity in Korea. In this context, Allen cautioned that missionaries take a gradual approach. His plan called for missionaries to bide their time until the government repealed the ban on Christianity. In this manner, ill will—on the part of both the government and the general populace—could be avoided. Allen insisted that missionaries, for the time being, focus on medical work. He argued that because they spread the Christian message by their very presence and actions, there was no urgency to engage in direct evangelism.[15] In contrast, Heron and Underwood were more willing to test the boundary of official toleration for the practice of Christianity. They claimed that tacit approval for their activities already existed, as local officials were well aware that they were missionaries and engaging in evangelism.[16]

The second issue that Allen, Heron, and Underwood contested regarded decision-making procedures. As noted above, the missionary enterprise was conducted as a bureaucracy. Missionaries received a handbook or manual detailing proper conduct and their rights and responsibilities. Yet the three earliest missionaries debated the interpretation of the handbook and its implementation on a practical level. In particular, the handbook stated that each male missionary had an equal vote on decisions made by the Northern Presbyterian Mission in Korea. Allen, however, came to dominate the decision-making process.[17] In one report to Ellinwood, Underwood complained that he had suggested to Allen that they start a program at the government hospital to teach English to officials and students. After some discussion among the missionaries, difficulties arose, and the topic was tabled. Thus, Underwood was surprised when a Korean official later contacted him and inquired when he would be prepared to take up his teaching duties. Underwood complained that Allen had apparently worked out the details for the course of study with the Korean government without consulting his colleagues.[18]

Underwood's frustration with Allen's actions and the tensions generated by the attempt to determine proper mission policy were both tied to the third issue under debate: Allen's control over Chejungwŏn.[19] Heron, a skilled doctor, complained to Ellinwood that though the missionaries were supposed to have equal rights, Allen acted as Heron's superior.[20] Particularly frustrating to Heron was Allen's monopoly over the allocation of mission funds earmarked for the hospital. Allen used these funds without any oversight, whereas Heron was required to provide detailed invoices and requests to Allen. Having "no voice" over the administration of the hospital, Heron lashed out at Allen and lamented that his subservient position was "humiliating."[21] The conflict between Allen and Heron at times devolved into petty claims of the other's moral failings. For instance, Allen accused Heron of calling him an ass, to which Heron responded that Allen had first levied this invective.[22] In addition, Underwood suggested that Heron disliked Allen because the former refrained from drinking, smoking, or partaking in frivolous activities; in contrast, Allen reportedly both drank and smoked.[23] Allen defended himself by asserting that Heron begrudged him the official titles and awards he had received from Kojong and that Heron was jealous because he had not had an opportunity to meet the king.[24]

The acrimony between the three reached a crisis in September 1886, when both Heron and Underwood tendered their resignations within one week of each other.[25] Before finalizing his resignation, however, Underwood made one last attempt to fulfill his pastoral charge by restoring harmony to the field. Calling together the Presbyterian missionaries, he put forth a set of proposals to reform the administration of the hospital. Particularly important, he proposed that the doctors working at the hospital form an advisory board with each member having an equal vote.[26] Moreover, a standing committee handling the administration of the hospital was to be established. In late January 1887, Allen, Heron, Underwood, and the other missionaries who had since arrived in the field all approved Underwood's plan.[27] While there would be other conflicts in the future, the first major crisis had largely passed.

Kojong and the Missionaries

The Home Board viewed the conflicts that beset the missionaries in Korea with dismay.[28] How was it that a work that seemed so promising, given the close relationship forged between Allen and the royal family, had so quickly unraveled?

A brief comparison with the Northern Methodist Mission provides clues to the underlying sources of the Presbyterian missionaries' problems. Both the Northern Methodist and the Northern Presbyterian mission boards hired relatively young men as their first missionaries. Most were still in their twenties. The boards placed these neophytes, who lacked any real knowledge of Korean culture or history and certainly did not speak the Korean language, in charge of starting new mission stations on the peninsula. The only one with experience in the field was Allen, who had served less than a year as a missionary in China. But the Methodists had one organizational advantage over their Presbyterian counterparts: the Methodist Church was structured with a clear top-down hierarchy. They had a clearly appointed superintendent in charge of running the Korea field. The Presbyterian mission, in contrast, was a more horizontally organized endeavor; whose voice would determine the structure and direction of the newly established work was unclear.

The lack of a clear leadership structure exacerbated another key difference between the Methodists and Presbyterians in Korea. Though Allen welcomed William Scranton, the first Methodist medical missionary to the peninsula, into service at the royal hospital, he vigilantly strove to ensure that the hospital remained within the Presbyterian sphere of control. Thus, Methodists were largely free of direct entanglement with the Korean court. At first glance, this appears to have put them at a competitive disadvantage in comparison to the Presbyterians. On closer examination, however, the situation turns out to have been liberating for the Methodists, who went on to establish their own private clinic in Seoul, build schools, and engage in open evangelism. By 1888, the Methodists boasted that they were seeing nearly the same number of patients as the Presbyterians were in Chejungwŏn.[29] Meanwhile, the Presbyterians, linked to the court by their work in Chejungwŏn, were subject to subtle pressures and restrictions imposed by the Korean government.

To better understand the early Presbyterian missionaries' conflicts, it is necessary to examine the role played by Kojong and the royal family. Scholars have ignored this factor because of their overreliance not only on personality flaws as an explanation but also on a persistent portrait of Kojong as a weak and ineffectual ruler. James Palais, for example, contrasted the dynamic leadership style of the

Taewŏn'gun with the passive style of his son, Kojong.[30] According to Palais, Kojong possessed an "inborn timidity, indecisiveness, and diffidence."[31] In line with this characterization, scholars of Christianity in Korea have maintained that Kojong foolishly overestimated both the missionaries' influence with the US government, as he sought potential allies, and his own ability to prevent missionaries from spreading Christianity.[32]

The portrayal of Kojong as a weak ruler stretches at least as far back as the first Protestant missionaries in Korea, who cast him and the royal family as naïve. For example, when Lucius Foote, who led the US legation at the time, first introduced Allen to the king, Kojong inquired whether Allen was a missionary. Kojong received the simple response that Allen was "physician to the legation."[33] In the conventional narrative, Foote's response masked Allen's true intention in the country and provided a back channel for the entry of a Protestant missionary. Missionaries perpetuated the relatively low estimations of Kojong and the royal family in their reports and letters. For instance, in describing his petition to establish a Western-style hospital, Allen stressed that he had indicated that his backer was "a benevolent society in America" that also ran hospitals in many of the major cities of China.[34] Allen assumed that if he emphasized China, Kojong would be more amenable to allowing this "benevolent society" to work in Korea. In other words, Allen believed that his cleverness, and Kojong's corresponding lack of cleverness, had paved the way for him not only to enter the country but also to establish a government hospital that could serve as a base of operations for the Presbyterian missionaries.

The portrayal of Kojong and the royal family as naïve and childlike continued in the writings of other missionaries. Annie Ellers was one of the first Western women to visit the court on a regular basis. A doctor, she arrived in the field in 1886 as one of the Northern Presbyterians. Allen secured her a position as Queen Min's physician. According to her reports, she often met not only the queen but also Kojong and the crown prince. She noted that the queen, Kojong, and the crown prince seemed to study her every move, and she characterized them as "child-like." Describing one visit, she noted how they all "rose" to say "goodbye" (in English) and how "amused as any little child at home" Kojong was to "count 1-2-3."[35]

Kojong may have been timid and unsure of how to transform Korea into a modern nation-state. However, the relatively low estimation of the royal family and the perception that they were "child-like" have obscured the ways both Kojong and the government attempted to control Western missionaries. Kojong played a pivotal role in placing first Allen and later Heron in a position of divided loyalties, demanding their allegiance, if not compliance, with the anti-Christian edicts.[36] This pressure in turn produced the conflicts within the Presbyterian mission community. This becomes clearer if we situate the establishment of Chejungwŏn in the broader context of Kojong's active efforts at modernization throughout his reign.

By at least 1881, with the dispatch of the "Gentlemen's Observation Mission" abroad, the Korean court had made the critical decision to explore the adoption of certain Western institutions and technologies. As with the *ti-yong* (Western Usefulness, Chinese Essence) debates in China, a growing number of reform-minded Korean elites advocated using Western technology while maintaining a Confucian cultural core.[37] By the second half of 1882, a number of petitions were presented at the court arguing that while Western religion (Christianity) was heterodoxy and needed to be strictly banned, Western technology had proven to be useful and good. In September, the court issued an edict ordering the destruction of steles the Taewŏn'gun had erected that excluded the West.[38] The edict explained that impressive technology had made Western nations wealthy and strong. Both China and Japan had succumbed to the pressures of the West and signed treaties with these nations based on the principle of equality. It was thus only prudent for Korea to do the same. Yet the edict stated that the country would adopt only Western technology. Those who maintained that if relations were established with the West, Christianity would enter and spread were gripped by an unfounded fear, the court asserted. Because the government had strictly forbidden this false teaching and because the country was steeped in the learning of Confucius and Mencius, there was no need to worry about the spread of heterodoxy. In particular, the edict emphasized that the government was equipped to control Christianity because it had in place the appropriate laws and possessed the will to mercilessly punish offenders. In short, the goal was to follow the example of the West for practical military and technological purposes but to control the spread of Western teachings—in particular Christianity.

Clearly, Kojong and the court were aware, before the arrival of the missionaries, of the dangers Christianity might pose if Korea pursued Western-style reforms. Despite its appellation of the "Hermit

Kingdom," the Korean court was cognizant of world events. For example, in 1883, *Hansŏng sunbo,* Korea's first modern newspaper, reported on everything from France's imperial conquest in Madagascar to Britain's military movements in Egypt.[39] In addition, the paper referred to the importance of religion in the West, its connections to state politics, and its cultural significance.[40] If the Korean court understood what was occurring on the other side of globe, it is a safe assumption that it had even better knowledge of issues in China and Japan. In particular, it would have observed a close connection between the "opening" of these two countries and the influx of missionaries. These foreigners not only proselytized but also started educational and medical projects. Moreover, of all Westerners, they stayed the longest, knew the language the best, and engaged local society the most. Missionaries were a ubiquitous presence in the region, and the Korean state could hardly have missed their status. Kojong's inquiry about whether Allen was a missionary at their first meeting signaled his understanding that missionaries often accompanied Western imperial expansion. Indeed, this inquiry was likely Kojong's warning to Allen that he suspected the latter's true intention in entering the country.[41]

Supporting this assessment is Robert S. Maclay's account of his journey to Korea in the summer of 1884. Maclay was a Methodist missionary stationed in Japan, and his wife was contacted to teach English to Koreans dispatched to the country as a part of the "Gentlemen's Observation Mission." Through this connection, Maclay met Kim Ok-kyun, who expressed a desire for the introduction of Western civilization to Korea. As a result, Maclay petitioned the Methodist board to open a station in Korea. After receiving approval, he approached Kojong to receive permission for missionaries to work in the country. Kojong consented on the condition that missionaries restrict themselves to educational and medical work. In short, Kojong intended to use missionaries to spread Western technology and medicine but sought to prevent them from spreading Christianity.[42] Kojong likely expected the Presbyterians to adhere to the same principles. Furthermore, the court used tactics to ensure that the missionaries stayed within the boundaries the Korean government had set. For example, Underwood once responded to an accusation by Allen that he had been using his position as teacher in the government school to preach by claiming this was impossible: a Korean official was always present listening to his lectures to prevent such an occurrence.[43]

Maclay's experience with Kojong makes it clear that Allen's "miraculous" treatment of Min Yŏng-ik was not necessarily the decisive factor that convinced Kojong of the efficacy of Western medicine and, in turn, spurred the decision to start a Western-style hospital. Intellectual elites in Korea had been aware of Western medical practices long before the "opening" of the country in 1876.[44] In fact, tracts regarding Western medical techniques, which had been translated into Chinese by Jesuit missionaries introducing Western concepts of the body and healing in China, had made their way to the Korean Peninsula by the late eighteenth century. After 1876, intellectuals increasingly began to investigate Western science and technology. Of particular interest were techniques related to health and sanitation, which was translated as *wisaeng,* meaning literally "to protect life." In May 1884, an article in *Hansŏng sunbo* extolled the virtues of Western sanitary practices.[45] The author explained that sanitation focused on the prevention of disease and reported that Western nations had a set of regulations allowing for the inspection of incoming ships, including quarantine of suspect items and passengers, to prevent the spread of communicable diseases. The article concluded by suggesting that the creation of a sanitation department would be of great benefit to the health of the people *(paeksŏng).*

Importantly, in Allen's original proposal to start a royal hospital, he wrote: "if the Government would grant me a few facilities, I think they would be amply repaid by having their sick cared for according to Western Science, and by having a place for wounded soldiers to be attended to. Also, it would be the means of instructing young men in Western Medical and Sanitary science."[46] Given the preexisting interest in the efficacy of *wisaeng,* Allen's offer to start a government hospital was likely viewed by the court as an unanticipated boon, especially in the face of the conservative officials who had risen to positions of prominence once the Enlightenment Party had been discredited as a result of the Kapsin Coup.[47] Despite the broader currents that opposed reforms, Allen's proposal offered Kojong not only an opportunity to start a modern Western-style hospital but also doctors whose salaries would be paid by an outside organization.

Meanwhile, for the Presbyterians, the establishment of Chejungwŏn turned out to be as much a burden as a boon. For one matter, as early as 1886 Heron reported that its status as a royal hospital prevented the Presbyterians from engaging in open evangelism.[48] For another, it was the hospital's entanglement with the Korean state that sowed discord in the Presbyterian mission community. Allen's appointment by the king to oversee the hospital acted as a prod for him to adhere to the Korean government's prohibitions on Christianity.[49] Allen had a moral duty to uphold the laws of the land and to serve the Korean state, and he felt an inordinate amount of pressure because Korean officials held him responsible for the actions of all missionaries, especially Americans.[50] However, differences of opinion in a mission field like Korea were bound to arise and were not unique to the Presbyterians; Allen's opposition to the policies of his fellow missionaries should not have endangered the overall health of the mission. The reality of the situation was that Allen acted as the sole power in the Presbyterian mission. How did he amass so much influence?

Two related factors worked to funnel power to Allen and give him controlling influence in the field. First, the Presbyterians had tied their work to the official approval of the court and the government hospital. Even Heron admitted the importance of this relationship and the missionaries' connection to the royal family in securing the presence of Presbyterians in the country regardless of whether religious freedom was ever granted.[51] The Northern Presbyterian Mission, thus, was heavily influenced by court politics and decisions. Second, Kojong's favor toward missionaries remained limited to Allen and did not extend, for example, to William Scranton.[52] In effect, Kojong made Allen a gateway to royal favor. Power flowed to and through this one individual.

To view this situation from a different perspective, Henry Kim has cited Ronald S. Burt's concept of a structural hole to explain how Allen gained influence.[53] A structural hole refers to an absence of connection between two groups or individuals. A third party that is able to link two disconnected groups gains social capital. Before 1884, the Presbyterians of the United States lacked direct access to the Korean state. Because of Allen's treatment of Min Yŏng-ik, he came to fill a structural hole. As the only missionary with direct access to the king, Allen was a valuable resource to the Presbyterian mission. Allen used this access to start a Western-style hospital, secure positions for Underwood and Heron, and gain a post for Ellers as the queen's physician. Allen possessed a great deal of social capital and influence because of Kojong's decision to make him the sole missionary gateway to the royal court. Kojong not only appointed Allen his personal doctor but also, in May 1886, bestowed official positions on both Allen and Heron. Several months later, Kojong elevated Allen to be an official of the second rank. While Allen viewed these appointments as signs of Kojong's favor, the position was curiously high and indicates the extent to which Kojong sought to establish control over Allen by incorporating him into the official bureaucracy, if only symbolically. In turn, this action created an imbalance of power relations within the Presbyterian missionary community.

In reviewing the early disputes in the Korea field, Martha Huntley has argued that one reason these conflicts reached a fevered height was that the mission board failed to fulfill its responsibility to offer proper mediation.[54] Having dispatched Allen, Underwood, and Heron to the field and committed to paying their salaries, the BFMPCUSA had the right to officiate major disputes and could even recall unruly missionaries. The board could have reprimanded Allen for monopolizing power in the field. Instead, it affirmed his right to exercise power over issues related to the hospital for at least two reasons. First, as discussed earlier, Allen played a key role in securing the Northern Presbyterian Mission's position in the country and control over the royal hospital. Reprimanding, demoting, or sacking Allen could have endangered the board's ties to Kojong and jeopardized its work in the country. Second, Chejungwŏn was an ambiguous space for the Presbyterian mission. On the one hand, it represented the source of its legitimate presence in the country. On the other hand, in petitioning Kojong to establish a Western-style hospital, Allen had unwittingly allowed the Korean government to enter the sphere of Presbyterian mission work. Those working at Chejungwŏn were employees of the state. Ellinwood's decision to side with Allen was an affirmation of the simple fact that the hospital was owned by the royal family.

Attempting to serve two masters, Allen, Heron, and the other missionaries who worked at Chejungwŏn had their loyalties split between the BFMPCUSA and the Korean government. Allen in particular found himself under tremendous pressure to abide by, if not obey, the demands of Korean officials because of his position as head of the hospital. Stated differently, the power that Allen derived from filling a structural hole did not make him all-powerful. Allen's position was dependent on Kojong's favor, and Kojong had a particular vision of the role of "missionaries" in Korea. By giving Allen an official title in the bureaucracy, Kojong had brought him, at least rhetorically, under the control of the state. Once an official,

Allen was honor bound to adhere to the laws of the land.[55] Thus, more than his personality flaws, it was Allen's sense of duty and Kojong's decision that sparked the battles that erupted among the missionaries. Allen's position, prestige, and honor were all tied to his ability to ensure that his colleagues adhered to the prohibitions against spreading Christianity.

A sudden outburst of conflicts between Heron and Underwood, starting in 1888, underlines the point that Allen's structural position in the official bureaucracy was more important than his personal failings. As described above, Heron and Underwood had been close allies in their criticism not only of Allen's domination of the field but of his vision for mission policy. However, in early 1887, Allen, tired of the constant fighting, accepted an offer from Kojong to accompany a Korean delegation to Washington, DC, for the purpose of establishing a diplomatic legation. With Allen gone, Kojong appointed Heron the court doctor and elevated him to the same official position in the Korean bureaucracy that Allen had previously held. As he took charge of the hospital's administration, Heron occupied the structural hole formerly filled by Allen. On the one hand, this gave him tremendous prestige and power. On the other hand, Heron now became tied to the wishes of Kojong and was held responsible for the behavior of the other Presbyterian missionaries. Though once an advocate of pursuing a more aggressive policy of evangelism, Heron made an about-face and argued that the missionaries needed to be circumspect and refrain from any activity that might incur the wrath of the Korean state.

Heron soon came into direct conflict with Underwood, who still believed in the necessity of pushing the boundaries of what was tacitly, though not legally, permissible. Heron was particularly critical of an evangelistic trip Underwood took through the interior in 1889.[56] Underwood had married a recent missionary to the field, Lillias Horton, and they decided that for their honeymoon they would take an extensive journey through the northern half of the Korean Peninsula. Before their departure, however, the Korean government reminded the diplomatic community that proselytization and the practice of Christianity were illegal. In light of this warning, the US legation required Underwood to swear that he would not engage in open evangelism or baptize during his trek in Korea before it would forward his travel documents to the Korean government for official approval.

Heron criticized Underwood's honeymoon plans, suspicious of his colleague's penchant for aggressively spreading the gospel at every opportunity.[57] When Underwood returned to Seoul and informed others that he had obeyed both his oath and his conscience by crossing the Yalu River and baptizing Koreans on Manchurian soil, Heron was livid.[58] He insisted that Underwood refrain from publicizing his missionary exploits.[59] Not surprisingly, Heron became furious upon learning that Underwood had published articles about his journey in missionary journals in the United States and complained that once news of the trip appeared in print, the Korean state, officials with the US legation, and other foreigners would view the Presbyterians with derision.[60]

By all accounts, bickering now beset the relationship between Heron and Underwood.[61] Just as had happened with Allen, the disputes between them devolved into petty personal accusations and slanderous remarks. Eventually, Heron attempted to flee his position by requesting a relocation to Pusan to start a new mission station.[62] Although in the end Heron remained in Seoul, his request indicates the degree to which his status as both a missionary and an official in the Korean bureaucracy strained his work and the work of the Presbyterian mission. Indeed, Horace Underwood and his wife complained that Heron was acting as Horace Allen had, consolidating power in his own hands and making unilateral decisions without consulting the other missionaries.[63] Not until Heron lay on his deathbed, in 1890, did some peace return to the field.

Lillias Underwood understood that both Allen and Heron felt that as the king's physicians, paid by the king and in charge of the government hospital with official rank, they were "honor bound" to maintain the "king's confidence."[64] As she astutely noted, Heron bore a heavy burden to follow government regulations in his position as head of the government hospital.[65] His letters to Ellinwood revealed that he was concerned not merely with what the actions of the other missionaries might do to the Presbyterian mission in Korea but also what their actions might mean for him.[66] Kojong had identified Heron as the head of the Presbyterian mission and applied pressure specifically on Heron to ensure compliance with the anti-Christian edicts. This pressure resulted in Heron's transformation from someone who endorsed open evangelism and enjoyed close relations with Underwood to someone who opposed aggressive proselytization and Underwood's actions in that direction.

Untangling the Hospital

In July 1890, Heron died suddenly after a bout of dysentery, and the Presbyterian missionaries were forced to consider what to do about the government hospital. Chejungwŏn had become a distraction from their efforts at evangelism and was a constant source of disagreement and dissension. The missionaries strongly believed that if they decided to continue their work at Chejungwŏn, the terms of their affiliation must be altered.[67]

In the first monthly meeting after Heron's death, the Presbyterian missionaries voted to form a committee to meet with the Korean official in charge of the administration of Chejungwŏn to negotiate new terms. At this point, however, the issue of who was actually in control of the hospital became a sticking point. Did the missionaries or the Korean government control the right to dictate the terms of the missionaries' involvement in the hospital and the right to appoint a head doctor? The majority of the Presbyterian missionaries asserted that they were in charge of the hospital. Opposing this viewpoint was Allen, who had returned to the field in 1889. After a committee meeting, Allen communicated privately to Underwood that Chejungwŏn was in fact a government and not a mission hospital. Underwood argued in response that regardless of the hospital's origins, the Northern Presbyterians' continued work with the institution despite the government's failure to fulfill its obligations, and in particular its failure to supply medicine, had demonstrated that Chejungwŏn was "under the Mission."[68] He asserted a right to negotiate new terms with the Korean government and claimed that missionaries had an ownership stake in the hospital equal to that of the state.

Following Underwood's reasoning, the missionaries formed a committee to meet with Korean officials and reserved the right to appoint a new doctor. Two factors, however, undermined the missionaries' efforts to claim ownership over the hospital. First, the Korean government insisted that Allen be given temporary control of the hospital and that he head the efforts to find a replacement for Heron. Second, the BFMPCUSA wrote the missionaries in Korea to inform them that Allen was to take charge of the hospital until a replacement arrived from the United States.[69] The latter point in particular damaged the missionaries' bargaining position, for the BFMPCUSA functioned as their boss.

Once again, the field devolved into a state of intense debate, and once again Allen was in the thick of things. With the backing of the Korean government, Allen wielded an inordinate amount of influence on the fate of the hospital. He was outnumbered, however, as an influx of new missionaries placed the vast majority against him. If the other missionaries could not seize control of the hospital, they would attempt at the very least to distance the mission from political alignments by attacking Allen's ambiguous status as both a missionary and a government employee. In particular, his colleagues remained adamant that Allen, who had accepted a position as secretary of the US legation, be prevented from serving as a missionary and be barred from serving on the committee to determine the future of the government hospital.[70] Facing such staunch opposition, Allen submitted to the board his formal resignation as a missionary, a move that he would later claim he had planned to make anyway upon officially accepting his position at the US legation.[71]

In July 1890, Allen transferred control of the hospital to Robert Hardie. Hardie occupied the post for only a few short months before ceding it to Cadwallader C. Vinton, who held it until November 1893. Vinton initially assumed his new post with vigor. He attempted to improve the missionaries' ability to do Christian work at the hospital and to control it by negotiating new terms with the Foreign Office of the Korean government. He later stated that he had received, on arrival, assurances from the Foreign Office that government funding for the hospital would be handed directly to him rather than to the Korean officials attached to Chejungwŏn and that he would take over full management of the institution.[72] Vinton believed that these two provisions would allow him to remake the hospital as he saw fit and would provide the means to engage in mission work. When neither of these promises came to fruition, Vinton grew tired of his duties at Chejungwŏn and steadily devoted less and less time to it, pursuing more direct evangelizing endeavors like those of his Methodist counterparts.

In May 1891, the Presbyterian missionaries attempted to change the basis of their work in the hospital. For a time, Vinton simply stopped attending the hospital—an action that he referred to as a strike.[73] He hoped to use the strike to get the Foreign Office to agree to give him direct control over the hospital's operations. In addition, Vinton and Daniel Gifford informed Allen that the mission had decided to end its association with Chejungwŏn. Allen quickly sent a letter to Ellinwood, complaining that the Presbyterians were in danger of losing its "first, last, and only success in Korea."[74] Allen then urged Augustine Heard, head of the US legation, to pressure the Northern Presbyterian Mission to reconsider its decision. Heard convinced Vinton to return to the hospital without redressing any of his grievances merely by informing him of the response of the Korean government: the Foreign Office already intended to entrust the administration of the hospital to Dr. Julius Wiles, who worked with the Church of England. Heard pointed out that the willingness of other foreigners to assume control of Chejungwŏn indicated the value of the institution.[75]

Vinton returned to the hospital, but only begrudgingly. Disgusted with Chejungwŏn, he disparaged it by writing to Ellinwood that it was in fact a mere dispensary, where doctors simply passed out medicine. Since the government prohibited missionaries from evangelizing at the "hospital," he had decided to spend only a few hours a day at this institution, preferring to devote the majority of his time to other more satisfying projects.[76] For the next three years, the government hospital languished, as both the government and the missionaries grew less committed to it. By mid-1893, the facility had become an eyesore and a source of embarrassment for the Northern Presbyterians. Likewise, Korean officials became less enthralled with the notion of financing a Western-style hospital. They ceased to provide for the upkeep of the facilities, supply medicines, or pay the staff the promised salaries. In short, within a decade of its founding, Chejungwŏn, which after the Kapsin Coup stood as a symbol of divine providence, had become an unwelcome burden for the Presbyterian mission.

Many Presbyterian missionaries were weary of their association with the hospital, and some were ready to see it die. In December 1893, William Baird, chair of the Northern Presbyterian Mission's Executive Committee, captured the sentiments of the field when describing this institution as an "enigma" that had failed to "fulfil the promise of earlier years." Prompting Baird's observations was the arrival of Oliver Avison, who was to take over the administration of Chejungwŏn. Baird predicted that the coming years would either witness a "death struggle of a lingering project or the beginning of a much hoped success."[77]

During his first six months of working at Chejungwŏn, Avison became increasingly frustrated with the corruption of the government officials connected to the hospital, the lack of support, and the poor facilities. The final straw, however, was his discovery, after a short journey through the countryside, that the Korean officials attached to the institution had decided to rent part of the building to a Japanese doctor. Incensed, Avison informed John Sills, head of the US legation in Korea, that he had decided to resign from Chejungwŏn. On May 10, 1894, Sills in turn notified the Foreign Office of Avison's resignation.[78] Though Vinton had attempted a similar tactic in 1891, he had ultimately returned because of "the prestige which accrues to our mission from its connection with the official medical work of the government, and from the introduction afforded by it to many of the higher class of Koreans."[79] Further, Vinton reported that not a few of his fellow workers desired that he return to Chejungwŏn under the "original conditions" to see if he could improve the situation from within the system. In contrast, Avison remained steadfast in his refusal to return to the hospital, despite repeated requests by Korean officials, and he had the unanimous support of his fellow missionaries. Here was the "death struggle" for Chejungwŏn that Baird had predicted. The missionaries were prepared to let the hospital die if they could not change the terms of the Presbyterians' association with it.

In August 1894, Avison forwarded to Sills a proposal concerning the conditions under which he would return to the hospital. In brief, Avison demanded that the management of the hospital be put completely in the hands of the American Presbyterians, that a piece of property at the back of the hospital lot be given to the Presbyterians to build a doctor's residence, and that control of both the hospital building and all the equipment within it be turned over to the missionaries. In return, the Presbyterians would provide for all the expenses associated with running the facilities. The proposal included a provision that the Korean government could retake control of the hospital after a period of ten years if it paid the full sum of the costs of building and repairs that the Presbyterians had made until then. Sills agreed to forward the proposal to the Foreign Office with two important amendments. First, Sills replaced "American Presbyterians" with "Avison," arguing that the Foreign Office would never approve the proposal in its current wording, for to do so would give official recognition to the missionaries and their work. Second, he replaced the ten-year clause with a period of one year. Sills reasoned that the Foreign Office would not approve a ten-year period; however, he assured Avison that experience had demonstrated that the Korean government would not want to expend financial resources to recover the hospital, and in practice the hospital would be forever in the control of the missionaries.[80]

On September 26, 1894, the Foreign Office informed Sills of its approval of Avison's proposal and stated that Chejungwŏn was now fully under his control. The next day, Avison penned a letter to Ellinwood with the good news that the Korea mission would resume "work on a new and we think improved basis."[81] He noted with further glee that this was the missionaries' first official contract with the Korean government; he believed it augured a turning point in the Presbyterians' work in the country.

Tied to the State

Allen's treatment of Min Yŏng-ik appeared fortuitous to the Presbyterian missionaries. Through his actions, Allen had supposedly proven the efficacy of Western medicine and gained the good graces of the court. In turn, he attempted to manipulate his newfound influence to advance the Presbyterian missionary effort in the country. These were calculated moves on Allen's part. Indeed, he explained to Ellinwood that Min had paid him a visit shortly after recovering and insisted on paying for the medical treatment. Though Allen hesitated, he offered to donate his services and charged Min only for the cost of the medicine with the thought that "it would be better to leave him [Min] in my [Allen's] debt."[82] As this statement reveals, Allen, a man of common origins, felt adept enough to manipulate the Korean court to secure concessions and a foothold for the Presbyterian missionaries on the peninsula. But the Korean court had much experience in trading favors, and the thought that Allen, both new to the field and lacking any diplomatic training, could easily manipulate the royal family was naïve. Allen on his own was no match for the royal family.

The Presbyterian missionaries' partnership with the Korean state in the royal hospital impinged on their ability to engage in open evangelism to Koreans. Moreover, the court's decision to appoint only one missionary as an official created a power imbalance within the Presbyterian missionary community. Though in theory the missionaries shared power, in practice Allen and later Heron dominated the decision-making process during their tenures as the head of Chejungwŏn. Moreover, they found themselves duty bound to obey the dictates of the Korean state prohibiting the spread of Christianity. Thus, both men were put at odds with those in the Presbyterian mission who sought to challenge this restriction. Further still, when the leaders of the Northern Presbyterian Mission of Korea attempted to break free of these entanglements with the Korean state after Heron's death, they found that their prestige was tied to the hospital and were unwilling to simply give up their connection. Only over time would their work at Chejungwŏn become a less important component of their mission. Later heads of the government hospital learned to be careful about the relationships they formed with Kojong.[83] More broadly, starting in the early 1890s, missionaries sought to distance themselves from the central government and to ensure that their relationships with the state remained untangled.

Chapter 2

Creating Separation

Moving Beyond Treaty Ports

Chejungwŏn serves as a reminder that from nearly the very start of the missionary movement in Korea, potential for conflict and friction existed among missionaries, who needed to balance competing religious and political demands. Politics was, in short, a potentially destabilizing element in the missionary movement. But, balanced differently, politics could also serve to advance the religious aims of the mission societies. To begin with, missionaries were not transient figures simply passing through the peninsula. Instead, they were "residents," and they planned to spend years of their lives in Korea. Put differently, Horace N. Allen, Horace G. Underwood, and John Heron not only represented the first generation of Protestant missionaries to the country; they also represented the first generation of Westerners to reside in Korea as expatriates.[1]

The missionaries' presence in Korea was based on legal rights secured through treaty provisions. They were permitted to land, reside, and work in "open ports." However, these provisions only provided a broad framework. How the rights and privileges outlined in existing treaties would be put into practice was yet to be determined when the missionaries first arrived. For instance, the 1882 treaty between the United States and Korea had included a clause that a cemetery for Americans would be designated by the Korean government. It was not until Heron suddenly passed away in 1890 that this clause required action. The US legation and Korean government engaged in a brief contest over establishing a suitable plot for the foreign community. Frustrated over a perceived lack of urgency on the part of the Korean government, the mission community—without objection from the US legation—decided to bury Heron at his residence. In response, and in haste, before the burial took place, the Korean government offered Yanghwajin.[2]

As this brief conflict over creating a foreigner's cemetery reveals, the place of missionaries and, more broadly, the expatriate community was ambiguous during the late nineteenth century. Missionaries actively turned to their legations to bring clarity to how their treaty rights would be instituted in practice. For example, were there limits to the missionaries' "right" to travel and to own property in the country? Were there limits on how they interacted with or employed Koreans? Did they have the right to voice opinions regarding the reforms the country required to become a modern nation? In seeking answers to these types of questions, missionaries demanded that their legations advocate on their behalf. These forays into the political sphere as private citizens seeking to define treaty rights put into place a pattern of interaction with their legations that would play a key role in allowing missionaries to expand beyond treaty ports and advance their religious endeavors during the late nineteenth century.

Missionaries, Modernity, and Extraterritoriality

Many missionaries to Korea came to feel a deep attachment to the country and developed strong opinions regarding how it should be reformed. Their interest reflected the fact that King Kojong had explicitly invited missionaries to serve as educators and doctors in order to modernize the country. With the approval of government officials, missionaries established hospitals, schools, orphanages, and other social institutions. Through these institutions, they shaped a rising generation of Korean men and women and were a part of the general discourse regarding the future of the country. To this extent, individuals like Allen, Underwood, and Heron were a part of local society. Yet, as a comparison with the Independence Club (Tongnip hyŏphoe) will reveal, missionaries and Korean reformers occupied different positions in relation to the state.

During the late 1890s, the Independence Club was one of the major nodes of discourse for Korean intellectuals around modernity. Established in 1896, the club sought to facilitate the modernization of Korea through public debates on contemporary sociopolitical issues of concern for the country and other public projects. It both supported and clashed with the early efforts of Kojong to centralize power and create a modern state.[3] For example, a modern Korean nation-state required articulating equality with China.[4] Along these lines, one of the first efforts of the Independence Club was to destroy Yŏngŭn Gate, which was where Korean officials had greeted envoys from China for much of the Chosŏn dynasty (1392–1910). The gate was a symbolic reminder of Korea's tributary relationship to China and thus of Korea's supposed inferior status. As a gesture to Korea's equality with China, then, club members advanced the project of not only tearing down this gate but also building a new structure, dubbed the Independence Gate, on the same site. The Independence Club ran a drive to collect the funds necessary to achieve this goal. Because this project originated outside formal state structures—though a number of officials were members of the club—and because of its private funding, Kojong could justifiably point to it as popular support for his regime. Indeed, the creation of the Independence Gate supported his own attempts to assert the country's equality with China, as he took the title of emperor and declared the establishment of the Taehan Empire.[5]

The Independence Club also, however, pursued measures that undermined Kojong's efforts to strengthen the power of the monarchy. In particular, the club sought to create a legislative assembly. Bolstered by the addition of high-ranking officials as members, the club gathered in late October 1898 for what it called the Assembly of Officials and People (Kwanmin kongdonghoe). It submitted six articles to the throne, which together demanded a constitutional form of government and the establishment of an elected legislative body. At this point, Kojong permitted officials who had been critical of the Independence Club to take action. By January of the following year, the club was disbanded, and many of its leaders were arrested.[6]

Often overlooked in studies of the emergence of the Independence Club is the fact that at the same time its members were discussing the need for modern reforms, missionaries in Korea were also speaking of the reforms the country needed to become an "enlightened" nation. They shared many perspectives with the Independence Club. In fact, prominent club members such as Sŏ Chae-p'il, Yun Ch'i-ho, and An Ch'ang-ho were Christians and had close ties to the missionary community.

Missionaries and members of the Independence Club used similar means to spread their ideas to the general populace. For example, the first newspaper to be published in pure vernacular Korean script was the *Independent (Tongnip sinmun)*. The paper started publication in April 1896, several months before the founding of the Independence Club, and continued publishing after the club was disbanded, until September 1899. Though not technically an organ of the club, the paper was established by Sŏ Chae-p'il and thus quickly became associated with the Independence Club and its progressive ideals. Discussing topics such as civil society and Western knowledge, this paper drew a clear connection between Western modernity and Christianity. Roughly one year after the *Independent*'s founding, Underwood started to publish the *Christian News (Kŭrisŭdo sinmun)*, which was also written in pure vernacular Korean script.[7] The readership of this paper, as with other papers at the time, is unknowable, but it is reasonable to assume that the audience of the *Christian News* was comparable to that of the *Independent*. Those Korean intellectuals, reformers, and officials who were interested in the latter would likely have perused the former, as Underwood included articles on topics such as the theory of time, cartography, horticulture, and the political systems of the world. In addition, because Underwood published the paper, a large number of Christians, both in the city and in the countryside, looked to its pages for information.

Although often running articles urging Koreans to be loyal to the state, Underwood's paper promoted similar ideas as the *Independent* and offered its Korean audience a vision of modern society that at times diverged from what Kojong sought to advance. The *Christian News* set a tone with the opening editorial of its inaugural issue. This editorial first criticized Koreans for blindly memorizing the Confucian classics and lacking comprehension of things even a child in the West grasped. It continued by arguing that knowledge included an understanding of such things as the principles of creation, the political systems of other nations, and the customs of different cultures, an understanding that would benefit the people *(paeksŏng)* and country *(nara)*. It thus called for Koreans to break free from two thousand years of tradition and pursue enlightenment *(kaehwa)*. The *Christian News*, the editorial declared, would give the people of Korea this needed knowledge.[8]

In actions as well as words, missionaries could both support and diverge from the interests of the state. Underwood organized a large celebration in honor of Kojong's birthday in 1897, the first year of the Taehan Empire. Lillias Underwood, Horace's wife, boasted that nearly all the missionaries in the city and a large contingent of officials attended the event.[9] The celebration included prayers and the singing of Christian hymns. In this sense, it was designed to portray Christianity as a religion that supported the Korean state and emperor. But Underwood's celebration also had the potential to clash with Kojong's visions for his new government. Indeed, in preparation for the official establishment of the Taehan Empire, Kojong constructed the Ring Hill Altar (Wŏn'gudan), which was modeled on the Temple of Heaven (Tiantan) in Beijing, the site where the emperor of China offered sacrifices biannually.[10] These rituals solidified his right to rule as the "son of heaven," the link between heaven and earth. The attempts by Underwood and his colleagues to advance Christianity as a religion that buttressed the Taehan Empire conflicted with the rituals that Kojong saw as supporting his rule.

Kojong disbanded the Independence Club because its vision of modern reforms clashed with his own. Missionaries promoted similar ideas. However, because of the missionaries' status under extraterritoriality, government officials were unable to directly suppress missionary discourse and actions. Extraterritoriality has long been considered important in the study of nineteenth-century missions. For example, one common scholarly explanation for the tremendous growth of Christianity in Korea during the late nineteenth century is that missionaries effectively proved the power of their religion by using this treaty provision (and diplomatic pressure) to bend local officials to their will. They supposedly manipulated their status as beyond the reach of the Korean judicial system to win favorable verdicts for their converts. Their intervention allegedly ranged from indirectly pressuring local officials to side with Christians to actively inserting themselves in local disputes. This "proof" of the efficacy of Christianity is said to have attracted large numbers of converts.[11]

The argument that extraterritoriality granted missionaries power has oversimplified the complex relationship that existed between missionaries, their legations, and the Korean government.[12] First and foremost, Protestant missionaries were vocal in maintaining that they adhered to a strict principle of separation of church and state. In large part, this was in response to the history of anti-Catholic persecutions that marked nineteenth-century Korea. American missionaries were well aware of these violent occurrences, and they attributed the Korean government's disdain for and aggressive treatment of Catholicism to the actions of Roman Catholic missionaries, who supposedly transgressed local laws and directly challenged state authority. Henry Loomis, who was stationed in Japan, explained to Francis Ellinwood that Catholic missionaries had a long history of defying Korean laws and that one Korean convert even went so far as to invite foreign powers to invade.[13]

To Protestant missionaries, this history demonstrated the inherent unreliability of the Catholic Church and confirmed that Catholics lacked a true national identity. In contrast, though their actions would later contradict their claims, Protestant missionaries in Korea argued that they respected the right of local governments to rule and that the adoption of Protestant Christianity did not undermine existing political structures. Indeed, Protestant missionaries contended that instead of challenging the state, Protestantism would ultimately produce loyal subjects. They were confident that once the government recognized this fact, it would actively promote the adoption of this religion.[14] Indeed, in 1896, Horace Underwood reported with pride a local magistrate's comment that the Protestants in the region were the best-behaved Koreans.[15] With this in mind, missionaries generally eschewed the use of extraterritoriality as a means to circumvent the Korean state or to provide protection for converts. In fact, as will be examined in more detail in chapter 3, because of a fear that many coming to the church possessed impure, materialistic motives, missionaries insisted in their reports to their friends and superiors that they consistently reminded those seeking conversion that a believer was expected to observe all laws.

Purchasing Property

Extraterritoriality placed Western legations in positions to mediate disputes between missionaries and the Korean government.[16] Importantly, Western legations and missionaries were two separate and distinct sets of actors, and the latter were subordinate to the former.[17] Diplomatic support for Christian activities was not guaranteed. Instead, missionaries had to convince their legations to advocate on their behalf. At least initially, missionaries turned to their legations not to secure a right to proselytize or even express opinions that ran contrary to the government but rather for help simply to reside in Korea. For example, they complained about the lack of safety and the problem of theft. In one early instance, an official from the US legation wrote to the Foreign Office of the Korean government, stating that thieves not only had stolen various items from the home of William Scranton but had even gone so far as to steal the doors. The official requested that security be extended to include the residences of all Americans—not just diplomats—living in Seoul.[18]

By the early 1890s, the focus of the missionaries' complaints turned toward difficulties in purchasing property. As established by treaty law, American citizens were permitted to purchase property in "open ports" and Seoul. According to prescribed procedure, after the signing of a contract, the purchaser had to send it to the US legation, which in turn would submit the document to the Foreign Office. If the agreement was found to be without fault, the Foreign Office would affix its seal and return the document to the US legation, which would hand the deed over to the purchaser. In practice, missionaries often encountered problems in purchasing property. For instance, in one early case, the Foreign Office wrote to the legation requesting that the deed to a piece of property purchased by Homer Hulbert in Seoul in 1888 be revoked on the grounds that the Korean seller was not the legitimate owner of the property. Hugh Dinsmore, who was in charge of the US legation, protected Hulbert's interests, responding that because Hulbert had legally purchased the property and possessed a certified deed, fully approved by the Foreign Office, the legation had no authority to strip Hulbert of his ownership.[19]

Initially just a personal matter, as time wore on, the issue of property ownership came to form a fundamental and critical aspect of the missionaries' efforts to expand their evangelistic efforts. As noted in chapter 1, by the late 1880s, individuals such as Horace Underwood were increasingly challenging Horace Allen's conservative strategy regarding evangelism. Underwood believed that the Korean government was aware of their activities and willfully turned a blind eye to their work. Meanwhile, missionaries reported that Koreans seemed eager to convert. Starting in 1886, missionaries had taken advantage of a provision in France's treaty with Korea granting French citizens the right to travel in the interior with valid passports. Because the US-Korea treaty included a most-favored-nation clause, this right extended to Americans. Missionaries embarked on itineration trips throughout the Korean countryside and reported that Koreans seemed receptive to the gospel. Given that pockets of Korean Christians already existed in the northern half of the peninsula, both Methodist and Presbyterian missionaries became increasingly confident that Koreans would convert in large numbers if only given an opportunity. In October 1890, the Presbyterian camp decided to pursue a "more aggressive, systematized evangelistic work," part of which included establishing bases of operation outside Seoul.[20]

Starting in 1891, the Presbyterians moved to purchase property in various parts of the peninsula. However, the missionaries' difficulties in purchasing property increased the farther they traveled from Seoul. In February, William Baird, Horace Underwood, and Samuel A. Moffett approached Augustine Heard, head of the US legation at the time, regarding the purchase of property in Pusan. They informed Heard of their plans to acquire land and requested that he approach the Foreign Office for a letter of approval before they began their trip south. Heard suggested that these three travel to Pusan and "arrange everything 'locally,'"[21] arguing that the Foreign Office would be less likely to reject a sale that was already an "accomplished fact." However, contrary to Heard's prediction, Baird, Underwood, and Moffett found the local officials unwilling to approve the purchase of property without sanction from the Foreign Office. They again requested assistance from Heard, who sent a message to the Foreign Office the next day. But the Foreign Office did not officially respond to Heard until late March (well after the missionaries, perhaps tired of waiting, had returned to Seoul). Citing the fact that a foreign settlement in Pusan had yet to be established and claiming that the right to purchase property in "open ports" pertained only to merchants, it rejected the missionaries' request.[22]

The subsequent history of this attempt illustrates the nuances of the relationships between the missionaries, the US legation, and the Korean government. After the missionaries' initial request was rejected, Heard responded in protest, arguing first that no distinction was made in any treaty provision concerning the occupation of foreigners wishing to purchase property in treaty ports. Thus, as American citizens, Underwood and his colleagues possessed every right to purchase property and reside in Pusan. And second, Heard pointed out that although there was no established foreign concession in Pusan, the grounds of a British consul site had been "designated." The property that the missionaries sought to purchase was close by; surely that property would fall within the radius of the foreign concession stipulated by treaty provision, whenever the consulate was established.[23]

Several days after this protest, the head of the Foreign Office visited Heard. He stated that his main fear about the Pusan sale was that the missionaries were attempting to establish a school. In support of his argument, he noted that the plot of land was much too large for a residence. Heard consulted with Baird, who informed him that the property was intended for two houses, not one. Armed with this information, Heard explained the situation to the Foreign Office and demanded that the deeds be approved. The Foreign Office conceded.[24] But in another twist, Heard later learned that the size of the property was much greater than what the missionaries had originally told him, which called into question the claim that the property was for two houses.[25] Heard chastised Baird and lamented having abused the power of his office against his Korean counterpart.[26]

The outlines of this encounter complicate the overly simple narrative of Westerners wresting concessions from a naïve foreign government. First, the Korean government correctly assessed the missionaries' intention to spread Christianity outside Seoul. Horace Allen later explained to Ellinwood in a private letter that officials were wary of Underwood and his aggressive efforts at evangelism.[27] They thus forcefully resisted the sale of land to the Presbyterians, using any means at their disposal—objecting to the missionaries' "nonmerchant" status, referring to a need to first establish a local foreign concession, and finally questioning the size of the lot for the missionaries' stated purpose. Second, the missionaries attempted to advance their work by using their treaty rights as citizens of the United States. Baird, Underwood, and Moffett knew that whatever his feelings about their mission, Heard was obligated to assist them as US citizens. Finally, Heard's defense of the missionaries was circumscribed to interpretations of existing treaty laws and was not a blind endorsement of their arguments or their desire to spread Christianity. Indeed, as his response on learning of the missionaries' deception regarding the size of the property suggests, Heard would not have campaigned on their behalf had he been fully aware of all the facts.

P'yŏngyang Persecution

In the case of treaty ports like Pusan, the missionaries could make a relatively solid case for the rights to purchase property and to reside in the city. Their attempts to secure land elsewhere would prove more difficult. Though missionaries could travel freely outside "open ports," they had no legal right to purchase property in the interior. Not surprisingly, when they attempted to circumvent this problem through a manipulation of existing statutes, conflicts erupted between missionaries and the Korean state. The first major conflict was the P'yŏngyang Persecution of 1894.[28] For many critics of missionaries, the P'yŏngyang Persecution represents an abuse of extraterritoriality, and the missionaries' "victory" over the state supposedly demonstrated the power of Protestant Christianity in the eyes of the local populace—leading many to flock to the church in order to take advantage of the missionaries' strength.[29] More important to this inquiry, however, is the light the P'yŏngyang Persecution sheds on aspects of the missionaries' conflict with both the Korean government and their respective legations.

During the first half of the 1890s, the missionaries became more aggressive in itinerating through the Korean countryside. But these trips were costly, tiresome, and dangerous. Thus, both Methodists and Presbyterians sought opportunities to establish bases outside Seoul. In particular, the Northern Presbyterians had long believed that P'yŏngyang was a strategic location. However, their knowledge of the city was limited. Moffett, who arrived in 1890, was scheduled to make a month-long trip through the northern half of the peninsula as a part of his language training during his first year in the field. Taking advantage of this timing, the Northern Presbyterian Mission tasked him with investigating P'yŏngyang and the surrounding vicinity.[30] Moffett would become a strong advocate for choosing the city as the site of the Presbyterians' station in the northern provinces of Korea.[31] In 1893 the Presbyterian missionaries in Korea decided to act on Moffett's recommendation. However, P'yŏngyang was not an "open port," and thus missionaries could not legally purchase property there.

It was apparently the Catholics who provided the Presbyterians with a strategy to circumvent Korean restrictions. In 1891, as Baird was attempting to start a new base in Pusan, an "open port" city, he had reported that Catholic missionaries were residing in the Korean countryside. Unsure whether they had bought property in their own names or had done so in the name of a Korean follower, Baird suggested to his superiors that the Northern Presbyterian Mission consider purchasing property in the name of a Korean convert.[32] While no record that Moffett conversed with Baird regarding this strategy exists, Moffett put it into action.[33] After initially failing in his attempt to purchase property in P'yŏngyang, he secured a building in the name of a Korean Christian, Han Sŏk-chin, in July 1893.[34]

The Methodists gained a foothold in P'yŏngyang in the same year using similar tactics. William Hall, a Methodist missionary and doctor, made an initial foray into the city in the spring of 1892 but found the edicts against Christianity very firm. He made another trip in September of that year and later reported that his tireless medical treatment of patients had succeeded in securing the goodwill of not only the general populace but also the governor. As evidence, he stated that the governor had appointed several guards for his protection. In fact, this protective measure more likely reflected the governor's desire to avoid an international incident should Hall be harmed by crowds. Nevertheless, in part because of this appearance of goodwill, Hall pushed the Methodist mission board to open a station in P'yŏngyang. They assented and appointed him in charge. In April of the following year, he purchased two pieces of property in the name of his Korean assistant.[35]

Both the Methodist and the Presbyterian missionaries in P'yŏngyang went about their business without incident until May 1894. Hall offered a firsthand account of the early days of the government crackdown:

> About one o'clock Thursday morning we were awakened by two of the native Christians, who informed us that our faithful helper, Chang Si-key, and the former owner of the house we were stopping in, had been cast into prison. . . . Early in the morning I went to the governor's, but he was sleeping, and I could not see him. I then went to the prison and found that, in addition to our men, the helper of Mr. Moffett, of the Presbyterian Mission, and also the former owner of the house that the helper lived in, were both in prison; and that same night policemen had gone to where Mr. Moffett stopped when in Pyong Yang and cruelly beat all the native Christians that were there.[36]

Hall reported that the local officials continually threatened to have these Christians executed and that his efforts to persuade the governor to intervene were fruitless. He later learned that this was because the governor himself had approved the arrests. Hall telegraphed Scranton, who notified his Presbyterian counterparts and the US legation. Because Hall, a Canadian, was technically a British subject, the British consul-general took charge in an attempt to pressure the Korean court to release those imprisoned.

The missionaries reported that the Foreign Office had informed them that the Koreans had been imprisoned for "preaching Christianity." Both the British and US legations protested, insisting that no laws had been broken. They demanded that these Korean Christians, some of whom were employed by the missionaries, be released. Although the Korean government was reluctant to give in, the Korean Christians were temporarily freed. Despite this victory, the missionaries initially feared that the final resolution of the conflict would involve a protracted diplomatic struggle among the Korean, British, and American governments. According to Daniel Gifford, a Presbyterian missionary working with Moffett to establish a base in P'yŏngyang, at issue were two points: missionary residence in the interior and the right to preach Christianity in Korea. On the first point, the missionaries assumed their governments would insist that their citizens should enjoy the same rights as French priests, some of whom allegedly resided outside treaty ports. On the second point, Gifford wrote that "it is too late in the day to stop it [preaching]." Though cautiously optimistic that missionaries would eventually be able to expand their work on the Korean Peninsula, he concluded that fighting for these rights would take time and slow their entry into non–treaty port cities.[37]

The situation suddenly shifted, however—not once but twice. Gifford's initial letter reporting that the conflict would take a great deal of time to resolve was written on May 12. Only five days later, he penned a follow-up letter stating that the matter would be settled shortly.[38] Both the British and US legations indicated to the missionary community that neither was prepared to fight for the "right" of their subjects or citizens to reside in the interior if the Korean government insisted on this point. Thus, Hall was required to vacate the property he was "renting" in P'yŏngyang and hand it back to the Korean Christian whose name was on the deed. In this manner, the British legation ordered the Methodists to withdraw from the city and, at least temporarily, halt their proselytization efforts. The missionaries' initial foray into the city appeared to have been rebuffed.

But the summer witnessed another major event, tilting the situation back in the missionaries' favor. In closing his letter regarding the refusal of the British and US legations to support the missionaries' efforts to reside in the interior, Gifford noted in passing that trouble was brewing in the southern half of the peninsula. He described the unrest as fomented by "over-taxed people" who were "arising against the officials."[39] Here he was referring to the beginnings of the Tonghak Peasant Uprising, which will be covered in more detail in chapter 4. For now, the importance of this uprising was that it served as the pretext for China and Japan to send troops to the peninsula and so catalyzed the First Sino-Japanese War (1894–1895). Not incidentally, P'yŏngyang became the scene of a major land battle between Chinese and Japanese forces in mid-August. The chaos produced during this period allowed missionaries to return to P'yŏngyang during the second half of 1894.

Briefly stated, though the British legation had required Hall and the Methodists to withdraw from P'yŏngyang, the Presbyterians still controlled their property, and Moffett was not prepared to abandon the city without a contest. In late May, he took a new approach to convincing John Sills, head of the US legation, to intervene on the Presbyterians' behalf: he insisted that the Korean government had violated their treaty rights. Moffett made five points: (1) he had provided money for a Korean to purchase the property but never claimed ownership; (2) he had never acted as though he were residing at said property but stayed in a room as he would at an inn; (3) the deeds were recorded at the required office; (4) the property was held in trust by three Koreans residing in Seoul; and (5) because Min had not demanded the return of the "Presbyterian" property, Moffett preferred that Sills refrain from broaching this issue. In making this argument, Moffett certainly stretched the truth. In particular, though his Korean helper technically owned the property, the missionaries kept the deed in their possession. Glossing over this inconvenient fact, Moffett insisted that at no time did he overtly or even indirectly transgress "treaty or law" in the matter of the residence. He allowed that on the issue of evangelism and the practice of Christianity one could potentially make the case that the missionaries were breaking the law, but as a caveat he added that neither the Korean government nor the governor was making any such claim. Because there was no transgression of the law, Moffett concluded that the Korean Christians had been arrested solely because of their employment with the missionaries—although treaty law permitted American citizens to hire Korean subjects. Thus, because there was no legal basis for imprisonment or torture, Moffett argued that Korean officials had violated the missionaries' legal rights, and he insisted that Sills intervene on their behalf.[40]

Moffett argued to Sills that the events in P'yŏngyang were in reality a persecution of Christians. However, the missionaries did not seek redress for the imprisonment and torture of Korean Christians. He indicated a firm understanding that the US legation would not support the mission community on the issue of religious freedom.

Thus, in regards to the fate of those arrested Korean Christians who were not employed by the mission, Moffett wrote:

> On the subject of Christianity it is evident from the position of the legations as to our having no treaty right to preach the Gospel . . . that we can look for no protection for the native Christians. Leaving them to the care of Him who cares for us all we will confine ourselves just now to seeking protection for our employees and the preservation of our right to employ them. . . . You will find us ready to obey all laws and treaty provisions in every respect and ready to make reparations wherever and whenever we may contravene them but at the same time ask that all our rights be carefully guarded and that so far as possible all privileges granted to other nations be secured for us.[41]

Importantly, in making this argument, Moffett felt that he was plotting a conservative course. In later justifying his tactics, he readily admitted that some might view his response as slowing the Presbyterians' penetration of the Korean interior. However, he stressed that neither the British nor the American legation was willing to press for the spread of Christianity and that he desired to remain above reproach in the eyes of both the Korean and American governments.[42]

For most of the summer, the Korean government ignored Sills's calls that the officials responsible for the arrest of the Korean Christians be punished and that Moffett be compensated for the violation of his treaty rights. However, in late July 1894, the Sino-Japanese War erupted, and in mid-August, on the eve of the Battle of P'yŏngyang, the Korean government suddenly satisfied Sills's demands. Gifford suggested this change was because Korean officials sought US diplomatic support. Whatever the reason, the central government ordered that those responsible for the imprisonment and torture of Moffett's employees be punished. In addition, the governor was required to pay a fee to compensate Moffett both for his travel to the city and for the telegrams the missionaries sent between P'yŏngyang and Seoul as a result of this incident.[43] With this verdict in hand, after the Battle of P'yŏngyang, both the Presbyterian and Methodist missionaries quietly returned to the city.

The Taegu Incident (1900)

The P'yŏngyang Persecution failed to resolve the issue of missionary residence in the interior. Sales via proxies increased after 1894, practiced by missionaries and other foreigners. From 1896 to 1900, magistrates noted on numerous occasions that foreigners were, in violation of treaty laws, residing outside of "open ports."[44] These officials submitted relatively similar complaints to the center, typically containing three points. They commenced by citing treaty law, which stated that foreigners could not reside, rent, or own property outside a zone of ten *li* (roughly three miles) from treaty ports. They continued by describing the refusal of foreigners to vacate property. Finally, they concluded by bemoaning their inability to prevent foreigners from violating treaty provisions and penetrating the interior. The uniformity and number of these reports suggests a concerted effort on the part of the central government both to regain control over local society and to instruct magistrates how to restrict the movement of foreigners. However, the inability to prevent foreigners from living in the interior was a constant reminder of the central government's ineffectiveness in controlling their spread outside of treaty ports. Perhaps because of the frustration generated by this situation, local officials became more aggressive in their treatment of missionaries and Christian communities. Beginning in 1900, the US legation fielded complaints from missionaries in areas with large Christian populations, such as Sŏnch'ŏn, Suwŏn, Ŭiju, P'yŏngyang, and Taegu, concerning veiled threats and crackdowns.[45]

Although it was neither the first nor the only conflict, the situation in Taegu became the most significant. Horace Allen—who was in charge of the US legation at the time—decided to make the city the basis of his protest of all similar cases in the country. Though the missionaries of Taegu and the governor of the province disagreed about what exactly had transpired, the following can be stated with a degree of certainty. In 1896, the Northern Presbyterians purchased a house and established a new station in Taegu.[46] James Adams oversaw the Presbyterians' work in the city in the early decades. He soon came to believe that this location, as opposed to Pusan, should be the center of the Northern Presbyterian Mission's work in the southeastern portion of the peninsula,[47] and the station grew as he was joined by other workers. In early 1900, Adams purchased another piece of property in the name of his helper, Kim Tae-gyŏng. In April of that year, Kim Yong-ho, the governor of North Kyŏngsang Province and the acting magistrate of Taegu, wrote to the Foreign Office protesting this purchase, claiming that the missionaries desired to use it to spread Christianity; in fact, he accused the missionaries of building a church.[48] A formal complaint was then sent from the Foreign Office to the US legation. Allen responded, as he had when dealing with similar disputes in other regions of the peninsula, by maintaining that no treaty law had been transgressed because a Korean subject was the legal owner.[49]

In this instance, however, Allen's explanation proved ineffective. Some six months later, in November, officers were dispatched to the residence where Adams was staying. They entered without permission and arrested Kim Tae-gyŏng. The pretext for the arrest was a dispute between the missionaries and a local tile maker. In the fall of 1900, Kim had contracted a purchase of tiles on behalf of the missionaries. However, the tile maker later refused to honor the contract. When the missionaries applied pressure, the tile maker went to the governor, who then ordered the magistrate to arrest Kim. Following the arrest, the missionaries went to the jail and, after presenting the contract for the tiles, secured Kim's release. But Kim was arrested again in early December; this time, he was not only thrown into prison but also severely beaten. Though the governor ultimately ruled in favor of the missionaries and forced the tile maker to refund about half of the amount they had prepaid, he nevertheless found Kim guilty of having "aided foreigners" and ruled that his beating had been justified.[50]

The missionaries in Taegu were displeased that the governor had found Kim guilty, and they asked the US legation to intervene. Allen put his energies into winning a favorable resolution to the Taegu Incident. In his official protest to the Foreign Office, he reasoned that the missionaries' purchase of property through a proxy and residence in Taegu were in accordance with treaty law. On this point, Allen noted that American citizens were permitted to travel in the interior with valid travel documents. Logic therefore dictated that they were also permitted to secure suitable lodging and food. Given their special needs as Westerners, their desire to secure "appropriate" lodgings was reasonable, and there was nothing inherently illegal about forwarding money to a Korean to ensure a place suitable for their needs.[51] Allen then went further to argue that because other foreign nationals were present in Taegu and residing in the city in plain sight, the local magistrate and governor were unjustified in singling out missionaries. If Korean officials insisted on discriminating against Americans, he threatened, he would have no choice but to bring this issue of land ownership and targeted discrimination to his superiors at the US Department of State.

Regarding the dispute with the tile merchant, Allen protested that the officials in Taegu had transgressed treaty agreements. He cited section 9 of article 3 of the British-Korean treaty, which stated that Korean officials were not authorized to enter any domicile where a British national resided without receiving either consular permission or the permission of the British resident. Because the US-Korea treaty included a most-favored-nation clause, all provisions in the British treaty were automatically granted to all Americans. Glossing over the fact that Adams's residence was officially owned by a Korean, Allen argued that no such attempt was made by the officers when they entered the residence where Adams was staying. Further, he pointed to section 1 of article 9 of the US-Korea treaty, which stated that American citizens were permitted to employ Koreans. In this instance, the specific charge against Kim was, as noted above, that he had assisted the missionaries in their contracting of the clay tiles.[52] Allen maintained that the governor's judgment was in blatant violation of the treaty provisions, as Americans had a right to employ Koreans. Ultimately, based on Allen's complaint, the Foreign Office ruled in favor of the missionaries and ordered that they be compensated.

The incident at Taegu captures how, by the turn of the twentieth century, Presbyterian missionaries had distanced themselves from the Korean government. They did so both spatially, as they joined the Methodists in attempting to spread beyond "open ports" and establish outposts throughout the peninsula, and relationally, as they shifted the ways they interacted with the Korean state. Missionaries argued that they respected the political authority of the state and, at the same time, challenged state authority. That said, they did not directly call for religious freedom. Instead, they entered the political sphere as private citizens claiming their treaty rights. In practice, this strategy provided them a means to establish stations and expand their evangelistic work outside of treaty ports, where, as will be seen in the next chapter, they were pleased to discover that many were receptive to the gospel. However, this method of engaging the state as private citizens was not an enduring solution; as chapters 6 and 7 will show, it proved not only ineffective but a liability when approaching colonial officials.

Chapter 3

The Conversion Conundrum

The Nevius Method and the Problem of "Rice Christians"

The Presbyterian and Methodist missionaries pressed hard to extend their reach into the northern provinces during the 1890s in part because of the apparent eagerness of Koreans in these regions to convert. It seemed they had found "gold" in Korea.[1] They described how Koreans traveled miles to attend Sunday services, quit jobs that were morally questionable, and devoted themselves to studying religious tracts. Affirming these reports was Robert E. Speer, who visited Korea from 1896 to 1897. As a secretary with the Board of Foreign Missions of the Presbyterian Church in the USA (BFMPCUSA; Home Board), Speer received regular briefings from missionaries across the globe with stories of both success and failure; he was not predisposed to view modest gains with untempered optimism. In regards to Korea, however, he wrote glowingly of the tremendous inroads Presbyterian missionaries had made. Contrasting their treatment on the peninsula to that of their counterparts in China, he wrote: "Instead of being called 'devil,' as missionaries and all foreigners are in interior China, the Koreans use the words of the highest respect, and their bearing in the country leaves nothing to be asked in the way of kindness and courtesy."[2]

Nevertheless, Speer felt the need to address the question of whether this growth was real. He explained that missionaries in Korea were careful not to engage in political affairs or solve worldly disputes; those seeking conversion entered the church with "high and genuine motives."[3] Though he frankly admitted that no one could predict whether such growth rates could be sustained, Speer was confident that the numerous conversions were genuine:

> Instances of individual conversion which are as thorough and satisfactory as any that are seen here [the United States], warm church life full of brotherly trust and co-operation, ex-Confucianists weeping over their sins and crying in their prayers, giving without urging and in full measure, and preferring this to any mission aid, such activity in personal work, and such desire for souls as are not common at home, men and women saved from adultery, drunkenness, and gross sin, and made clean and pure, a fervent love of the Bible, and a keen desire for more teaching,—Mr. Grant and I saw enough of all this to satisfy us, even making allowance for all merely superficial and imitative experience, that this work is true.[4]

He thus verified with enthusiasm the missionaries' reports from the Korea field.

Speer's apparent need to spend ample time justifying his judgment of the reports from Korea indicates that success in the field—which might have been simply a sign of good fortune, or perhaps of God's favor—aroused missionaries' suspicions. This was the conversion conundrum: the more Koreans seemed interested in converting, the more missionaries feared that they sought entry to the church with impure, materialistic motives. This fear was at least partially based on the experiences of missionaries throughout the nineteenth century in other mission fields, such as India and China. Apparently sincere and devoted converts would rise to leadership positions only to be discovered to be corrupt. Such experiences elsewhere in the world prompted missionaries in Korea to exercise caution as they examined Koreans for baptism and pondered handing full church control over to Korean Christian leaders.

The missionaries needed a system to ensure proper belief. How could they address the nagging question: had converts, including leaders, truly transformed from heathens to Christians? To this end, the Presbyterian missionaries adopted the Nevius Method, which became known as the representative missionary strategy of Korea. Though it was officially adopted only by the Presbyterians, other mission boards borrowed the basic principles of this policy. In theory, the Nevius Method sought to cultivate a strong native church by requiring local believers to take control of the church from the very beginning.

In practice, this strategy institutionalized the power of missionaries and required Koreans to demonstrate a true Christian transformation through the performance of acts of obedience to their new faith.

The Problem of "Rice Christianity"

Horace N. Allen, Horace G. Underwood, William Scranton, and Henry G. Appenzeller, the first missionaries of the Northern Presbyterian and Northern Methodist Boards, figure prominently in any telling of the early years of Korean Protestantism. The impressive missionary careers they carved out, however, obscure the fact that they were mere novices when they arrived in the country. They looked to more established fields for models of evangelism.

China in particular was a key source of information. Many of the first evangelists to arrive in China held lofty goals of converting a sea of unbelieving Chinese, only to realize that mission work was arduous. Aside from adjusting to life in a foreign country, new recruits to the field had to become fluent in not only the local language but also the local culture and history if they were to communicate with their audience. Though many missionaries earnestly invested a great deal of time and energy in acquiring the skills necessary to be effective, they remained reliant on the help of Chinese agents, who were often paid for their services. As their native agents led other Chinese to the church, missionaries could send positive letters and reports back home to mission boards and churches detailing how their funds were bringing about the Christianization of China.

In part, the missionaries' fixation on church growth stemmed from the need to demonstrate that they were effective evangelists. As noted in chapter 1, a spiritual desire to be a missionary was a necessary but not sufficient condition for joining a major mission organization such as the BFMPCUSA. These institutions were massive bureaucracies, and missionaries were professionals whose chosen vocation was spreading Christianity. To justify their positions and salaries, they had to show results: missionaries submitted annual reports, counting their success in terms of churches built, converts won, and souls saved. Moreover, whether in China, Korea, or another field, missionaries often opened and operated hospitals, schools, and other institutions, which required a great deal of capital. To justify the expenses not only to the mission board but also to friends, churches, and private donors who supported the world missionary movement, missionaries needed to show that their investments would lead to spiritual yields. To give just one example from the Korea field, in December 1890, Francis Ellinwood of the BFMPCUSA officially approved the purchase of property in Pusan and effectively established a mission station in that port city; in commenting on this expansion, Ellinwood noted that generous donations from John T. Underwood (the brother of Horace Underwood) "seem(ed) to require a positive advance."[5]

But the pressure to demonstrate their effectiveness in "advancing" Christianity also led to a dilemma regarding the "truth" of the conversions the missionaries oversaw. The church, with its considerable resources, faced a problem when it appeared as a source of material gain in the eyes of the local populace—the problem of so-called rice Christianity.[6] Throughout Asia, rice was not only a food staple but also a form of currency. The term "rice Christians" referred to those who came to the church seeking worldly profit, whether in terms of a job or political favor. By the late nineteenth century, this term was a part of missionary vernacular everywhere, but especially among those sent to Asia.

To an extent, the missionaries' use of the term "rice Christianity" denoted their arrogance and disdain of the local population, calling into question the sincerity of their efforts to treat converts as equals. Indeed, the phrase seems to support the cultural imperialist critique that many missionaries harbored racist attitudes of superiority: natives were objects to be converted but would always be inferior in the eyes of their Western counterparts. Yet to reduce the use of the phrase "rice Christianity" to racism marginalizes the concern that led to its invention. Missionaries knew that many who sought conversion did so for material gain. These individuals would convert, secure positions of power, and eventually damage the church by inciting a scandal. And missionaries exacerbated the problem by relying on paid native agents to increase church membership quickly, thus making conversion a gateway to gainful employment. Though these workers might have been sincere in their own conversion and may have truly desired to spread the gospel, they were often employed without sufficient theological training and lacked the knowledge to provide effective spiritual leadership.

Employing unqualified and spiritually unprepared workers was particularly problematic when they met skeptics who posed difficult philosophical questions. For example, many missionaries in Asia were both aware and critical of Karl Gutzlaff's failed Chinese Union.

Believing that Chinese agents were better able than foreigners to convert their compatriots, Gutzlaff in 1844 had established a cadre of workers to spread the gospel outside established treaty ports. Critics, however, accused Gutzlaff's agents of lacking a solid grasp of concepts such as sin and of simply reciting, in their preaching, information they had memorized. When challenged on points of doctrine, these workers often reverted to interpreting biblical truths in terms of folk culture or Confucianism.[7]

In the case of Korea, the first generation of missionaries to the country assumed that the problem of rice Christianity would be even greater in their field than in China, given the Koreans' extreme poverty. Missionaries like Underwood, Appenzeller, and Scranton were concerned about rice Christians and viewed this subset of converts as potential sources of danger.[8] Indeed, less than a decade after the founding of the Northern Methodist Mission in Korea, missionaries noted that one of their first converts had severely damaged the reputation of their work in the country. After this individual's initial conversion, he apparently had a true awakening to his faith and quickly advanced up the ranks to occupy a position of leadership. The missionaries later learned that this man had been extorting money from those under his supervision. The Methodists lamented that this corruption on the part of a church leader recognized by missionaries, Korean Christians, and the general populace had cast their work in a negative light.[9] This case was not unique, and some missionaries went so far as to characterize many potential believers as having a "mercenary" spirit, seeking to learn how much they could gain from entering the church. Even when Koreans converted for purely spiritual reasons and gave up their former lifestyles, they often "backslid"; the realities of being a true Christian led many converts to return to their "heathen ways" when life became too hard.

Given this ongoing problem, determining sincerity of belief was important to build church communities that could have long-term success. Simply adding people to the membership roll might threaten not only the salvation of these individual "Christians" but also the salvation of *all* of the members of the church.[10] Assessing belief was difficult, however. Missionaries had to trust and work with Korean Christians while remaining ever vigilant for signs of insincerity or erosion of their initial commitment. Robert Speer captured this dilemma when describing a contradictory need to balance the "spirit of complete confidence and trust" with "the judgement of scrutiny."[11]

How could one simultaneously trust converts and suspect their motives? This riddle was a constant source of vexation.

Witnessing "True" Belief

The dual concern with growth and preventing "fake" Christians from damaging the health of the church posed a challenge to missionaries regardless of denomination. Even in the China field, where they had long battled "selfish elements," missionaries argued that to turn away those who came to the church on this basis was "un-Christian." Instead, they pointed out that rice Christianity was not a recent phenomenon. Rather, the practice of converting for material gain was as old as the history of this religion, and many believed that providing for the needy was a basic mission of the church. Some went as far as to question the validity of Christianity if faithful adherence to this faith did not result in visible, earthly gain. In other words, these missionaries pointed out that individuals came to Christianity for all types of reasons, and the purpose of the church was to "reform" their hearts and souls.[12]

Allowing rice Christians into the church, then, was a part of the missionaries' calling. They were responsible for the reform and transformation of each individual member who entered their church, despite the dangers they might pose. Yet the question remained: how could one trust the conversion of Koreans? Indeed, missionaries often complained that Koreans had no moral qualms about lying when it was expedient. In one case, Samuel Moore lamented that a convert shamelessly bragged about lying to avoid persecution from his non-converted compatriots.[13] Because of instances such as this, whether by questioning converts before baptism or by observing behavior, Protestant missionaries all sought signs of "sincerity."[14]

Catholics also realized that many came to the church for a myriad of worldly reasons. For example, Gustav Mutel of the Society of Foreign Missions of Paris noted that many Koreans who sought baptism lacked a true understanding of the religion and sought practical gain. While he expressed sympathy for these people, who were being oppressed by corrupt local officials, Mutel explained that he was doing his best to ensure that they would not damage the larger work of the Catholic Church.[15] The burden of discerning true faith rested on the shoulders of the priests who were stationed throughout the peninsula. One of these priests, who oversaw Catholic communities in Hwanghae Province from 1897 to 1903, was Joseph Wilhelm. He often wrote reports about individuals seeking to convert for selfish reasons and stated that he therefore avoided getting directly involved in most local political matters. He confidently boasted that many of these individuals left when they found that being Catholic was more onerous than the problems for which they had originally sought his assistance.[16] Wilhelm's confidence in the sincerity of the converts who remained stemmed from his observations of their actions. In his reports, he described Korean Catholics who stood up to various forms of persecution and approached their faith with seriousness. In one case, he recounted how a convert, during confession, asked to be forgiven for not attending weekly mass. This man explained that he lived forty *li*, approximately thirteen miles, away and thus could only attend every two weeks. Wilhelm marveled at this dedication, asking how many French Catholics would demonstrate remorse for failing to attend mass under such conditions.[17] As a Catholic priest, Wilhelm relied on his personal observations to assess his converts: he knew which followers were sincere because of their actions.

The concern over discerning true belief cut across the Catholic-Protestant divide. Missionaries, from Wilhelm to Underwood, observed potential converts to assess their motivations. Importantly, they sought to control not merely conversion but also membership in a church community. For example, Scranton reported to the Northern Methodist Mission Board that he carefully explained to potential converts the difference between baptism and church membership. He informed them baptism was a personal decision of individuals and a declaration of their desire to accept Jesus. Church membership, in contrast, he explained, was the decision of the church and a declaration of its satisfaction with the sincerity of believers.[18] In other words, while baptism represented an internal and private commitment to become members of a Methodist church community, Koreans needed to prove their sincerity to missionaries through external actions. Methodist missionaries spent time watching and observing Korean converts to ensure that they had experienced a true transformation in belief and behavior before accepting them as official church members.

The Nevius Method: A Hierarchy of Church Membership

Keeping abreast of developments in China, the Northern Presbyterians—at the urging of Underwood—invited John and Helen Nevius to

Seoul in 1890 to hear about a new method of evangelism that John had developed. The couple had arrived in China in 1853 and worked in Shandong Province. Some thirty years after his arrival, Nevius published a series of articles in the *Chinese Recorder,* the main missionary periodical in China at the time, detailing a new missionary method by which, after previous years of frustration, he had built a healthy congregation of Chinese Christians.[19] After listening to Nevius's presentation, Underwood and his colleagues decided to adopt this new mission strategy. Like the Methodists and Catholics in Korea, Northern Presbyterian missionaries also relied on visible evidence of a life transformed by Christian "truth." After their adoption of the Nevius Method, however, they differed from their colleagues in the systematic way they observed, tested, and categorized converts.[20]

In outlining his plan, John Nevius argued that missionaries were excessively concerned with quick growth.[21] As noted above, the need to produce results had the ironic effect of slowing church development by allowing converts with ulterior motives into the fold. Building on the missionary methods developed by Rufus Anderson and Henry Venn, Nevius sought to cultivate a strong indigenous church by requiring local believers to take control of their faith in three key sectors: church finances, church governance, and Christian evangelism. For example, missionaries were to refrain from providing money to build churches or other buildings. Rather, if native Christians desired to build a church, the responsibility to collect the funds to purchase land and erect a building lay with them. Though these church buildings would likely be modest, this method would prevent the problem of rice Christianity and allow native believers to take ownership of their newfound faith from the beginning.

In terms of governance and evangelism, the Nevius Method consisted of two interconnected parts: church membership and systematic learning and testing. In regards to the first part, Nevius outlined three levels of churchgoer. The first level lacked any formal association with the church. These were individuals who occasionally attended church events and services but had yet to declare a desire to convert. The second level consisted of catechumens. These were individuals who had expressed a desire to convert but were not full members of the church and had not yet received baptism. In general, missionaries sought to discern whether potential catechumens had demonstrated recognition of sin and a true commitment to Christianity. If accepted, they needed to obtain a catechism, a Bible, and other religious tracts to study. Typically within a year, missionaries gave catechumens a baptismal examination, at which time they judged the candidates' doctrinal grasp of Christianity and asked local church leaders whether the candidates had displayed a true knowledge of the faith as exhibited by their daily actions. If they passed, the catechumens were then baptized and finally considered full church members, the third level of churchgoer.[22]

In addition to these levels of membership, the Nevius Method outlined three basic relationships within the church. The first was between missionary and helper. Each missionary had a paid native helper. Helpers were supposed to have proven their sincerity over a long period and to have undergone a great deal of Christian instruction by attending Bible classes and studying under missionaries. They worked under the direct supervision of a missionary, acted as guides when missionaries made their itineration trips, and visited Christian communities to ensure that everything was in order. The second relationship was between leaders and members. Leaders were members of local churches who had received special training but remained part of the laity. They oversaw the local communities when missionaries and helpers were absent. The final relationship was between one member and another. Nevius envisioned members acting as both teachers and students to one another.[23]

In theory, the Nevius Method called for the cultivation of local leaders who would govern their churches and lead others to the Christian faith. In practice, it was a policy instituted and run by missionaries. Despite the language of creating independent indigenous churches, the Nevius Method afforded missionaries a great deal of power because it systematized their ability to test and categorize those seeking membership in the church. It thus effectively created a hierarchy of power. At the top sat the missionary, and each lower member had a designated set of responsibilities. Learning and testing occurred at each level of membership, and no matter one's sincerity as a Christian, the outside validation of someone higher up in the hierarchy was required to advance. For example, as noted above, those who desired to enter the church needed to demonstrate their knowledge and practice of the faith, first to be accepted as a catechumen, and then to pass the exam for baptism.

A quick look at two catechisms used in the Presbyterian missions—Horace Underwood's translation of John Nevius's tract for baptismal candidates and Samuel A. Moffett's translation of Helen

Nevius's tract for seekers and beginners—gives a sense of what Korean Christians were required to know. Underwood's translation was forty-six pages long and written in a question/answer format. What is striking is the thoroughness with which the catechism covers each topic and the immense amount of information catechumens were expected to learn. They studied everything from basic biblical facts, such as what was created on each of the seven days of creation, to deep theological issues, such as the underpinnings of the Trinity and the meaning of the Lord's Supper.[24] In contrast, Moffett's translation of Helen Nevius's catechism was divided into eight chapters that dealt with such topics as types of prayer, Bible study, Christian rituals, and church structure. If we characterize the catechism for baptismal candidates as an attempt to teach Koreans what they should believe, then the catechism for seekers and beginners was an attempt to teach not only *what* but also *how* to believe. For example, it included detailed information on (and sometimes examples of) family prayers, prayers of confession, and prayers for children. Moreover, when discussing Bible study, the tract for seekers and beginners exhorted readers not simply to read the words but to reflect on the meaning of what they read. Finally, it laid out a detailed order of worship for Sunday services. Through these catechisms, missionaries like Underwood and Moffett shaped the boundaries of both proper Christian belief and proper Christian practice on the peninsula.

Mastery of the catechisms, as well as of other study materials "recommended" by the missionaries, was required to pass the baptismal examination, which was rigorous. Candidates entered a room and faced at least one missionary, his helper, and the local church leaders, who posed a series of meticulous questions. Eugene Bell described the testing process for his parents:

> Each candidate for baptism is given a separate, private examination in the presence of the session and two Korean deacons, which is very thorough. At these examinations we generally ask about the following questions, and keep a record of the most important replies. 1. Name 2. Residence 3. Age. When did you hear the Gospel? From whom? What did you think of it then? How long have you believed? You say you "believe," what do you believe? Explain how and why you expect to be saved by Christ. Are you a sinner? What about your sins, have they been forgiven? What has Christ done for you? Do you sing when you pray to Him? Have you the presence and witness of the Holy Spirit

> with you? What makes you believe you are a Christian? Are your actions now different from what they used to be? How often do you pray? What do you say when you pray? Have you spoken to the other members of your family about the Gospel and tried to get them and your friends to believe (this is a very important question)? Do you keep the Sabbath day? How? What have you done with your household gods? Do you sacrifice to your ancestors? Have you a concubine? Or if a woman, are you the first or second wife? What is the meaning of baptism? Why do you wish to be baptized? If you truly believe could you be saved without baptism? What do you do for a living?[25]

Bell admitted that these questions were complex and hard but commented that experience had taught the missionaries that such thoroughness was necessary.

After baptism, missionaries subjected converts to continuous monitoring. To ensure the purity of the church, missionaries needed to know of malfeasance. Obtaining this knowledge was structurally built into the Nevius Method, which, regardless of its stated intentions, created a system of constant surveillance that funneled information to the missionaries.[26] For example, itineration constituted an important component of the Nevius Method. Missionaries were based at centrally located stations and traveled to the various Christian communities. The logic of this system was that it encouraged native Christians to take the bulk of the responsibility in their Christian lives while requiring relatively few missionaries to work with a large group of believers. On the surface, the obvious drawback was a decreased ability to oversee converts. However, the Nevius Method offset this problem by drawing *all* church members into the web of "teaching" and, by extension, "observing" others. The continual cycle of teaching-learning, which was a duty of each member regardless of rank, would further inculcate Christian doctrine.[27] In practice, the system created an incentive for members to demonstrate their own spirituality and commitment to Christianity by pointing out the flaws in others. In this manner, every catechumen, full lay member, and leader was both an object to be observed and a subject who observed.

Both catechumens and baptized members who were found to be lacking in their studies or not living "Christian lives" were disciplined.[28] For relatively minor offenses and first-time offenders, missionaries issued private reprimands. More serious offenses warranted public confessions of sin. And for major transgressions, missionaries suspended or even expelled members. Describing these disciplinary actions, Charles Allen Clark reported that Korean Christians could be expelled from the church in "only a few minutes."[29] Even after laboring to study Christian doctrine, change their daily habits, and receive baptism, Korean Christians could be expelled from the church for sliding back into proscribed behavior. Their need to demonstrate their spirituality to others was never-ending.

Korean Christians in leadership positions were not exempt from censure both direct and indirect. For example, one area in which Protestant missionaries believed that Koreans were unenlightened concerned gender roles and the oppression of women.[30] Missionaries believed that as Korean Protestants deepened in their faith, they would assume more "modern" views on gender relations. This mindset informed an interaction between Horace Underwood and Kim Yun-o. Kim was among the early leaders of the Sorae Christian community in Hwanghae Province. A local elite and a man of relative wealth, he was one of the first to receive baptism in the province and was active in spreading the gospel in Hwanghae. He was well known as a Christian leader not only in the region but throughout the peninsula. Despite his status and position in the church, however, during one visit, Underwood chastised Kim for simply standing by and watching his wife carry a jar of water from the village well. Embarrassed by this encounter, Kim took measures to dig a well closer to the house and improve the women's quarters of his home with modern comforts, such as clocks, lamps, and glass windows.[31] More significantly, however, Kim eagerly showed Underwood these improvements during his next visit to Sorae. It was not enough for Kim Yun-o to experience a change of heart; he needed to demonstrate his transformation to Underwood.

Missionaries recognized that their rules and regulations were stricter than those imposed on church members in the United States—and that the disciplining of members was also much harsher than in the West. But the missionaries held that both practices were necessary to determine "sincerity" of faith and to ensure continued diligence, given the Koreans' supposed penchant for deception and lack of spiritual awareness. Despite the challenges, a large number of Koreans flocked to the church.[32] For example, on one trip to Haeju, Underwood baptized 123 catechumens. Likewise, Graham Lee claimed that in 1898 he entered one thousand catechumens on the rolls and baptized three hundred during his itineration trips in Hwanghae.[33] It should be noted that these catechumens who received baptism represented groups that local leaders had already vetted and deemed ready to sit for the baptism exam; in other words, many more sought the opportunity to receive baptism.

Missionaries reported with pride the ways Christianity was transforming the lives of its members. In particular, they cited Koreans who faithfully observed the Sabbath regardless of the financial and physical costs, turned their backs on alcohol, and eschewed entrenched heathenistic practices like shamanism.[34] One missionary remarked that the process of creating a strong native ministry consisted essentially of transforming Koreans from a group of "*others* sacrificing, others-reliant, [and] others-respecting *self*-seekers" into a group of self-sacrificing, self-reliant, and self-governing Christians.[35] Samuel Moffett commented that converts differed from their compatriots in terms of their moral transformation.[36] Stated differently, these converts were no longer Koreans; they were now (Korean) Christians.

Because most Korean Christians at this time did not leave written records, their motivations for converting and subjecting themselves to such questioning in the baptismal examination remain unclear. However, once the desire was in place, they often spent valuable resources on their studies. They had no other choice if they wanted to increase their standing in the church community. A clear division existed between catechumens and fully baptized members. No one could participate in the Lord's Supper, for example, before receiving baptism. Thus, each time this sacrament was performed, the division between "church member" and "becoming church member" was reinforced; this division gave catechumens an incentive to pass the baptismal examination as quickly as possible. Moreover, unlike full-fledged church members, catechumens could be expelled without a formal church trial. Finally, as discussed above, the Nevius Method created a structural hierarchy of relationships in which each member was both a teacher and a student. Again, knowledge of Christianity was the currency of power.

Source of Power: Masters of Rites

The success of the Nevius Method lay in the missionaries' claim to superior knowledge of Christian doctrine and their monopoly over religious ceremonies like baptism.[37] An early episode in the history of Korean Protestant missions illustrates the importance of baptism. In 1893, Malcolm Fenwick published an article in a periodical called *The Truth* that criticized Underwood. He argued that Underwood had baptized Koreans without fully investigating whether they had a true grasp of the faith and recklessly converted the villagers of Sorae without giving them an adequate examination. This accusation was apparently grave enough to provoke a strong reaction from Underwood's wife, Lillias. Writing to Francis Ellinwood, Lillias took great pains to defend her husband's early work.[38] Moreover, Horace Underwood himself felt compelled to rebut Fenwick's claims in an article written for *Missionary Review of the World,* a major missionary periodical in the United States.

Underwood reported that in 1886, Sŏ Sang-ryun had come to Seoul and told him that some men from his village desired to be baptized. Sŏ was a colporteur, or book seller, who had worked closely with John Ross, a Scottish Presbyterian missionary stationed on the Manchurian side of the Yalu River. Sŏ had subsequently moved to Sorae, in Hwanghae Province. In part because of the anti-Christian edicts, Underwood refused to accompany this man, whom he had just met for the first time. Sŏ demonstrated persistence, returning with four residents of Sorae. After a discussion about how to proceed, the missionaries met with the candidates over the course of several days and rigorously examined them. Satisfied that they were sincere in their faith, Underwood baptized the four. Before leaving, these Koreans requested that Underwood visit Sorae, but he again refused. Several months later, another villager from Sorae came to Seoul seeking baptism. At this point, Underwood finally decided that he needed to travel to the village, where he examined a number of applicants over the course of a week and baptized four villagers, which he considered a very modest number.[39]

Fenwick's accusation, Underwood's response, and the persistence of the Koreans who desired to be baptized reveal several important issues. First, the charge of converting such a large number of Koreans was serious enough to warrant replies from both Horace Underwood and his wife. Baptism was a sacred ritual symbolizing, or in some quarters granting, the spiritual rebirth of an individual. Second, the missionaries monopolized the power to grant baptism and baptized only after potential converts demonstrated their sincerity and their understanding of the significance of this ritual. Finally, and perhaps most importantly, Sŏ's repeated trips to Seoul seeking baptism and his pleas for Underwood to visit Sorae indicate the importance of baptism. Without baptism, Christians lacked legitimacy. Thus, these Koreans had devoted both time and money to the pursuit of this Christian sacrament.

Baptism's importance as a ritual and as a means of preserving the missionaries' control is demonstrated in a story Lillias Underwood told in later years. She recounted that her husband and Oliver Avison once arrived in a village that no missionary had ever visited, only to find that the residents had not only already adopted Christianity but also baptized themselves:

> They found a little company of earnest simple-hearted believers, who had thrown away their idols, ceased their ancestor worship, and were in all things, as far as they knew, obeying the Lord. But "the washing rite," as baptism was translated, puzzled them. *"He that believeth and is baptized shall be saved."* What then was this? They pondered and studied. God showed them it was in some way a sign of washing from sin, and when after long waiting, no teacher came, they agreed that each going to his own home should wash himself in the name of the Father, the Son and the Holy Ghost, praying for himself and his brethren, that if in anything they had sinned in this rite, God would forgive them. And so the missionaries found them, and though for the sake of due order they were baptized in the prescribed way, it was felt that in God's sight it had already been done.[40]

On the one hand, this entire village was accepted into the church without being subjected to a strict examination. On the other hand, the rebaptism of this community reveals the extent to which missionaries desired to maintain control over the ritual. This double baptism was a potential heresy. According to the Nicene Creed, individuals require only one baptism. Offering a second baptism implies that the work of the Holy Spirit was somehow insufficient the first time. Yet, though Underwood and Avison believed that a true baptism had taken place when the villagers "washed" themselves, they still felt compelled to rebaptize them. In so doing, Underwood and Avison at least symbolically brought this village under the supervision of their mission.

Under the Nevius Method, the missionaries' power shifted from controlling access to financial resources to controlling church membership, as conversion became more difficult. Church membership and status in the Christian community were predicated not on sincerity of belief alone but on proving one's knowledge of Christianity to the missionaries. During the initial stages of Protestantism's history in Korea, missionaries were the only individuals with the power to grant baptism. Not surprisingly, they stood at the apex of the church hierarchy, judging who was sincere enough to advance in status.

Signs of Discontent

Missionaries may have dominated their relationships with Korean Christians, but native believers possessed the means to apply pressure to their foreign counterparts in two ways. The first was logistical. Despite John Nevius's cautions regarding the employment of local agents, missionaries continued to rely on Korean help—both through the formal employment of workers and through the assistance of volunteers. As the episode concerning Underwood and Avison's visit to the village that had chosen to "self-baptize" illustrates, the numbers of those who desired to convert outpaced the ability of missionaries to visit them, let alone oversee them. Thus, missionaries leaned on their helpers and local elders to provide oversight. Second, theoretical concerns also dictated that missionaries work with Koreans: because the stated aim of missions was to establish a strong native church, missionaries were dependent on Koreans to fill leadership roles to demonstrate the maturation of their work. In other words, a lack of Korean leaders indicated the stagnation and failure of the missionary effort.

Given that the ideal of the Nevius Method was for Koreans to take ownership of the church, some Koreans believed they had a superior claim to take control of the administration of Christianity on the peninsula. This proved to be a point of tension, given the continued presence and power of missionaries in the country. Many native believers moved up the ranks, even achieving the status of ordained pastor, only to discover that the missionaries' voices were still dominant. Stated differently, although missionaries preached common membership in a heavenly kingdom and demanded that Koreans take control of the administration of Christianity in Korea, in practice they hesitated to cede full power to their Korean counterparts.

One critic of this inequality was George Paik (Paek Nak-chun). Born in 1895, Paik was originally from North P'yŏngan Province. He received his master's degree from Princeton Theological Seminary in

1925 and his PhD from Yale in 1927. Paik's PhD dissertation, written under the direction of Kenneth Latourette, concerned the history of Protestant missions in Korea. A careful reading of this work reveals praise for missionaries, sprinkled with a critique of the missionaries' domination. In this sense, Paik's work captured the ambivalence that many Korean Christians felt toward their foreign counterparts.

Paik emphasized two problems of missionary policy in Korea. First, he complained about the dearth of educational opportunities for Korean pastors. As noted above, Nevius had originally lamented the reliance on native workers in China because they were often uneducated and lacked an ability to respond to theological questions. One of the goals of his method was to ensure that native leaders were well educated and possessed a deep knowledge of their faith. In practice, however, at least some missionaries feared that providing too much education to Korean leaders might be unwise. For instance, Paik specifically criticized an article written by W. D. Reynolds regarding the training of a native ministry. Expressing concern over the problem of rice Christians, Reynolds argued that Korean pastors should receive an education that was only slightly higher than what most Koreans received at the time.[41] He feared that providing Korean pastors access to higher education would only widen the gap between native ministers and the average Korean Christian. In response, Paik argued that this attitude was shortsighted and questioned its patent double standard, as missionaries to Korea were required to have, at a minimum, a college degree. Paik even criticized the first theological seminary established in P'yŏngyang in 1901. He argued that in its initial incarnation the seminary admitted individuals without academic ability and that the "theological" courses were no more than Bible classes. Somewhat condescendingly, Paik referred to this seminary as a Bible training school for Christian workers.[42]

Second, Paik criticized the missionaries' failure to quickly establish a fully independent Korean presbytery.[43] He cited Arthur Brown's comments on the missionaries' delay in establishing a presbytery in Korea after his inspection of the Korea mission field in 1901. Brown noted that in other mission fields ecclesiastical institutions had been established almost as soon as a handful of native believers had formed. Yet, in Korea, a Korean presbytery was still lacking. He argued that this situation was not ideal and that missionaries needed to make provisions for the creation of a Korean presbytery. Indeed, he was troubled by the missionaries' explanation that they needed to wait until more qualified men had been cultivated for leadership positions. He went so far as to suggest that if American elders had to abide by the same standards as Koreans, most presbyteries in the United States would have to be disbanded.[44]

It is important to note that Paik's assessment of missionaries was largely favorable. For most of his study, he praised the sacrifices that missionaries had made in Korea. Nevertheless, while claiming solidarity with these foreigners, Paik was displeased with their domination and unequal treatment of Korean Christian leaders. Missionaries remained in the country occupying positions of leadership and controlling institutions, from churches to hospitals and schools. The reluctance to hand control over to Korean leaders called into question the missionaries' oft-cited rhetoric of partnership.[45] In sum, Paik was not the only one disgruntled with missionary domination; many shared his feelings of ambivalence, both recognizing the importance of these foreign actors yet critical of the unequal relations between missionaries and Korean Christians.

The Great Revival of 1907

By the turn of the century, many Korean Christians had grown weary of the inequality in their relationships with missionaries. The constant requirement that they appear holy while being prevented from taking full control of the church became taxing. This was the context of the P'yŏngyang Great Revival of 1907. As commonly told by church historians, the Great Revival was one in a series of revivals. The first took place at a prayer meeting held in 1903 in Wŏnsan, Kangwŏn Province.[46] That meeting was led by R. A. Hardie, a medical missionary with the Methodists who were frustrated over a lack of success in attracting converts. During the meeting, he suddenly confessed that he held Koreans in contempt. Breaking down in tears, he asked for forgiveness from the Korean Christians in attendance, and this led to an outbreak of prayer and confessions from others. Hardie and the missionary community attempted to recreate this experience in leading revival meetings throughout the peninsula—having individuals publically confess their iniquities and testify to the working of the Holy Spirit to produce reconciliation and healing. The revival movement slowly spread to other parts of the peninsula, as missionaries and Korean leaders sought to bring about a renewal of the church through an honest confession of sins.

In January 1907, the revival movement reached the Presbyterian community of P'yŏngyang. As part of a Bible training class called for by the Nevius Method, Christians from the region gathered in the city. At the end of each night, missionaries invited participants to confess their sins. While some responded, the missionaries noted that these confessions lacked sincerity and remarked that there was a spiritual deadness.[47] On the second-to-last night of the class, the leader dismissed those who wished to depart and invited those who wished to confess their sins to remain. The five hundred to six hundred who stayed behind became both witnesses to and participants in the start of the P'yŏngyang Great Revival. Suddenly, Korean men began to rise and confess their sins. Grown men broke down in tears, and the wailing of voices praying in unison was so intense that one missionary described it as "frightening." On the following and last night of the training meeting, missionaries waited with anticipation to see if the confessions and revival would continue. Much to their satisfaction, the scene of the previous night was not only repeated but repeated with greater intensity and vigor.

People have evaluated and debated the significance of the Great Revival at P'yŏngyang ever since it took place.[48] For many, the Great Revival represents a development in the spirituality of the Korean church and marks a shift in power from missionaries to Korean pastors. Sung Deuk Oak has argued that the great outpouring of confessions and the very evident working of the Holy Spirit taught missionaries that Korean Christians possessed a level of faith equal to that of Americans. With this demonstration, foreign evangelists were able to break free from cultural imperialism and paternalism.[49] As an example, Oak cites an article penned by John Z. Moore for the *Korea Mission Field.* Moore first confessed that he had held a "contemptible" belief that the East and West were fundamentally different, sharing little common ground. But after witnessing the religious transformation of Koreans during the Great Revival, he learned that "the Korean is at heart, and in fundamental things, at one with his brother of the West."[50]

Though perhaps sincere, this statement by Moore does not mean that equality had suddenly materialized between missionaries and Korean Christians. Indeed, the inequality that existed between the two groups was subtle and systemic. For instance, Moore's preconceived views of Christian orthodoxy served as his standard in reassessing his affinity with his Korean brothers. The events in P'yŏngyang were not unheard of in revivals held in the United States. Although certain elements of the Great Revival may have been uniquely Korean, the missionaries witnessed Koreans behaving as Holy Spirit–inspired Americans were expected to behave. In this subtle manner, while recognizing that Koreans possessed a unique spirituality and expression of Christianity, the missionaries still evaluated their Korean partners' faith by using the American experience as a standard.

The shift that resulted from the Great Revival did not mean that missionaries immediately viewed Koreans as having reached spiritual maturity. Instead, the outpouring of confessions throughout the night and into the early hours of the morning must be understood in the context of the Nevius Method. This conversion strategy was intended to ensure that those entering the church not only had an intellectual understanding of their faith but had also been spiritually transformed. For nearly twenty years leading up to the P'yŏngyang Great Revival, missionaries had spoken confidently of the effectiveness of the Nevius Method and the tremendous gains made in Korea for the kingdom of heaven. But throughout the night, Korean Christians confessed to cheating, lying, stealing, adultery, and even murder. The missionaries now had new reason to question the sincerity of the Koreans' conversion and the thoroughness of their transformation.

But the intensity of the Great Revival also revealed the level of frustration, or even animosity, that lay hidden in the hearts of Korean Christians against missionaries. Though the Nevius Method claimed to give Koreans control over the administration of Christianity in the country, in fact missionaries occupied positions of influence, as they judged what behavior fell within the borders of Christian orthodoxy. The Great Revival provided a space for Koreans to voice their anger without fear of reprisal. Indeed, it is significant the actual content of the multiple confessions was not as significant as the *act* of confessing. In detailing the "evil" they harbored and seeking forgiveness, Korean Christians acted in accordance with the Nevius Method's demand that they demonstrate a "true" understanding of the Christian faith and "repent" of their ways. In this manner, they were not merely reintegrated into the church community; they could even claim that they had reached a higher plane of spirituality. However, the fundamental issue of the inequality of the relationships between missionaries and Korean Christians was not resolved—and would surface again.

Chapter 4

Christian Oasis

Church Growth in Hwanghae Province

The Nevius Method may portray Korean Protestants as passive actors, simply in positions of weakness in their relations with missionaries. This characterization, however, presents too narrow a view of the vast web of relations in which Korean Protestants operated. Church membership and adherence to Christian precepts, while certainly having spiritual motivations, also held practical benefits regardless of Nevius's original aim. Hwanghae Province offers an early example of how Christianity—both Catholicism and Protestantism—could have material benefits for Koreans and restructure nodes of influence.

Up to 1942, the locus of Protestantism's strength in Korea, both in terms of numbers and theological vibrancy, was in the northwestern provinces of North and South P'yŏngan and Hwanghae. Hwanghae, in particular, would capture the early imagination of the first generation of missionaries, and the wider Western Protestant world, because of the village of Sorae. This location was home to the first major cluster of Protestant converts in Korea and the first church building constructed by Koreans. Likewise, it served as an early destination for many of the first generation of Protestant missionaries to the country and was touted in the West as a stronghold of Protestantism on the peninsula. Yet before its rise to fame, nothing about Sorae, in terms of location, wealth, or historical significance, suggested that it would become a center of Christianity or an influential village in the region. Tucked away in the northwestern corner of Hwanghae Province, by the Yellow Sea, it was approximately 180 miles from

Seoul and nearly fifty-four miles from Haeju, the capital of the province. To get to Sorae, one had to travel off the main road that ran from Seoul to Haeju and then on to P'yŏngyang. According to Maria Kim, who was born in the village and later became a prominent figure in the Korean nationalist movement, the only "road" into Sorae when her grandfather first arrived was a dirt path wide enough for just one cart to pass at a time.[1]

Key to the transformation of Sorae into what would become known as the "cradle of Protestant Christianity in Korea" was the partnership that formed between the Kwangsan Kims, a local elite family that controlled the village, and the brothers Sŏ Sang-ryun and Sŏ Kyŏng-jo.[2] Through the efforts of these two families, Sorae became known in the region as a "Christian village" and a location where interested parties could learn more about this religion. As conversion to Christianity became increasingly popular in Hwanghae, the influence of Sorae grew. Sorae's rise demonstrates that although missionaries occupied superior positions of influence in their relations to Korean Christians, this relationship did provide material benefits to the latter. Koreans took advantage of the materials provided by their association with missionaries to transform the nodes of sociopolitical power in the province; no wonder the state was concerned over the subversive potential of Korean Christians.

Transforming Sorae

The story of Sorae's rise as a Christian village starts with the arrival of Sŏ Sang-ryun and Sŏ Kyŏng-jo. The former was a merchant who converted to Christianity in Manchuria through his encounters with missionaries stationed at a location known as the "Corea Gate." He assisted in the translation of the Bible into native Korean script and also served as a colporteur, distributing religious tracts that he had smuggled into Korea. Sŏ's success in spreading Christianity, however, soon incurred the ire of local officials in his hometown of Ŭiju, on the border with China, so in 1883 he and his younger brother, Sŏ Kyŏng-jo, decided to relocate to Sorae. There they again evangelized and formed a small Christian community. The following year, Horace N. Allen arrived in Korea, and in 1886, as discussed in chapter 3, Sŏ Sang-ryun traveled to Seoul to ask a missionary to come to Sorae to administer baptism. Because of the anti-Christian edicts, the missionaries at first refused, but eventually Horace G. Underwood resolved to visit; in 1887, he became the first of many missionaries to travel to Sorae.

The basic outlines of this narrative have been well documented by many scholars of Korean church history.[3] What has been largely glossed over, however, is what the move from Ŭiju to Sorae involved. When the Sŏ brothers came to Sorae, they faced the influence of an established elite family, a branch of the Kwangsan Kim clan. The Sŏ brothers' presence in the village and the practice of Christianity required the tacit approval, if not the outright blessing, of Kim Sŏng-sŏm, the patriarch of the lineage in Sorae. As it happened, they received not only approval but also participation. In particular, two of Kim Sŏng-sŏm's sons, Kim Yun-bang and Kim Yun-o, entered the church and received baptism when Underwood visited in 1887.[4] With this cooperation, a partnership was established between the Sŏ and Kim families. Especially during the next three decades, they worked closely with each other to spread Christianity first in the village and eventually throughout the province.

A major factor in the Kim and Sŏ families' opportunity to raise the status of Sorae was, ironically, the "unequal treaties" Korea signed with Japan and Western nations. These treaties required that the Korean government designate a number of ports as "open"; these were where foreigners could land, reside, and conduct business. At first, missionaries and other foreigners were restricted to these "open ports" and Seoul. The inability to move freely about the peninsula meant that missionaries could engage with only a limited number of Koreans. This situation diverted a great deal of influence to individuals like the Sŏ brothers. The relationship between the missionaries and the Sŏ brothers was somewhat analogous to the relationship between Korean intermediaries and Japanese merchants after the signing of the Treaty of Kanghwa (1876). Though Japanese could trade on the peninsula, they were restricted to "open ports." As a result, they had to rely on Korean intermediaries who acted as purchasing agents. This system was extremely beneficial for Korean landlords and middlemen, as the latter facilitated the formers' business dealings with Japanese merchants.[5] In much the same way, Korean converts were crucial for missionaries seeking to gain access to the interior. Even after foreigners could travel outside treaty ports with valid travel documents, most missionaries lacked sufficient knowledge of the country, cultural fluency, or language skills to travel on their own. Koreans like the Sŏ brothers served as guides, translators, and mediators for the missionary community. They were middlemen, and as a result, they were prime beneficiaries of mission work, in terms of the financial wealth, political clout, and cultural capital that accumulated as they spread Christianity throughout the peninsula. Sorae, as their home base, likewise benefited.

Up to the mid-1890s, Sorae was a destination for Protestant missionaries to visit and served as a strategic way station for missionaries traveling north.[6] Though other Protestant centers in Korea, most notably in P'yŏngyang, eventually overtook Sorae in terms of prominence, the village—which was located on the coast of Hwanghae—remained important to the missionary community as the home to a summer resort. By the early twentieth century, missionaries in not only Korea but also China and Japan flocked to the nearby beach to rest and recuperate.[7] In short, from the vantage point of missionaries based in the "open ports" and Seoul, God had miraculously placed a Christian oasis in what was otherwise heathen territory.

During the 1890s, the Sŏ and Kim families made efforts to convince Underwood and others of the need for a permanent missionary in Sorae by promising housing and a small plot of land, which the villagers would farm. Moreover, Kim Yun-o built quarters that were suitable—in size, furnishings, and hygiene—for a foreigner.[8] In 1894, William MacKenzie settled in Sorae with the intention of remaining in the village as a permanent resident missionary. His stay was cut short by his death the following year. This event, however, gave the Christians of the village an opportunity to be proactive in attracting another foreign evangelist. Shortly after MacKenzie's passing, Sŏ Kyŏng-jo submitted a letter to Horace Underwood and requested that he translate and send it to MacKenzie's alma mater, the Presbyterian College of Halifax. In this letter, which eventually appeared in *The Theologue*, a periodical published by the college, Sŏ first extolled MacKenzie's work in transforming Sorae from a heathen to a moral village. He then requested that the college provide another missionary to continue the work and ensure that MacKenzie's death would not have been in vain.[9] Though this letter ultimately failed to attract another permanent missionary to Sorae, it is significant that Sŏ not only advertised for a missionary to be stationed in Sorae but even expanded the scope of his search abroad. The story of MacKenzie's untimely death also inspired the Canadian Presbyterian Mission to formally enter the Korea field and placed Sorae in the view of the North American Christian world. Put differently, because of the efforts of the Sŏ brothers and the Kim family, Sorae gained a measure of fame in the 1890s that was incongruent with its size, resources, or location. The Korean Christians of Sorae literally put the village on the map for Christians around the world.

The promotion of Sorae to the international community as a budding site of Christian strength was not unjustified. Sorae's leaders made a concerted effort to spread Christianity in the province.[10] At first, this itineration was not based on any particular schedule or fiscal backing. Eventually, however, perhaps in response to a growing receptivity to Christianity in the region, the leaders of Sorae organized a society to promote systematic proselytization in the region.[11] Specifically, they organized a group of men and targeted non-Christian villages in surrounding counties. The members of this society were to travel weekly to one of these villages. Moreover, they were to meet regularly to discuss progress and strategy.[12] In short, the missionary endeavor in the province had two layers. Westerners led the first. Because of the restrictions imposed by the resources at hand and their decision to employ the Nevius Method, however, their physical presence in Hwanghae was limited. Koreans led the second layer of endeavor. They outnumbered the missionaries and had a wider geographical reach, and they performed an important function in mediating between Western missionaries and local Christian communities.

Acting in this manner, the leaders of Sorae made their village a center not only for missionaries but also for other Christians living in the area. Limited time and resources meant that missionaries could not visit every village in the province. Thus, for residents of unvisited villages seeking baptism, traveling to a known center like Sorae was an expedient way to obtain knowledge of Christianity and gain access to a missionary. Stated differently, missionaries often complained of an inability to satisfy the masses who sought baptism in the northern provinces. Those who wished to receive baptism or meet a missionary often had to travel to centers like Sorae, where local leaders provided the first line of testing. Individuals like Sŏ Kyŏng-jo and Kim Yun-o not only evangelized and instructed but also determined who was ready for a baptismal exam. This afforded them a great deal of influence and prestige in the eyes of those who wished to convert and remain in good standing in the church.

By the end of the nineteenth century, Sorae had become known as the representative Christian village of Korea not only among foreigners but also among other Koreans throughout the peninsula.

For example, in the inaugural edition of the *Christian News (Kŭrisŭdo sinmun)*, in 1897, Underwood devoted space to extolling the virtues of Sorae and its residents. He described the readiness with which the villagers had adopted Christianity and its influence in improving morality, fostering political order, and advancing modernization.[13] In subsequent issues, Underwood continued to single out Sorae as a model village and even mentioned Kim Yun-o as a leading figure in the church community in Hwanghae Province. Implicit in these praises were the messages that Sorae was a modern village and that Kim was a model modern man. In this manner, the village was introduced to would-be reformers, officials, and Korean Christians throughout the country, and Kim achieved a level of fame that would otherwise have been impossible. Appearing in the newspaper in such a manner must have been a source of pride for the residents of the village, and it reinforced the notion that Sorae was where Koreans could go to learn more about Christianity.

As conversion became more attractive, for either purely spiritual or more worldly reasons, inhabitants of the surrounding villages continued to travel to Sorae. One particularly important example involved the town of Ŭllyul. According to missionary reports, this was a fairly large town, with a significant number of wealthy elites. Initially resistant to Christianity, by the late 1890s the leaders of the town were demonstrating an interest in converting. In 1898, the magistrate of the county requested that Horace Underwood visit. Underwood agreed, with the understanding that he would be allowed to evangelize.[14] By the following year, Underwood reported that a strong and vibrant cluster of Christians had formed in Ŭllyul. But instead of taking credit for this sudden growth of Christianity, Underwood pointed to the proactive spirit of the town's residents. He explained that even before the magistrate's request, a wealthy resident had traveled to Seoul to purchase an office. While at the capital, he had learned of Christianity. He decided to spend his money to purchase Christian tracts instead of an office. Returning to Ŭllyul, he distributed these tracts. The residents then sent a delegation to Sorae to request further instruction. Describing the status of Christianity in the town, Underwood wrote:

> they [the Christians of Ŭllyul] have now a gathering of earnest students of the Bible and an average attendance on church services of 75 to 100, some eight out-stations at which regular work is carried on,

> and 150 people who call themselves Christians. They have purchased entirely unaided a large building where they have a sarang waiting room, church, and leader's dwelling, and every thing is in a most satisfactory condition.[15]

Underwood's report revealed two important points. First, in the initial stage of their adoption of Christianity, the leaders of Ŭllyul dispatched a delegation to Sorae for instruction. That a group of wealthy elites would dispatch a fact-finding mission to a relatively poor group of Christian leaders in a village of about 280 underlines the extent to which Sorae had become known as a center of Christianity in the region. Second, in a period of about a year, Ŭllyul transformed itself into a major Christian center, at least in Hwanghae. Primarily because of the relative wealth of its members, Ŭllyul's Christian community was able to quickly build a church, construct a residence for a missionary, and establish substations to which it sent its own evangelists. In short, it was becoming a rival of Sorae.[16]

As the situation with Ŭllyul suggests, there was a great deal of competition among Christians in Hwanghae. As individuals converted, entire villages strove to build churches and implored missionaries to visit. William Baird complained that in the northwestern corner of the province, where Sorae was located, there was a ten-to-thirteen-mile stretch with at least ten separate places of worship.[17] Reporting one year later on the same region, William Swallen noted at least two cases of splits within church communities. He cynically remarked that in one instance, the villagers held worship services less than a half a mile from each other.[18] Even within the village of Sorae, Underwood noted that the church had been, for a period of time, troubled by division and dissension.[19] The adoption of Christianity did not erase hierarchies or competition between communities for resources. Rather, it added another variable to local society, and the successful manipulation of missionaries and claims of legitimacy were crucial factors in determining the ownership of this new avenue to influence. In many respects, then, Christianity was incorporated into local social structures.

The large numbers flocking to the churches in Hwanghae indicate that converting to Christianity was seen as advantageous in the region. One reason may have been that association with this religion granted access to many of the benefits provided by the "opening" of Korea to the West. Converts often parlayed their relationships with missionaries and membership in a world community of churches into opportunities to reach beyond the borders of their villages and sometimes even of Korea. For instance, Sŏ Sang-ryun became Underwood's language instructor after 1887 and accompanied him on trips through the countryside. He then became an assistant to other incoming missionaries and traveled to areas such as Ŭiju, his hometown; Pusan, in the southeast of the peninsula; and Wŏnsan, in the northeast. Likewise, Sŏ Kyŏng-jo also served as a missionary assistant. He subsequently moved to P'yŏngyang to attend the newly established Presbyterian seminary and was part of its first graduating class in 1907. He eventually became the first Korean pastor of Saemunan Church, located in Seoul and originally established by Underwood. While the Sŏ brothers were atypical in the distances they traveled and the positions they attained, many other converts achieved a degree of mobility when they engaged in evangelism, attended Bible classes, or participated in revival meetings; these events afforded opportunities to visit major cities and important sites that would not otherwise have been available.

Training classes and itineration enabled only temporary absences from Sorae. Those who left returned. Christian communities also, however, opened avenues for people to leave on a more permanent basis, especially through education. Scholars have long noted the important roles missionaries played in spreading modern education in Korea. But in many instances, the Korean Christians sought out new educational opportunities without the missionaries' intervention. One early example occurred in Sorae. As noted above, William MacKenzie died in 1895. Before his death, he had turned over to Sŏ Kyŏng-jo a sum of money to be distributed to the poor. Unsure what to do with this sum after MacKenzie's sudden demise, Sŏ handed it to the British legation, which duly returned it to Sŏ to use as he saw fit. The villagers of Sorae decided to purchase a plot of land and use the income from tilling it to endow a village school.[20]

The Sorae school gave the children of the village a way to leave. For instance, Maria Kim was perhaps the most famous descendant of Kim Sŏng-sŏm. Born in Sorae in 1892, she moved to Seoul to attend Chungsin Women's School (Chŏngsin yŏhakkyo). In 1914, she departed for Japan to attend Tokyo Women's College. She took part in the preparations for the March First demonstrations and helped organize the Korean Patriotic Women's Society (Taehan Aeguk Puinhoe) in April 1919. The colonial government arrested Kim for her role in organizing and participating in the demonstrations. She was released after five months and eventually made her way to the United States. She studied at both the University of Chicago and Columbia University, Teachers College. She later returned to Korea, where she continued to participate actively in the nationalist movement.[21] All of Maria Kim's travels, studies, and activities started with her primary education in Sorae, which opened a conduit for her to access the educational opportunities provided by missionaries in the major urban centers of the peninsula.[22]

Importantly, the decision to establish a school in Sorae rested in the hands of the local leaders and not of the missionaries, and it was they who chose to educate both boys and girls. Given Sorae's beginnings as a small, isolated village in a corner of Hwanghae Province, the opportunities for not only male but also female villagers to receive a Western education and, in the case of Maria Kim, to leave the village and even the country are noteworthy.

Perhaps more surprising than this physical migration beyond Sorae were the ways the villagers, who were predominantly peasants, entered into a new set of relationships with the worldwide Christian community. As noted above, Sŏ Sang-ryun and his brother contacted MacKenzie's old school to request another missionary to serve in residence in Sorae. Another important episode demonstrating how Korean Christians linked themselves to the global Christian community occurred in 1897. The October issue of the *Christian News* reported on famine conditions in India. Several issues later, the paper reported with pride that the residents of Sorae, on reading of the suffering in India, had forwarded money to Seoul to aid their fellow Christians.[23] This sparked similar acts of benevolence from other Christian communities throughout the peninsula. The interest in India continued; the *Christian News* later published a letter from a missionary in India grateful for the contributions, and the paper published updates on conditions in that country for years afterward.

As this episode reveals, the residents of Sorae gained a view of the world that allowed them to think beyond their village. For some reason, they identified enough with those suffering in India to pool money in their support. This action reinforced the status of Sorae as the representative Christian village in Korea and was a statement of power. Further, this donation for India represented a claim of equality with Western churches and membership in a universal community of Christian believers, only ten years after Underwood's first visit to Sorae.

Catholic Growth in Hwanghae

Protestantism was not the only branch of Christianity to experience rapid growth in Hwanghae. Catholicism likewise found the province to be fertile ground. For example, in 1896, the number of Catholics in the region numbered slightly more than five hundred. The following year, nearly three hundred entered the ranks of the baptized. The church continued to grow rapidly, and by 1903 its membership rose to about seven thousand.[24]

To explain the Catholic growth in the region, scholars have focused on the relationship between An T'ae-hun and the priest Joseph Wilhelm. An T'ae-hun was born in 1862 to an elite family in Haeju, the capital of Hwanghae Province. Years later, after passing the provincial-level civil service exam, An left for Seoul, where he became associated with the Enlightenment Party. Although he did not personally participate in the Kapsin Coup, after its failure he quickly left the capital to seek safety in his home province. An settled in the village of Ch'ŏnggye, in Sinch'ŏn County. While the surrounding mountains offered protection from outside invaders and attacks, this area was far poorer and more remote than An's hometown. Yet Ch'ŏnggye proved to be a strategic location. When the Tonghak Peasant Uprising broke out in 1894 a group of supporters formed in Hwanghae. An wrote to the provincial governor requesting permission to raise a "righteous army" *(ŭibyŏng)* to battle the Tonghak. Permission was granted, and once the Tonghak neared Ch'ŏnggye, An led his forces to meet the incoming threat. Over the course of the next several months, he won successive battles.[25]

During one battle, An seized a large amount of rice that a Tonghak force had taken during a raid on a local government office. In early April 1895, officials demanded that An return the grain. Either unwilling or unable to comply, An fled to Seoul. At first he attempted to enlist the help of Protestant missionaries; when that failed, he took refuge in Myŏngdong Cathedral. During his stay, An studied Catholicism, and eventually the Catholic priests of the Society of Foreign Missions of Paris interceded on his behalf with the Korean government. In the meantime, he chose to convert, and when he returned home, he brought with him sacks filled with Catholic tracts and study materials.[26]

An's path soon crossed Wilhelm's. Interest in Catholicism grew in Ch'ŏnggye to the point that An T'ae-hun wrote to the priest about it. While Wilhelm was suspicious, he set out to examine the area, and much to his surprise, he found that the letter was accurate. After a period of instruction, Wilhelm decided to baptize thirty-three individuals, many of whom were related to An, on January 1, 1897. But An was not satisfied with merely having members of his family baptized. The Catholic missionaries had long established an institutional presence in Hwanghae Province, with a station located at Maehwa, Anak County. Individuals such as the priests Wilhelm and Charles Joseph Ange Le Gac operated from this station, overseeing the growth and development of Catholicism in the region. An T'ae-hun strove to establish an additional station at Ch'ŏnggye and continually petitioned Wilhelm to relocate to his village. In April 1898, Wilhelm acquiesced. Despite its relative isolation, Ch'ŏnggye became a major center of Catholic activity in Hwanghae as a direct result of the measures An T'ae-hun had taken.

In discussing the rise of Catholicism in Hwanghae, Yumi Moon has characterized the activities of Korean Catholics in terms of opposition or resistance to the Korean state.[27] She noted numerous government reports that criticized the Catholic Church for serving as a safe haven for former Tonghak rebels in the province to continue their "riots" against the state. For instance, in 1896 Min Yong-ch'ŏl, the governor of Hwanghae Province, complained of the abuses perpetrated by Korean Catholics. Min complained that old evil elements (that is, Tonghak) were hiding under the protection of the Catholic Church. In addition, he stated that in his province, even if only five out of ten households in a village were Catholic, the Catholics would demand contributions from the other villagers, regardless of faith. Min argued that despite recent efforts by the government to prevent corruption, the Catholics, who relied on the power of Western missionaries, flaunted their strength in the face of local officials.[28]

Certainly, many former Tonghak members found refuge in the Catholic Church. However, this observation must be properly contextualized. For one thing, the main figure who spurred the growth of Catholicism in Hwanghae was An T'aehun, who first came to the attention of the central government because of his suppression of Tonghak forces in the province. To label him and his family members as former Tonghak adherents is obviously incorrect. For another, while the sudden explosion of Catholic Church membership in the region may appear startling when viewed in isolation, when considering the expansion of Protestantism, this growth, though impressive, was not unique. Given that conversions were witnessed all over Hwanghae and across the various social classes, it is not surprising that some of those converting were former members of the Tonghak religion. Koreans throughout Hwanghae Province were converting to Christianity for diverse reasons, which were not limited to relying on missionaries to intervene in local disputes or resist state power.

The criticism of officials like Min of Catholicism reflected the complex realities of the communal identities Christians form through conversion. For example, in 1902, the governor of Hwanghae submitted a report claiming again that many Koreans converted only for material gain and lacked a true understanding of their faith. He was particularly critical of Korean Catholics, who were allegedly stating that they obeyed the dictates only of their priests and not of local officials.[29] But the very idea of Korean identity and citizenship was in a process of formation during the late nineteenth century. Thus, the suggestion that at least some converts gave primacy to their identity as members of a universal religious community would have been threatening to government officials no matter what the converts' backgrounds were. Put differently, the claim of Korean Catholics that they listened only to the orders of their local priest should not be immediately viewed as a reliance on extraterritoriality or a sign of abuse by Korean Catholics. The various anti-Catholic campaigns in Korea during the nineteenth century had been rooted precisely in these communities' refusal to reject their faith and abide by the dictates of the state.[30] Though identifying oneself primarily with a religious community, as opposed to a political one, has historically been a legitimate and common practice around the world, it has often provoked suspicion and retaliation from government officials. With this fact in mind, maintaining allegiance to a priest should be seen as neither idiosyncratic to Korean Catholics nor necessarily as a sign of abuse. Indeed, contrary to the governor's assumption, it may indicate a deep understanding on the part of converts of the demands of their faith.

Whether Catholics in Hwanghae were "truly sincere" and understood the nature of their conversion is open to debate and, not incidentally, presents the same challenges in discerning "true belief" that confronted the first generation of Protestant missionaries to Korea, covered in chapter 3. What can be stated with more certainty is that the status of Christian actors was often ambiguous because they actively courted and negotiated the advantages of being members of a universal church. At the same time, as with Protestantism, conversion to Catholicism did not erase the preexisting social relations. The significance of Min Yong-ch'ŏl's observation that even if half of a village was Catholic, the other half was coerced to pay "tribute" lies in the fact that half of a village could be Catholic. If villages in late Chosŏn Korea are best understood as collectives, where villagers were expected to contribute time or money to projects that would benefit the whole, what happened when half, or the majority, of a village adopted a new religion? Were the remaining villagers expected to contribute regardless of faith? From Min's perspective, the Catholics were corrupt extortionists. But in many respects, Korean Catholics were simply carrying on established social practice. In one particular conflict, a Catholic explained to an official inspector dispatched by the central government why the local Catholics had required others in the village to provide labor to construct a church. He argued that when a villager sought to build a new house, it was the custom for others to assist. He reasoned that the construction of a church was no different.[31] As this example suggests, discerning the line between corruption and the continuation of a social practice was a difficult task.

The Kabo Reforms: State Making and The Hwanghae Church Cases

At the same time that Christianity was spreading and growing in Hwanghae, the central government was embarking on a quest to centralize power and create a modern sociopolitical system, one that would deeply affect everyday life in the province. The catalyst for the reforms was the Tonghak Peasant Uprising, which broke out in the spring of 1894 in the southwestern portion of the Korean Peninsula over issues of taxation and charges of local corruption on the part of officials. These protests eventually expanded, and the peasants steadily moved north toward the capital. The Korean army proved ineffectual in suppressing the peasant army, and King Kojong requested military aid from China. The dispatching of troops from China to Korea gave Japan a pretext to likewise send troops to the peninsula. Internationally, one result was the start of the First Sino-Japanese War (1894–1895), which would have tremendous ramifications for both Japanese and Chinese history. The presence of Chinese and Japanese troops, the latter of which occupied Seoul, caused an urgent crisis for the central government.

During the initial stages of the war, the Japanese foreign minister to Korea, Ōtori Keisuke, demanded that Korea institute a series of reforms. Within the Korean government, opinions on reforms had long fallen along a spectrum, ranging from opposition to change to support for reforms that would maintain a Confucian base and support for Western-style modernization. As we have seen, King Kojong was open to a moderate course of Western-style reforms, but the presence of the Japanese army in the capital was troubling. Thus, Korean officials demanded that Japan first withdraw its troops before pursuing further modern reforms. In the face of this opposition, on July 23, Ōtori ordered Japanese forces to seize control of the palace. Kojong was effectively removed from power, though he maintained his title, and pro-Japanese officials took control of the government.

As Young Ick Lew has demonstrated, Ōtori and other Japanese officials did not seek to control Korean affairs directly. Instead, Korean officials such as Kim Hong-jip oversaw what would be known as the Kabo Reforms.[32] In late July, they established a special deliberative council, which from 1894 to 1896 passed a dizzying number of edicts introducing radical changes to the political, social, and cultural systems of Korea. For example, in its first phase, from July to October 1894, the council passed over two hundred edicts. The changes included redrawing provincial boundaries, abolishing the social status system, and permitting women to remarry. Taken together, as Kyung Moon Hwang has argued, these reforms sought to "rationalize" the state and its relationship to local society.[33] Yet, as with other efforts at state making around the world and through history, the central government was limited in its ability to simply increase its power to rule, as local society resisted. For this reason, an examination of how state making and the "rationalizing" process took place is necessary.

On a practical level, a major aspect of increasing the power of the state over local society often concerned the extraction of wealth, or, put differently, taxation. Because of preexisting sociopolitical and economic practices in Hwanghae, the reform of taxation in the province would have unintended consequences. Since the start of the Chosŏn dynasty, the state had assigned certain lands, known as postal and military station land *(yŏktunt'o)*, to pay for the maintenance of local armed forces, postal stations, and tributary roads to China.[34] The funds from postal and military lands came in the form of rent. Because the tributary route to China ran through Hwanghae, a large percentage of the province was considered postal and military land. Furthermore, because of its proximity to the capital, Hwanghae was also home to royal family land, which operated on a similar basis.

During the Kabo Reforms, the central government sought to rationalize the administration of postal and military station land and property belonging to the royal family. This process included separating the finances of the royal family from the state, assessing the value of the land, and deciding how to collect taxes and rent. In theory, one of the goals of the Kabo Reforms was to ease the tax burden on peasants through such measures as eliminating the collection of miscellaneous taxes. These reforms, however, often had the opposite effect in Hwanghae. For example, technically, taxes were to be paid by the landowner. Yet in the case of the properties under discussion, the landowner was either the central government or the royal family. Rather than forgo receiving taxes, both the state and the royal family required those tilling their lands to pay not only rent but also any taxes owed on the lands. This led, not surprisingly, to a series of protests and lawsuits.

State making in Hwanghae generated social unrest, which set the stage for a series of clashes—collectively known as the Hwanghae Church Cases (Haesŏ kyoan)—centering on Catholic communities but also involving Protestants.[35] Starting no later than 1900 and lasting until 1903, these clashes eventually became so frequent and outlandish that the central government took notice and dispatched a special inspector, Yi Ŭng-ik, to investigate and resolve them.[36] Precipitating these incidences of violence was a prolonged drought in the region. Coupled with the Kabo Reforms, the drought imposed a huge financial burden on peasants. Not surprisingly, many chose to leave the land. For example, Homer Hulbert noted that in Anak and Yŏnan Counties of Hwanghae, 1,952 and 1,900 houses had been deserted, respectively.[37] Meanwhile, many peasants who remained petitioned the government to reduce their tax burden during the first years of the 1900s, often noting the amount of land left barren because of the departure of other peasants. In one particular suit, the petitioners complained that the rents were so high that 70 to 80 percent of the families in the surrounding villages had left.[38] In other words, Hwanghae Province was characterized at this time by extreme poverty, disease, and a roaming population of ex-tenants who had abandoned their land.

The Hwanghae Church Cases were not, however, simply protests against the state. Though some of the incidents concerned the collection of taxes, many of the cases were struggles between Catholic and non-Catholic villagers over the appropriation and use of local resources and called into question communal identities. In one instance, the main point of contention was a Catholic village's request to cut down trees located in another region for the purpose of constructing a church.[39]

Given the escalating competition over resources in the region, it is significant that Protestantism was also associated with extortion or corruption. For example, in 1896, several months after his initial criticism of Catholicism, Min Yong-ch'ŏl issued a report concerning abuses perpetrated in the name of Protestantism. Two Koreans in Hwanghae, with the surnames of Pak and Ch'oe, were wearing Western suits and falsely claiming an association with Horace Underwood to commit a litany of crimes, which included extorting money from the local populace.[40] Min used this incident to criticize Christianity for providing a haven for criminal elements seeking to flee his jurisdiction. But, this criticism captures only a small piece of the broader picture.[41] That this extortion was possible simply because Pak and Ch'oe wore Western-style suits and claimed to work for Underwood reflects the power Underwood's name held in the province. Hwanghae fell within Underwood's zone of responsibility, and the con artists' credibility indicates the extent to which Korean Protestants in Hwanghae traversed the countryside. It is reasonable to assume that individuals such as Kim Yun-o mentioned Underwood's name when meeting the magistrates of unfamiliar counties. Moreover, the collection of tithes and other funds, the contribution of which was a sign of "true" faith, was a standard practice of the Nevius Method. It was so common for Korean Christians to use Underwood's name to collect funds and proselytize that the magistrate and the local populace were easily fooled by Pak and Ch'oe.

Meanwhile, to outsiders, even legitimate tithing could appear as a form of corruption. The following is Horace Underwood's description of the collection of the yearly tithe in Sorae:

> Nearly all the Christians in this section have adopted the tithing principle and at harvest time nearly all without waiting send their tenths to the church authorities. It was my privilege to witness the taking up of one of the special annual collections and a more orderly and systematic method I have witnessed ever in church offering. Elder Saw [Sŏ] quietly announced the need of the special collection, the

> amount desired, which was large and then appointed various deacons, stewards and leaders, who had been previously assigned their places. They passed around among the church members, quills writing down the amounts which were whispered to them.[42]

Underwood's example of the villagers' "orderly" collection of tithes reveals the power that Sŏ Kyŏng-jo and the leaders of the church at Sorae held to extract wealth from their parishioners. This power takes on special significance in the context of the Kabo Reforms, which forbade tax collectors and local officials to collect miscellaneous fees—fees that had formerly funded the daily administration of the provincial government. The sight of Christians siphoning off surplus wealth must have been frustrating, if not infuriating, for local officials, who were finding their own operating budgets suddenly reduced. Tithing could be construed, in other words, as a form of miscellaneous tax. Hwanghae had pockets of wealth that Protestant and Catholic leaders could tap but local officials could not.

Portrayals of Christian communities as having access to wealth must be contextualized against the general poverty caused by the prolonged drought. For example, in 1901, the Protestants of Sorae organized an open thanksgiving celebration for all to attend. Of this event, Mary Barrett described the shock of visitors from surrounding villages, who had trouble comprehending the generosity of the meal set before them.[43] In reality, however, it is not hard to imagine that upon seeing the church building, the school building, the lodging suitable for a Westerner, and the enormous amount of food, visitors sharing in this free meal would have assumed that there was a great deal of wealth in Sorae.

The conflicts between Catholic and Protestants in Hwanghae often centered on issues of wealth. The first case that caught the attention of the Korean elites and the state involved Yi Sŭng-hyŏk and his ox.[44] According to Yi Ŭng-ik's report, in May 1902, Yi Sŭng-hyŏk, a Protestant, had lent an ox to Sin Kyu-jin, who lived in a neighboring village, to plow his field. One night, Sin came to Yi and reported that the ox was sick. The ox died shortly thereafter. Yi was then visited by a Catholic named Kim Sun-myŏng. Claiming that the village had until then been free of any cattle disease, Kim demanded that Yi promise to pay for the losses if any other oxen died. Left without a choice, Yi agreed. Some time later, the ox of a fellow Catholic, with the surname Ch'oe, died. Thus, Ch'oe, Kim, and others called on Yi to collect payment. When Yi was unable, or perhaps simply unwilling, to pay, they beat him almost to the point of death. Yi crawled back home, but once Yi had sufficiently recovered, they returned. This time they took turns beating him with sticks. Yi was hurt so severely that other villagers protested, and the beating ceased. But the assailants returned days later and, insisting that in the commotion one member had lost a valuable hairpin, demanded that Yi compensate him for the loss.[45]

The death of Yi Sŭng-hyŏk's ox and the demand that he make amends if any other oxen in the village died speaks to the severe drought and rampant disease conditions in the province. Yi's beating suggests the level of desperation Ch'oe felt at the prospect of farming without the aid of an ox. More importantly, however, the demand for compensation also indicates a belief that Yi possessed the capacity to pay, whether out of his own pocket or by calling on others to pay for him. Protestants like Yi belonged to communities that had demonstrated an ability to amass funds to build churches and school buildings and even hold feasts open to all during a drought.

The multiple beatings indicate that Kim and his fellow Catholics did not fear official repercussions. Indeed, the case involving Yi continued after his beating. The local magistrate dispatched officers to arrest Kim Hyŏng-nam and Kim Sun-myŏng in connection with the beatings and other charges. However, right before the arrest, both Kims allegedly declared that they were rebels and did not follow the laws of the Korean state but only the orders of their priest. They then claimed that the officers lacked the authority to arrest them.[46] During this exchange, the officers suddenly found themselves surrounded by another group of Catholics, who had apparently hastily assembled to assist the two Kims. They were taken to Le Gac's residence, where they were threatened. Adding insult to injury, Le Gac informed the officers that for wasting the time of these Catholics, they had to pay an indemnity.

The Catholics' defiance of official repercussions was predicated on two factors. First, they trusted that their priests, Wilhelm and Le Gac, would intercede on their behalf. But second, they possessed superior force in comparison to the local magistrate. Indeed, one defining feature of the Catholics' activity in Hwanghae was the speed with which they could assemble in large numbers. As early as Min Yŏng-ch'ŏl's first criticism of Catholicism, the term *tang* (黨), which can be translated as "gang" and has a negative connotation in the

Confucian worldview, was used to describe the mentality and nature of the Catholic community. In one deposition, a Korean declared that if Catholics from a different region were gathering to protest, it was his duty, as a fellow church member, to participate.[47] In nearly all of the cases cited by Yi Ŭng-ik, Catholics appeared in groups. For example, in one instance, the magistrate ordered around thirty local patrolmen to a local village to arrest Catholics on the charge of ignoring his order to refrain from chopping down trees belonging to a neighboring village. These officers, however, found themselves confronted by some hundreds of Catholics.[48] The magistrate and his men were unable to deal with the numerical strength of the Catholics in the region. In fact, they could never match the Catholics' forces. As a part of the Kabo and Kwangmu Reforms, a series of edicts were passed that sought to establish a modern police force. These edicts placed strict limits on the number of officers assigned to local magistrates and the provincial governor. Moreover, the separate forces of the magistrates and governors were not to be combined.[49] As a result, local officials were always at a numerical disadvantage when facing Korean Catholics in Hwanghae.

Curiously, in contrast to the Catholic crowds that assembled in relatively short order, Yi Sŭng-hyŏk stood alone. This was not an aberration: in most of the Hwanghae Church Cases, Korean Protestants faced their Catholic counterparts either alone or in relatively small numbers. For example, in 1901 and 1902, two related cases arose concerning the construction of a Catholic church in Sinhwanp'o, which was located in Chaeryŏng County. Under the leadership of Kim Pyŏng-ho, the Catholics in the area started to collect funds to build a church. They ordered Yi Ch'i-bok, who was originally a Protestant but had converted to Catholicism, to contribute money. Yi refused to pay, claiming that he had recently converted back to Protestantism. He sought the assistance of Han Ch'i-sun, a local leader of the Protestant community, who informed Kim that Yi, as a Protestant, was not required to contribute. But the following year, Catholic leaders ordered Han Ch'i-sun and other Korean Protestants to appear before them and demanded that they contribute. When they refused, Han and the other Protestants were beaten severely by a large group of Catholics.[50]

The only case in which Protestants were directly accused of extorting wealth involved Kim Yun-o. In 1901, he became the object of a lawsuit lodged by a Catholic, Cho Pyŏng-gil. Cho claimed that Kim, acting as *hyangjang*, a head of the local village association, had misappropriated village funds. In his defense, Kim Yun-o claimed that the local association lacked sufficient funds to carry out its duties, and thus the surrounding village leaders had all agreed to contribute money to make up for the shortfall.[51] The suit was dismissed at the local level, so Cho went to Seoul to submit another suit to the central government the following spring. The higher court ruled in Cho's favor. But getting Kim to pay these funds proved to be another matter. Thus, a group of Catholics accosted Kim Yun-o at his home on the order of the priest Wilhelm. He was taken to Ch'ŏnggye, where he was confronted by Wilhelm and Le Gac. The priests allegedly had Kim beaten and imprisoned and demanded that he pay Cho for both the expenses related to the lawsuit and the cost of gathering the Catholics to deal with him. Given the situation, Kim felt he had no choice but to agree.

This particular case became a point of contention between Wilhelm and Protestant missionaries once the official investigation into the violence in Hwanghae commenced. For example, Underwood held that the matter should be resolved in a court of law, whereas Wilhelm was insistent that Kim Yun-o be brought to swift justice. The surviving materials prevent us from knowing whether Kim Yun-o was guilty of the charges brought against him. However, earlier petitions submitted by Kim and the suits brought against him shed light on the reason he was targeted. First, in November 1900, Kim Yun-o, Ch'oe Yun-mun, and Kim P'il-sun presented a petition to the Royal Treasury (Naejangwŏn) complaining about difficulties in collecting taxes in Yŏnan County.[52] In turn, in January of the following year, residents of Yŏnan County complained that Kim Yun-o was corrupt. Significantly, in one petition to the Royal Treasury, Kim Yun-o identified himself as *marŭm*.[53] *Marŭm* were agents who, following the Kabo and then the Kwangmu reforms, were appointed by the central government (as opposed to the local magistrate) to assess land value and collect taxes. Thus, it appears that Kim Yun-o had gained enough prominence to receive one of these positions. As many resented the role he played in the new systems of taxation and local administration, he was regarded with animosity. Indeed, Wilhelm was vehement in his assertion to Underwood that Kim was a corrupt official. Whatever Kim's actions, it was likely his positions as *marŭm* and as a local village head that motivated this condemnation.

Kim Yun-o operated within the strictures of the newly formulated state-society system because he was a part of the official system.

Just as early Presbyterian missionaries and the Korean state had overlapped via the government hospital, so now there were points of overlap between Korean Christians and the state bureaucracy. Kim Yun-o's ability to become a part of the establishment rested, at least in part, on the prestige and fame he had gained via his association with Protestantism. Stated differently, as Sorae rose in prominence, Kim Yun-o—whom Horace and Lillias Underwood identified as a leader of the Christian community—also gained prominence, ultimately penetrating the state structure.

Korean Christians, Christian Universalism, and the State

Scholars of both Catholicism and Protestantism have cited the phrase "relying on the power of the great Westerner" *(yang taein chase)* to explain early Korean interest in Christianity. Supposedly, many Koreans turned to Christianity because missionaries offered material benefits or protection from local officials.[54] Yet whatever powers Koreans believed missionaries had—political, economic, or otherwise—Koreans were not passive agents. Those who turned to Protestantism or Catholicism attempted to attract Western missionaries and support by cultivating the image of their communities as centers of Christianity. In the case of Sorae, the Sŏ brothers and Kim family were able to translate conversion and their relationship with missionaries into new avenues of advancement. Moreover, through their active promotion, they transformed Sorae from an unimportant village into a major Protestant site, known far beyond the borders of the Korean Peninsula.

The true advantage of associating with "the great Westerner" was not necessarily missionary intervention in local society. In fact, in the case of the conflicts between Catholics and Protestants in Hwanghae, missionaries were unable to provide meaningful assistance. Put differently, as detailed in chapter 2, though professing a commitment to avoiding political entanglements, missionaries often became involved in political matters to advance their religious work in the country. The clashes in Hwanghae were no exception. As early as 1899, missionaries remarked in their personal reports of stagnation caused by Catholic oppression in Hwanghae.[55] Not surprisingly, they petitioned Horace Allen, who was in charge of the US legation, to intervene on behalf of their converts. However, with a tinge of disbelief that Wilhelm would knowingly allow for such tales as he was being told, he informed his former colleagues that nothing could be done as this was a domestic issue.[56] Thus, rather than focusing on the supposed power of "the great Westerner," attention must be paid to how native actors—whether Protestant or Catholic—proactively used the language of partnership and their connections to the world Christian community to take advantage of the new opportunities provided by Korea's opening to the West.

In 1894, with the Kabo Reforms, the central government may have embarked on the path of state making and rationalizing state-society relations, but implementing these new laws and regulations at the local level proved challenging. In the case of Hwanghae, the steady rise of Christian communities was a matter of concern for the state. Christians formed structured, extrabureaucratic organizations that collected money (tithes), opened schools, and meted out punishments. Furthermore, Christians were so ubiquitous that pretenders could simply don a Western-style suit, traverse the countryside, and demand funds. How were officials to know which activities were legitimate and which were illicit? For these reasons, even though many Korean Christians, both Protestant and Catholic, may have claimed to be patriots loyal to the state, the fact remained that they also represented potential challenges to state power. As will be explored in the following chapter, the issue of Christianity's relationship to the state and their connections to the missionary community became areas of concern for Japanese officials after the establishment of the Protectorate Treaty in 1905.

Chapter 5

Redefining Relations

Missionaries and the Japanese Colonial Government

At the turn of the twentieth century, missionaries had just cause to feel confident about their work to date and the prospects for Christianity in Korea. Within fifteen years, they had entered a country with a history of crackdowns on the religion, engaged in a successful diplomatic contest with the state to secure the "right" to reside in the interior, and parlayed this right into thriving mission stations throughout the peninsula. Koreans appeared to be extremely receptive to the gospel, and the number of new believers willing to turn their backs on their former "heathen" lifestyles gave many missionaries hope that the day when Korea would become a Christian nation was not far off. In 1905, however, the Japanese government announced that Korea had agreed to hand control of its foreign affairs over to Japan with the signing of the Protectorate Treaty. A mere five years later, Japan annexed the country. With the emergence of the Japanese colonial enterprise in Korea, the missionaries had to reconfigure and redefine their relationship to the state.

Japanese colonial officials were wary of both missionaries and Korean Christians. The Hwanghae Church Cases (1900–1903), discussed in chapter 4, served as a reminder that Christian groups possessed subversive potential. Perhaps more concerning, however, were the ties Korean churches had to Western missionaries and international Christian communities. Korean converts such as the residents of Sorae had actively used these ties to traverse the countryside, go abroad, and advance their own interests. Meanwhile, missionaries had proven in their conflicts with the Korean government that they were willing to manipulate legal channels to advance the spread of Christianity. Thus, to implement their colonial vision, Japanese officials moved to dislodge missionaries from their position of dominance over Korean churches.

Most scholarly narratives hold that for most of the first decade of the colonial period, missionaries remained largely silent regarding Japanese rule.[1] Not surprisingly, this supposed lack of action has troubled church historians. One common explanation asserts that missionaries refrained from active protest because they feared that politicizing the church would endanger the gains they had secured. They thus called for Korean church leaders and adherents to observe the principle of separation of church and state. But there are two problems with this interpretation. First, a narrow focus on the political situation in Korea misses how the broader international context exerted pressure on missionaries to reconsider the interaction between church and state. Second, as this chapter will illuminate, missionaries did in fact protest against aspects of Japan's colonial rule of Korea, but their protests were ineffective. In engaging the state, they once again entered the political realm as private citizens claiming individual legal rights. However, the Japanese colonial government fiercely asserted its authority over the political sphere. At the same time, missionaries found themselves once again entangled in a problematic relationship with the state, as colonial officials claimed a right to regulate all schools engaged in secular education—including those run by the various missions.

The Boxer Uprising and the Problem of Separation of Church and State

To understand the missionaries' early response to the colonization of the Korean Peninsula, it is crucial to consider the Boxer Uprising (1898–1900). Arising first in the northwestern corner of Shandong Province, China, during the 1890s, the Boxers were a secret society claiming to give special powers to practitioners of their martial arts. As Joseph Esherick has demonstrated, socioeconomic conditions particular to the region and severe drought during the closing years of the 1800s precipitated widespread violence against Christians, who were both hated for upsetting local customs by relying on foreign powers to coerce officials into ruling in their favor and blamed for causing the drought by angering local deities.[2] Violence eventually erupted as the Boxers, using the slogan "support the Qing, destroy the foreign," attacked Chinese Christians and foreigners in Shandong. Gaining in numbers, they soon pushed toward Beijing. Eventually, Western powers and Japan dispatched troops to quell the Boxers and ensure the safety of their citizens and subjects.

Two factors combined to burn this event into the minds of Westerners. First, the level of destruction and animosity directed at foreigners in general and missionaries in particular was shocking and led to a tremendous loss of life and property. Second, improvements in communications made this one of the first major international events to receive relatively instantaneous news coverage.[3] Western readers thus kept abreast of the events in China and were drawn into a discussion concerning the causes of the Boxer movement.

In the discourse that arose, missionaries attracted the ire of Western governments and the general public. Many charged that missionaries had incited the uprising through their disregard for local customs and quick recourse to political means to secure "satisfactory" rulings for their converts. For example, one reporter claimed that the Chinese, while tolerant of Christianity, resented the meddlesome behavior of missionaries, who flaunted their power and lived in opulent Western housing. More frustratingly for the Chinese, missionaries were said to protect converts, who allegedly represented the base elements of Chinese society and entered the church only for practical gain. According to the reporter, Chinese Christians lived lives of wealth and comfort at mission compounds, not wanting for food, clothing, or shelter.[4] Because of such claims, missionaries were on the defensive in the aftermath of the Boxer Uprising, and many came to doubt their roles and purpose. Major missionary periodicals like *Gospel in All Lands* and *Missionary Review of the World* published articles questioning the roles that foreign evangelists played in inciting animosity in the fields where they worked and whether, more controversially, missionaries were still needed.[5]

On the Korean Peninsula, missionaries read newspaper reports and listened to rumors about the Boxers both out of concern for their colleagues and out of fear that the calamity could spread to Korea. In 1901, the Protestant missionaries met to clarify the relationship between the church and the Korean government for their members and published five points on the matter in the *Christian News (Kŭrisŭdo sinmun)*. First, missionaries stressed that they did not interfere in the political or official affairs of the Korean or any other government. Second, even though treaty laws established a relationship between Western countries and Korea, the church and Western governments represented two distinct bodies. Third, even when Koreans converted to Christianity, they were still subjects of the country and bound to follow its laws, pledge allegiance to the emperor, and obey officials. Fourth, the church did not prohibit its Korean members from performing state duties; by the same token, if accused of a crime, a church member must be prosecuted. Finally, the church was a holy place, and thus neither a church nor any related space, including a missionary's home, could be used to discuss political affairs.[6] Scholars such as Yun Kyŏng-no have pointed to this meeting as an indication of the missionaries' apolitical orientation and desire to maintain separation between church and state.[7] However, these five points were constructed at a particular historical juncture. In reaction to the criticisms that arose in the aftermath of the Boxer Uprising (that foreign evangelists had interfered in political affairs for the benefit of their converts and that native Christians viewed themselves as standing above the law of the land), the missionaries in Korea sought to ensure that all converts understood the proper boundary between church and state. Being a Christian did not erase an individual's loyalty to a political state, nor would missionaries shelter those who sought to use the church as a vehicle for political protest.

In sum, the violence and aftermath of the Boxer Uprising provoked discussions about how Christians were to act as members of a distinct political community. Despite the seeming clarity of the five points regarding the relationship between church and state, however, the situation on the ground was not straightforward. Arthur Brown, who had visited Korea in 1901, noted that the Christian community in Korea was in an extremely "delicate and difficult position." On the one hand, missionaries upheld a commitment to obeying state authority and sought to avoid "embarrassing" local officials. On the other hand, he also argued that "the Gospel always has been and always will be a revolutionary force in a corrupt nation. It tends to develop in men a sturdy independence, a moral fiber, a fearless protest against wrong, which in the end make them what the Puritans were in England and what our revolutionary sires were in America."[8] As Brown's statement suggests, even for missionaries, the place of Christianity in the political sphere was ambiguous. Japanese officials would manipulate these ambiguities to regulate Christianity on the peninsula.

Missionary Views on the Japanese Empire

When the Protectorate Treaty was first announced, missionaries to Korea were unsure how to interpret the rise of Japan's power in the country. At first, they shared with many of their compatriots a high regard for Japan's level of civilization, and many held hope that Japanese influence would positively advance their religious work. Their initial impressions of the actions of the Japanese army during the opening stages of the Russo-Japanese War (1904–1905), which was partly fought on the peninsula, suggested that a fruitful relationship could be established with Japanese officials.[9] Carl Kearns remarked that the Japanese were critical to protecting missionaries at the start of the war and that they had exhibited "infinite patience" in dealing with the "lying" and "blood sucking" Korean government.[10] Soon, however, Kearns and others came to view the Japanese with suspicion. Signs of tension surfaced even before the conclusion of the Russo-Japanese War.

Given that missionaries worked closely with Korean Christian communities, they had a relatively clear understanding of how Japanese control over Korea affected the lives of Koreans at the grassroots level. In August 1904, Samuel A. Moffett wrote the US legation on behalf of the missionary community in P'yŏngyang, expressing a degree of apprehension, if not disgust, with the outlandish actions of the Japanese in the region. In particular, the Japanese forcibly rounded up Koreans to work on the railroad and even shipped some of them off to Manchuria to act as coolies. These men were beaten and poorly paid, if at all. In one village, when a group of Christians refused to work for the Japanese, soldiers allegedly assaulted the leader of the church and forced a written agreement that thirty-five men would be dispatched as laborers. While not openly demanding that US officials put diplomatic pressure on the Japanese government, Moffett suggested that anti-Japanese sentiment would grow if action was not taken.[11]

Over time, more and more missionaries took a stance critical of the Japanese colonial enterprise. By November 1905, the situation had deteriorated to the point that Hunter Wells reported to Arthur Brown he was, to his knowledge, the only "out and out pro-Japanese" missionary in the country.[12] The reasons for the missionaries' criticism varied. One missionary commented that the Japanese policies, in practice, were of an antimissionary and anti-Christian tenor.[13]

Another told stories of Japanese soldiers breaking up all meetings where politics were discussed.[14] Still another lamented that the numerous "blunders" committed by Japanese officials had led to "restlessness and disquiet."[15]

In short, the missionaries' initial positive evaluations of Japanese officials quickly gave way to more critical assessments. Even Kearns had a change of heart. In March 1905, he wrote to Horace N. Allen, head of the US legation, complaining that a squad of Japanese soldiers had seized lumber that he had purchased for the purpose of building a new church.[16] Allen responded that he had spoken with Japanese officials and had been told that payment had been forwarded. Despite this assertion, even as late as November 1905, according to Kearns, the payment had not been received.[17] Because of this situation and other stories of Japanese violence, Kearns's assessment shifted radically. Criticizing those in the United States who viewed Japan as a benevolent power in Korea, he claimed that those in the country could tell such tales as Japanese viciously beating Koreans and destroying villages for insignificant offenses.[18] While not all missionaries felt as strongly as Kearns, many missions found the activities of Japanese officials troubling.

Kearns's unpaid-for lumber was a relatively minor irritant in comparison to the Japanese military's appropriation, in part or entirely, of missionary property. The missionaries' inability to defend their land ownership rights or failure to secure an equitable solution stands in stark contrast to their earlier legal successes with the Korean government, as covered in chapter 2. The best advice that US officials could muster was that missionaries should register their properties with the US legation and post notices, written in both Korean and Japanese, stating that the buildings were owned by Americans.[19] These measures proved ineffective. Neither being an American nor possessing a legal claim to a piece of property was enough to ensure that missionaries could successfully defend their possessions. As these multiple conflicts suggest, far from having simply welcomed colonial rule, many missionaries were wary of the Japanese imperial presence in Korea.[20] They were uncertain what the future held but believed that regardless of any personal misgivings, the Japanese government would be a permanent figure in the country. Thus, the question that lurked in the minds of missionaries was what the future held for Christianity in Korea under the rule of Japan.

The *Seoul Press* and the Rhetoric of Cooperation

Japanese officials took a multifaceted approach when engaging missionaries and religion more generally. To begin with, in November 1905, using the argument that the Protectorate Treaty had placed Korea's foreign affairs under Japan, the Japanese government requested that all foreign countries route their diplomatic missions to Korea through Japan. The United States was the first to comply, thus downgrading their diplomatic presence on the Korean Peninsula. Significantly, Japan had successfully negotiated with Western nations the end of extraterritoriality by 1899. For this reason, after annexation in 1910, citizens and subjects of the United States and other Western nations in Korea now fell under the jurisdictional control of the Japanese empire.[21]

In general, the Japanese colonial government believed that achieving equality with the West required cultivating the appearance of being "civilized."[22] With this in mind, Itō Hirobumi, who served as the first head of the Residency-General of Korea (RGK), disseminated an image of Japan's presence in Korea as "modern." From the very beginning, Itō sought to spread to the Western world the message that Japan was playing a positive role on the peninsula. For example, in December 1906, he invited George Ladd to view Japan's work in Korea. Ladd was a former Yale University professor who held a teaching post at the Imperial University of Japan and had served as an advisor to the Japanese government during the 1890s. Not surprisingly, he had close ties to a number of Japan's ruling elites and held a favorable opinion of Japanese civilization. Ladd accepted Itō's invitation and traveled to the peninsula in 1907, publishing his observations the next year as *In Korea with Marquis Ito* (1908). Two broad themes ran throughout this work. The first was the tremendous advances the Japanese were achieving in bringing civilization to Korea; the second was the contrast between the supposedly rash and puerile missionary attitudes toward Japanese rule and the patience of Japanese officials in dealing not only with Koreans but also with missionaries.

Escorted by Japanese officials during his stay in Korea, Ladd concluded that missionaries were uncharitable and prejudiced in their assessments of Itō and his administration. He stated that anyone who knew "the practice of Korean robbers, official and unofficial, toward their own countrymen, or who recalls the sight of a Korean mob tearing their victim limb from limb, or who credits the reports of the unutterable cruelties that have for centuries gone on behind the palace walls" understood that the Japanese were a civilizing force in Korea. Importantly, Ladd implied that the missionaries operated in a small, sterile bubble and that the great numbers of conversions to Christianity had lulled them into forgetting the inherent "dishonesty" and "impurity" of Koreans.[23] Missionaries were, in other words, poor judges of character and unreliable sources of information.[24] Nevertheless, Ladd remarked, despite these foreigners' repeated unfavorable reports of Japanese rule in Korea, Itō steadfastly treated them with "patience and sympathy."[25]

Though Ladd's critical attitude toward missionaries was likely adopted from his hosts, Itō and Japanese officials did attempt to convince missionaries and other Westerners residing in Korea of the good Japan was doing in the country and that both missionaries and Japan shared a common goal. Starting in 1905, the RGK subsidized the *Seoul Press*. In 1907, officials purchased this newspaper outright. Under the leadership of Zumoto Motosada, who was also an official for public information under Itō, the *Seoul Press* became a daily paper and served as the mouthpiece of first the RGK and then, after annexation, the Government-General of Korea (GGK). Published in English, this newspaper strove to shape the views of the English-speaking population in Korea. In particular, the *Seoul Press* often ran articles emphasizing that Japanese officials appreciated and supported the work of missionaries, not only on the peninsula but also around the world. These articles claimed that the Japanese government supported Christianity and that it believed in the civilizing benefits this religion afforded benighted areas of the world. Furthermore, the *Seoul Press* stressed that Japanese officials in Korea felt unity with Christian leaders.[26] In fact, whereas their colleagues in Japan criticized missionary behavior, the editors defended the missionary enterprise in Korea as performing a vital role and argued that the criticisms of Korean missionaries levied in Japan were unjustified.

In praising missionaries, the *Seoul Press* engaged in a subtle struggle to define the role of these foreigners. While the Korean government had never officially recognized or treated missionaries as religious actors in Korea, the *Seoul Press* stressed the religious function of missionaries. In so doing, however, the paper asserted that these foreigners should not enter the political realm. For example, the editors implied that the success of Christianity in Korea stemmed from the missionaries' commitment to focusing solely on the spiritual and moral development of the country—whereas their counterparts in other countries often became engaged in the political realm. Stated differently, the various articles on Christianity that appeared in this paper underlined that the proper role of missionaries in Korea was limited to the reform of the country's moral, cultural, and social systems. They were not to become involved in politics, which was the legitimate sphere of state action.

A series of articles on P'yŏngyang that appeared in the spring of 1907 advanced the message that a fruitful partnership could be achieved if missionaries observed the principle of separation of church and state. For those Japanese officials concerned with the subversive potential of Christianity, P'yŏngyang's status as a Christian stronghold was disconcerting. As noted in chapter 2, both the Methodists and the Presbyterians had established bases of operations in P'yŏngyang in the early 1890s, and the city quickly became a major hub for Protestantism after the P'yŏngyang Persecution (1894). Moreover, with the outpouring of confessions during the Great Revival of 1907, P'yŏngyang could rightfully claim to be the center of Korean Protestant spirituality. An incident that occurred two months after the Great Revival intensified the fear that these Korean Christians could potentially rise in protest against Japanese rule. As reported by the *Seoul Press,* a rumor circulated in the city on April 8 that the Japanese intended to annex Korea. In response, a small group in P'yŏngyang allegedly attempted to incite the population to "massacre" all the local Japanese residents. According to the *Seoul Press,* disaster was averted largely thanks to the calmness with which the Japanese residents of the city confronted these rumors, the firmness with which missionaries attempted to dispel the idea that Japan sought to annex the country, and the "good sense" of the "more intelligent section of the native Christians."[27] The *Seoul Press*'s unequivocal praise of the Japanese settlers and missionaries stood in stark contrast to the qualified praise of Korean Christians. The implication was clear: as a group, Korean Christians possessed questionable moral fiber, judgment, and intelligence and thus required careful oversight. The editors of the *Seoul Press* would exploit these ideas in subsequent articles.

Beginning one day after reporting on the alleged massacre attempt on the Japanese residents of P'yŏngyang, the paper ran a series of articles on the city that together delivered a three-part message: the Japanese were bringing civilization to Korea, the Japanese and the missionaries shared a common goal, and missionaries should not act in the political realm. The first installment discussed the changes wrought by the Japanese settlers. After the conclusion of the Russo-Japanese War, they had flooded into P'yŏngyang, bringing capital that they used to transform the physical appearance of the Japanese settlement by constructing modern streets and buildings. This transformation ultimately benefited the local Korean population.[28] The second installment focused on the positive changes missionaries had brought to the city. The *Seoul Press* commended missionaries for improving the moral fiber of Koreans residing in P'yŏngyang. Significantly, this issue specifically broached the "problem" of rice Christianity, arguing that many early converts entered the church for material gain but that this was to be expected given the corruption of the Korean government. For the same reason, missionaries often had to intervene in the political realm to secure justice. But, as demonstrated by the Great Revival (1907), P'yŏngyang was now home to a committed community of Korean Christians. The article implied that the missionaries' continued intrusion in the political realm risked reviving the problem of Koreans entering the church for nonspiritual reasons.[29] Having established the impressive economic and spiritual changes that Japanese settlers and missionaries had wrought in the city, the editors turned their attention in the third installment to the proper relationships among Japanese settlers, missionaries, and officials. Japanese settlers were enriching the city and, by extension, lifting Koreans from abject poverty. Missionaries were providing for the spiritual and moral welfare of Koreans. The RGK in turn was providing a safe and stable social and political environment in which Japanese, Koreans, and missionaries could operate harmoniously.[30]

Subsequent articles in the *Seoul Press* reiterated the point that the legitimate sphere of missionary work was moral whereas that of the Japanese government was political; because the RGK had established a civilized and modern government, there was no need for missionaries to interfere in politics. Even two years later, after the assassination of Itō in Harbin, China, by a Korean Catholic, An Chung-gŭn, the *Seoul Press* emphasized its belief in the importance of Christianity in Korea. But it warned of the dangers if the separate responsibilities of missionaries and the Japanese government mixed.[31]

In one of the most clearly worded statements concerning the separation of the two spheres, the editors wrote:

> If these two great interests, religion on the one hand and honest civil government on the other, work side by side in their *own sphere, neither one interfering or infringing upon the rights and responsibilities of the other,* but each working out their own great purposes, abundant proof will soon be forthcoming that no "tragedy of a nation" is being enacted in Korea other than a magnificent "tragedy" which the world will yet applaud.[32]

In sum, the resident-general attempted to relegate missionaries to a religious-moral sphere of action.

Korean Conspiracy Trial

A little more than a year after the annexation of Korea, Japanese colonial officials claimed that they had discovered a nefarious plot. According to the officials, in the fall of 1911 the police had arrested a Korean, Yi Chae-yun, on a random burglary charge. In the course of his interrogation, Yi revealed knowledge of an alleged plan to assassinate the governor-general. This confession was the catalyst for what is known as the Korean Conspiracy Trial. The police arrested over seven hundred Koreans on suspicion of taking part in this plot. A large percentage of those arrested were either Christians or students at schools run by the missionaries. In June 1912, 123 of the arrested went to trial. Because of the number of those on trial, and also probably because a large number of foreigners were expected to attend, the Japanese built a special courthouse for the event. Much to the GGK's dismay, instead of exemplifying Japan's efficient judicial system and proving the malfeasance of the Christians in the peninsula, the case became an international fiasco when nearly all of the defendants declared that their confessions, which formed the basis of the case against them, had been given under torture. Even more appalling, at least for the missionaries, was the discovery that these confessions had named Samuel A. Moffett, George McCune, and other prominent missionaries as providers of crucial assistance in planning and guidance. One by one, the defendants rescinded their confessions.

The first trial concluded in controversy in late August as the court prevented the defendants from calling any witnesses who would discuss the issue of torture. Furthermore, the court barred the implicated missionaries from taking the stand to prove their innocence. The tales of torture, the drama of the defendants' recantations of their confessions, and the allegations of missionary involvement sparked international interest and widespread criticism of Japan's legal system. A trial of appeal commenced in late November of the same year, and at this new trial, all but six were exonerated.

Many scholars have argued that the GGK manufactured the Korean Conspiracy Trial simply to remove the obstacles missionaries and Korean Christians presented to their rule.[33] But another and equally important way to view the trial is that the Japanese authorities procured confessions that matched their fears of what was happening in the countryside, particularly in the northern provinces. Indeed, given that only two years had elapsed since An Chung-gŭn's assassination of the former resident-general, Itō Hirobumi, the notion that a group of Christians was plotting to assassinate the governor-general was not entirely farfetched. In short, officials may have believed that these confessions were for the most part true, even if they were procured under torture. Indeed, at the time, some missionaries in Japan and some members of the mission boards in the United States were inclined to give the Japanese authorities the benefit of the doubt.[34]

Both colonial officials and missionaries in Korea manipulated the language of separation of church and state to present contesting characterizations of the trial and whether missionaries could become involved in protesting the arrests. In the initial stages, missionaries entered the political sphere to advocate on behalf of those arrested. For example, the Presbyterian missionaries in Sŏnch'ŏn were particularly concerned with the Korean Conspiracy Case, as students studying at their schools constituted a large percentage of those arrested in the first wave.[35] Alfred Sharrocks, who was in charge of the Sinŭiju station, located on Korea's northern border, traveled to Seoul in December to ascertain the nature of the arrests and charges. There he met the director of the Bureau of Foreign Affairs. Sharrocks tactfully attempted to complain about the arrests of Christians while at the same time emphasizing that the missionaries did not seek to interfere in Japan's legal right to enforce its laws. Sharrocks's trip was ineffectual, however: the arrests continued, and rumors of torture persisted. Similarly, on January 8, 1912, the leaders of the Northern Presbyterian Mission submitted a letter to Governor-General Terauchi.[36] Not only was this effort unproductive, but the missionaries reported that Terauchi took a hostile position.

Because of these attempts by missionaries to intercede on behalf of those arrested and their accusations of malfeasance on the part of colonial officials, the *Seoul Press* became more critical of missionary behavior in Korea for illicitly entering the political realm and attacking the Japanese government. In one editorial, published not incidentally on the day the first trial ended (August 28, 1912), Yamagata Isō wrote with a sense of betrayal that even after the assassination of Itō, the paper had been firm in casting missionaries as allies and had defended them against those who suggested that they sought to topple Japanese influence in the country. But recent events had challenged "the sweet belief that the missionaries were constant and loyal to our [Japanese] authorities."[37] Subsequent editorials from August 29 to 31 refuted the charge that the GGK was anti-Christian.[38] Instead, the *Seoul Press* claimed that the root of the problem was that the missionary body was anti-Japanese.[39]

The *Seoul Press* had attempted to keep missionaries from the political realm through a carefully plotted argument and interpretation of the history of missions in Korea. It maintained that early missionaries had no choice but to become involved in politics because of the corrupt Korean government. Now that Japan, a modern and civilized state, had assumed control, missionaries needed to leave the political sphere. In contrast, in justifying their efforts to assist those who had been arrested, the missionaries turned this argument around, asserting their right to act in the political sphere because of Japan's advanced level of civilization. They argued that since Japan possessed a "modern constitutional government," which guaranteed freedom of press, missionaries could freely disseminate news of the activities of the colonial government, even if this had political ramifications.[40] With this mindset, they remained vocal in protesting the arrests of their students and other Korean Christian leaders throughout the trial.

The Korean Conspiracy Trial revealed an important structural change in the relationship between missionaries and government officials. In the missionaries' prior conflicts with the Korean government, the US legation had acted as a powerful third-party arbiter, able to adjudicate the conflicts between missionaries and the Korean state.[41] The downgrading in status of the US's diplomatic presence in Korea and the cessation of extraterritoriality rights placed missionaries under the jurisdiction of the Japanese colonial regime.

From the United States, the various mission boards stepped in to advocate on behalf of the missionaries. For example, although the Board of Foreign Missions of the Presbyterian Church, USA (BFMPCUSA; Home Board) at first hoped not to become involved, the widespread reports of the trial in the newspapers required a response. Arthur Brown dispatched a letter to the Japanese ambassador to the United States, Chinda Sutemi, in May 1912. After laying out the facts of the case, Brown emphasized that the missionaries upheld the right of Japan to govern and that the BFMPCUSA "loyally" accepted the right of "the constituted Governments of the countries in which mission work is carried on, to do everything in their power to keep the missionary enterprise free from political movements, to avoid any interference with a Government or its courts of justice." The letter then proceeded to assert that Western nations admired Japan for its modern and just legal system and its "reputation for the humane and enlightened rule of a subject race." However, given the "misinformation" that had been reported concerning the involvement of missionaries in the plot against Terauchi, Brown concluded the statement by requesting that Chinda understand the BFMPCUSA's decision to publish statements submitted to the board by the various missionaries concerning what was occurring in Korea.[42]

As Brown's letter suggests, the missionaries and their respective mission boards lacked real power. Indeed, Brown's tone was apologetic, requesting that the Japanese officials not take offense at the BFMPCUSA's pending statements about the trial. In other words, Brown's letter indicated weakness, not strength. The Korean Conspiracy Trial was not an isolated incident, and the BFMPCUSA's inability to apply pressure on the colonial government in favor of the missionary community would continue for much of the 1910s.

Separation of Church and Schools

The Japanese colonial government's attempts to regulate private schools during the 1910s caused missionaries more consternation than the Korean Conspiracy Trial. Education constituted an important means of cultivating loyal subjects in Japan during the Meiji Restoration. Not surprisingly, then, it was also an important component of Japan's colonial enterprise. After the signing of the Protectorate Treaty in 1905, Japanese officials sought to assert their authority over education on the Korean Peninsula. To begin, the RGK passed a private school law in 1908 and required missionaries to register their schools. The missionaries generally complied without complaint.[43] In August 1911, the GGK issued its first set of ordinances designed to reform education in Korea. Now to meet the registration requirements, schools had to submit reports, adopt a standard curriculum, and teach the Japanese language. Any courses that fell outside the GGK's established curriculum needed to be approved. These regulations posed challenges to the mission schools. Most obviously, the majority of missionaries to Korea could not speak Japanese, so adhering to this new set of regulations necessitated hiring Japanese instructors. In addition, and more pressingly, Bible or Christian instruction required official approval. Though concerned, the missionaries quickly attempted to register their schools.

The Japanese colonial government's efforts to regulate mission schools did not meet true resistance until it issued a new set of regulations on private education in 1915. The revised code contained two additional provisions that alarmed the missionaries. First, private schools had to wholly adopt the official curriculum. Second, religious teaching during school hours was strictly prohibited.[44] Those schools that held official permits issued before April 1, 1915, would have a ten-year grace period to come into compliance with the new ordinances. All other schools would have to be organized along the new lines. Though a number of mission schools possessed the proper permits, others did not. Regardless of status, however, all schools would eventually have to comply.

The GGK took to the various presses to convince the missionary community of the necessity and legality of these measures. Making the case for the state's right to regulate private education was Komatsu Midori, minister of education for the GGK. Writing in the *Seoul Press,* he argued that while the Japanese government upheld the principle of religious freedom and appreciated "all religions which render good service in maintaining and promoting morality," the historical and racial relationship between Korea and Japan made education a critical arena for the assimilation of Koreans and the cultivation of loyal subjects. Moreover, Komatsu reasoned that instruction in Christianity during school hours violated the principle of freedom of religion, for it would require students, regardless of personal belief, to study Christian doctrine. To allow people both to receive an education and to believe freely, schools had to be controlled by the state. He further claimed that these regulations were not fundamentally different from those followed in the West. In particular, in the United States, the government had taken control of "common" education, both because providing wide-scale education was so expensive and because the government needed to cultivate citizens. Returning to the case of Korea, Komatsu argued that education had become a part of the government's sphere of influence, and therefore religion should not be taught in schools. In sum, Komatsu concluded that both the GGK and the missionary community had their respective duties and that "holding each its own field activity, neither of them must enter the domain of the other."[45]

These new regulations sent shockwaves through the missionary community. Many grew concerned that the colonial government harbored a secret anti-Christian agenda.[46] The removal of religion from mission schools challenged the justification for financial support from mission boards and other organizations. As a method of "indirect evangelism," these schools represented a significant activity of the Protestant missionary movement in Korea. For instance, in the 1914–1915 academic year, the Protestant mission societies oversaw over seven hundred primary schools with an enrollment of nearly twenty thousand students. Furthermore, the missions ran thirty-seven higher institutions with an enrollment of more than two thousand students. Indeed, educational work constituted approximately 22 percent of the various mission boards' annual budget.[47]

The GGK was well aware of the stake that the missionary community had in education and the uproar these regulations would incite. Thus, Komatsu also took the step of writing to Arthur Brown, who represented both the BFMPCUSA and the Committee of Reference and Counsel Representing the Foreign Missions Conference of North America, to explain the logic of the new regulations. Along with a brief letter, Komatsu forwarded a translated copy of the new regulations and a copy of his article in the *Seoul Press* justifying the need for a strict separation of religion from secular education.

Komatsu's letter to Brown provided an opportunity to protest directly to the GGK. Given the severity of the situation, Brown took extreme care in crafting a response, first circulating Komatsu's letter, the new regulations, and the *Seoul Press* article to various experts in the field of education, asking for their assessment.[48] Armed with their thoughts, Brown typed and dispatched a twenty-one-page reply on June 16, 1915. He opened the letter diplomatically by praising Japan's level of civilization and the necessity of its work of uplifting the Korean people. He emphasized that missionaries not only lauded Japan's presence in Korea but also fully recognized Japan's right to govern the colony as it saw fit. However, Brown argued, Komatsu misunderstood the principle of separation of church and state, at least as practiced in the United States and Great Britain, where private schools retained the right to teach religious topics. To give further weight to his position, Brown included long quotes from leading US educational scholars reacting to Komatsu's letter.[49] Brown then closed his letter by suggesting that if the regulations were not modified, Western nations would view the situation in Korea as out of line with "modern" education as practiced in the West, and Japan's status as an enlightened nation would be damaged.

Brown's response to Komatsu is reminiscent in tone and approach of communications by the US legation during its property disputes with the Foreign Office of Korea in the 1890s. In its implication, backed up with expert opinions, that Komatsu was incorrect in his understanding of Western civilization, the letter was pedantic in tone. Perhaps because it cast him in such a negative light, Komatsu refrained from responding until early November 1915. In his reply, he essentially reiterated the points he had made in his original letter and emphasized that the situation in Korea could not be compared to education in the civilized nations of the West. Furthermore, Komatsu stressed that Japan had the legal right to oversee secular education within its colonies as it saw fit.[50]

As Komatsu's tepid response indicates, Brown was not a strong advocate on behalf of the missionary community in Korea. Brown's position was further weakened by fractures within the Home Board regarding how to approach the Japanese colonial enterprise. Particularly noteworthy was Robert Speer's appraisal of the situation in the country. When Brown's letter to Komatsu arrived in Korea, Speer happened to be in Korea on a trip to inspect conditions in Asia. He wrote a letter chastising Brown for his haste, stating that he and Ransford Miller, the US consul-general in Korea, had met with a number of Japanese officials to discuss the new regulations. It appeared that progress had been made, and these officials had appeared responsive to the concerns Speer laid out until Brown's letter arrived. Speer wrote: "I can see daylight on all our problems if only some of our dear warrior friends out here will not want to work with a bludgeon, and if you, Arthur dear, now that you have annihilated Mr. Komatsu, or at least blown him to smithereens with that unanswerable letter, will gather up the fragments with a very soft and gentle hand."[51]

Brown relented. In a memorandum to the missionaries in Korea, he pointed out the contradiction between the clear "no religious teaching" clauses of the new regulations and the private assurances given by officials to missionaries that the GGK adhered to the principle of freedom of religion. The question facing missionaries, thus, was whether they could trust these assurances without the benefit of an official, authorized record.[52] Brown insinuated a distrust of Japanese officials, remarking that many missionaries had attempted to get officials to verify private understandings by submitting memorandums summarizing their conversations but had met with the reply that there were "some corrections to be made." Nevertheless, in January 1916, the Home Board advised the Korean Presbyterian missions to take measures to convince the GGK that the missionaries supported the regime and would maintain the status quo. It was hoped that by the end of the ten-year period, the situation would have changed to the point that this issue could be revisited.[53] However, the colonial government remained steadfast in insisting that mission schools would need to comply with the new directives.[54]

Subverting Missionary Unity

The Japanese colonial government's policies on private school education had the consequence, intended or otherwise, of undermining a growing movement among Protestant missionaries in Korea to cooperate in the spirit of Christian unity. Since at least the late nineteenth century, the trend in the international, or rather Western, Protestant world had been toward overcoming denominational or national differences to promote ecumenicalism. Korea, as a relatively young mission field, developed in step with this movement, though it was not without both inter- and intradenominational competition. The first decade of the twentieth century proved crucial to this trajectory. In 1905, the major Methodist and Presbyterian mission boards, in addition to a smaller number of Christian societies, established the General Council of Protestant Evangelical Missions, which would later be renamed the Federal Council of Protestant Evangelical Missions in Korea. A major purpose of this council was to work together in order to establish one united Korean church. However, though the council repeatedly announced an effort to remove "any possibility of friction in our interdenominational relationships," many questioned how the denominations could cooperate, given the theological differences that divided them.[55]

Perhaps as important as theological debates, the administration or advancement of evangelistic enterprises proved a stumbling block to ecumenical cooperation. For instance, the early mission societies to Korea established various territorial comity agreements in order to avoid unnecessary competition and more effectively evangelize in the country. The first agreement was established in 1892 between the Northern Presbyterian and Methodist missions. As more denominations entered the field, more agreements were contracted. But until 1905, there was no single comity arrangement that covered all the mainline denominations and the entire peninsula. Thus, the General Council set the establishment of a joint agreement as an early goal. In 1908, the various denominations finally agreed on how to divide up the territory. As the lateness of this agreement suggests, the mainline missionaries hotly contested issues that affected their respective enterprises, despite the rhetoric of Christian unity that had driven the establishment of the council. In fact, out of consideration for the many mission boards that represented separate interests, distinct practices, and unique theologies, the decisions of the council were nonbinding.

One sector in which the denominations believed union could be quickly achieved was education.[56] In line with the establishment of the Federal Council of Protestant Evangelical Missions, the major Protestant mission societies also established the Senate of the Educational Federation of Missions in Korea.[57] Contrary to expectation, however, education proved to be a prominent point of contention between the various denominations during the 1910s.

It is worth noting that the Presbyterians maintained numerical advantages in Korea in terms of both missionaries in the field and church members.[58] Because representation in the Senate of the Educational Federation, as in the Federal Council, was based on the number of missionaries in each mission society, the Presbyterians held an overwhelming majority. Moreover, among the four Presbyterian mission societies operating in the country (Northern Presbyterians, Southern Presbyterians, Canadian Presbyterians, and Australian Presbyterians), growth was uneven. The Northern Presbyterians held the largest share and occupied the northwestern corner of the peninsula, which included P'yŏngyang.[59] Significantly, by 1905 they moved to establish a united college program in the city. William Baird reported that the college was to be open to students of all denominations and indicated a hope that all the major mission societies in Korea, both Presbyterian and Methodist, would eventually join this work.[60]

One of the first actions the Senate of the Educational Federation took was to establish a united Christian college, which would be known as Chōsen Christian College. The mission societies in Korea had discussed this endeavor since at least 1905. One major point of contention had been the location of the school, and when the Senate of the Educational Federation formally proposed a united college, conflict erupted. Should the senate expand the work already established in P'yŏngyang, establish a new college in P'yŏngyang, or establish a completely new college in another city? The latter two choices would have required the Northern Presbyterians to choose between funding two colleges or shuttering their existing program in P'yŏngyang. Not surprisingly, the Northern Presbyterians were on the whole adamant that the location of the college be in P'yŏngyang. In contrast, the Methodists, who had a foothold in P'yŏngyang but lacked a strong presence in the city, held that Seoul was the most appropriate location for a united college.[61] Not only was Seoul the political, economic, and cultural center of the country, but it was more centrally located than P'yŏngyang.[62]

From the outset, voting on whether to establish the new college in Seoul or P'yŏngyang fell mostly along denominational lines. A major exception was the Northern Presbyterian missionaries based in Seoul, who agreed with their Methodist colleagues that the capital was the ideal (and fairest) location for an ecumenical college. Led primarily by Horace G. Underwood, the Seoul station broke from the rest of its Northern Presbyterian Mission colleagues and petitioned the Home Board to intervene. When the Home Board agreed, siding with the Seoul station in the argument that the new college should be established in Seoul, the Executive Committee of the Northern Presbyterian Mission was incensed.[63]

In the midst of the controversy, the colonial government issued its 1915 regulations, which fractured the already stressed relations between and among the mission societies in Korea. At first the groups seemed in agreement: in September 1915, the Federal Council passed a resolution to take advantage of the ten-year grace period afforded by the rescript to continue providing religious education in their schools. The hope was that the colonial government would eventually agree that its new policy conflicted with the principle of freedom of religion and that these new requirements would be modified.[64] In a letter to John Mott concerning the Federal Council's discussions on how to respond to the new regulations, Frank Brockman boasted that there was only one dissenting vote. He closed, "I was delighted with the spirit shown throughout the entire conference. Loyalty to the Government and a desire to cooperate in every way possible was shown by every delegate."[65] However, the Northern Methodists soon broke ranks with the Federal Council, agreeing to have Paejae, the mission's flagship school for boys in Seoul, comply with the new regulations. In August 1916, at the Federal Council's next annual meeting, William Noble, representing the Methodists' interests, gave a detailed address not only justifying this decision but also criticizing his Presbyterian counterparts. Noble expressed surprise over the animosity and misunderstanding generated by the Methodists' decision, as they believed it would not affect the other missions. Instead, their only focus was advancing their evangelistic endeavor. Noble stressed that after the Methodist missionaries' numerous discussions with Japanese colonial officials, they firmly believed that colonial officials would permit registered schools with a population consisting predominantly of Christians to engage in Bible studies at a location close to, though not on, school grounds. Thus, Noble reasoned that the Methodists were not acting in a manner contrary to their Christian principles.[66]

More significantly, Noble used this opportunity to criticize the inequity of the Federal Council's composition. Likely referring also to the controversy surrounding the establishment of Chōsen Christian College, he noted that the Presbyterian missionaries, who outnumbered the Methodists, dominated the Federal Council and complained that "when the Presbyterian members advocated a policy the final vote has always been for the policy advocated because they have had the numbers to carry the vote."[67] In short, the Federal Council, Noble insinuated, was in reality a Presbyterian institution. The Methodist missionaries thus asserted their right to pursue a policy in their own best interests. Indeed, Noble closed by citing the constitutional clause stating that no action of the Federal Council was binding and by claiming that the Methodists had been faithful to both the other missionaries and their own mission.

Contrary to Noble's claims, the Methodists' decision directly affected Presbyterian interests. To begin with, though the revised regulations granted a ten-year grace period for those schools already possessing official permits, in reality the colonial government applied continuous pressure on noncompliant institutions; it pointed to the Methodists as evidence that missionaries could follow the order without violating the Christian charge of their schools. Second, the government did not automatically recognize the degrees of graduates from schools that did not conform to the GGK's new demands. Presbyterian institutions therefore lost a number of students. For instance, in 1918, John Genso, reporting on the situation in P'yŏngyang, noted that the Methodist academy in the city had swelled to 230 students, whereas Presbyterian school enrollment had decreased steadily since 1915. If the trend continued, he feared that by 1921 they would have to shut down.[68] In part as a result of this pressure, the Northern Presbyterian missionaries stationed in Seoul attempted once again to break ranks and petitioned to have their two schools conform to the new regulations.[69] When the Northern Presbyterian Mission voted against this effort, the Seoul station appealed to the Home Board for the right to begin negotiations on the matter with the GGK.

Equally troubling to Presbyterian solidarity was the status of Chōsen Christian College. The Methodists' decision to let Paejae conform to the new regulations raised the question of whether they would push to have the proposed interdenominational college follow suit. Again, the Presbyterians split: the Northern Presbyterian Mission community on the whole opposed the idea, while the missionaries located in Seoul were supportive. Arthur Brown and the Home Board sided with the Seoul station, further agitating the Executive Committee of the Northern Presbyterians. Ralph Reiner, for one, accused Brown of misunderstanding the situation in Korea and of having been "lulled" into a belief that the GGK had ceded ground to the mission community regarding Chōsen Christian College.[70]

The Executive Committee of the Northern Presbyterian Mission now sought to establish clearer lines of autonomy from the Home Board. As early as 1915, upset with the Home Board's intervention over where to establish Chōsen Christian College, the Executive Committee had drafted a motion to petition for more independence, but that motion was tabled to deal with the crisis surrounding the 1915 regulations on private school education. It was resurrected in November 1917, when, on orders from the Executive Committee, James Adams submitted a brief regarding the need to readjust the relationship between the Home Board and the Korea mission field.[71] Among his many points, he noted that the Presbyterian system was a "representative democracy" and that each congregation, session, or presbytery held jurisdictional autonomy in regards to its individual operation. Likewise, in Korea, each missionary had the right to vote, with the majority determining the decisions of the mission. The Seoul station, the brief maintained, had attempted to circumvent majority opinion by appealing to the Home Board; the majority of missionaries stationed in Korea viewed the Home Board's actions as an autocratic and inappropriate intervention in the Korea field. The Executive Committee thus asserted a right to increased autonomy. More specifically, the committee asked that the Korea Mission be granted the right to vote on issues vetoed by the Home Board, which had "review and control" (that is, veto) authority over actions taken by the various mission fields. If two-thirds of the mission again approved the issue, it would be able to act despite the Home Board's objections. The Home Board replied several months later, chastising the committee and calling the proposal both infeasible and a misinterpretation of the democratic system of governance. In particular, likening the relationship between the BFMPCUSA and the mission field to the relationship between the US central government and ambassadors, the Home Board argued that the latter must follow the direction of the former.[72]

The March First Movement

By 1918, the situation looked bleak for even the staunchest Presbyterian missionary. The unity expressed by the various comity agreements and the establishment of the Federal Council appeared to exist in name only. Not only did the Methodists and Presbyterian disagree, but even among the Presbyterian missions there was dissension over how to respond to the restrictions on private education. On the whole, the missionaries were on the defensive, and perhaps they would have eventually capitulated or shuttered their schools if not for the March First Movement. This episode, a key event in the history of Korea's struggle against Japanese colonial aggression and the development of a Korean national consciousness,[73] also proved a pivotal moment for Christian missions in Korea. The March First Movement provided a common platform on which all mission societies could once again take a collective stand and placed missionaries in a stronger negotiating position in relation to government officials.

In January 1919, Kojong died, and the GGK planned to hold a funeral procession on March 3, 1919. Korean nationalists both inside and outside the peninsula decided to seize this opportunity to hold a peaceful demonstration calling for Korea's independence. However, fearing that the Japanese colonial officials had caught wind of their plans and intended a preemptive strike, they moved up their actions to March 1. On that day, twenty-nine of the thirty-three signers of the Declaration of Independence gathered for a private meeting in Seoul. After reading the declaration, the leaders turned themselves in to the Japanese police authorities. The declaration was also read at Pagoda Park, in the center of Seoul, and a peaceful demonstration ensued. The subsequent three days passed without incident. Then suddenly, on March 5, renewed demonstrations broke out not only in Seoul but throughout the peninsula. The demonstrators included Koreans from numerous backgrounds and sectors of society. The number and scale of the demonstrations apparently shocked Japanese colonial officials. Breaking with its previous tendency to round up, question, and prosecute offenders, the government first reacted by violently suppressing the demonstrations. The colonial police force particularly targeted Christians, both missionaries and Koreans, apparently on the assumption that they had played a leading role in sparking these events.

In part because of their experiences in the Korean Conspiracy Trial and then the fight over the revised private-school regulations, missionaries took the stories about Christians who had been targeted with the utmost seriousness. On March 13, Oliver Avison telegrammed A. E. Armstrong, a secretary with the Canadian Presbyterian Mission, to come to Seoul immediately. Armstrong, who happened to be in Yokohama, Japan, on a visit, arrived on the morning of March 16. He was told that he had been summoned to witness firsthand what was occurring in Korea and to receive reports of the situation. The missionaries of Korea had chosen Armstrong because he was scheduled to return soon to Canada. Armstrong departed for Japan the following night and within a week left the country. On April 5, he met with Brown in the United States, handed him a detailed summary of the events on the peninsula, and discussed his own observations.

Brown and other members of the major mission boards viewed the situation in Korea with concern. Yet they wished to avoid making it appear as merely a mission or Christian issue. Responding cautiously, on April 16 they tasked the Commission on Relations with the Orient of the Federal Council of Churches with collecting reliable accounts of the atrocities allegedly being committed in Korea.[74] It published these accounts in two pamphlets, "The Korean Situation" and "The Korean Situation, Number 2." In addition to this centralized response from the mission boards, individual missionaries in Korea also wrote to newspapers, periodicals, and home churches with stories of Japanese violence. These accounts shocked the Western public and cast serious doubt on the Japanese government's carefully honed message that it represented a modern and civilized government. Indeed, the March First Movement seemed to offer clear evidence that Japan was incapable of being a civilized or modern imperial power.

The March First Movement reveals a number of important aspects of the complex interactions between missionaries, Koreans, and colonial officials. To begin with, at least temporarily, this event switched the power relations between missionaries and Korean Christians. After the outbreak of the protests, many missionaries sought to keep their schools open. However, the insistence of their students on participating in the movement and their subsequent arrests forced all mission schools to remain closed until the following year. Although missionaries might have preferred their students to remain free of political involvement, they were unable to enforce such a demand. The power to act was in the hands of Korean Christians. Indeed, many missionaries had a sense before the March First declaration that something was afoot. One station reported: "As the day approached for the public funeral . . . no one seemed able to find out just what was brewing. One missionary was told upon asking a leading pastor for his confidence that it was best that he should not know."[75] The Korean Christian organizers of the March First Movement kept missionaries in the dark, even when they sought information as to what was to occur.

While neither participating in the planning for the March First Movement nor necessarily approving of the participation of their students, missionaries did benefit as their relationship with the colonial government improved. On the one hand, officials were concerned over the missionaries' continued reporting and dissemination of this event to the international community. On the other hand, they assumed that missionaries could influence the Korean Christian community. Thus, the colonial government turned to mission societies in an attempt to defuse the volatile situation on the peninsula. In particular, the protests precipitated a change in colonial policy, as the Japanese government sent Saitō Makato to replace Hasegawa Yoshimichi as governor-general of Korea. Saitō soon instituted a set of political reforms and ushered in a period of cultural rule. In addition, seeking missionary support, the Saitō administration repealed or revised many of the measures on education and propagation that hindered the spread and practice of Christianity in the country.[76] In particular, it altered the 1915 ordinances on private school education. Private schools once again had the freedom to include religious education in the daily curriculum. Moreover, the colonial government passed a set of regulations permitting missionaries to receive "designation" for their schools. "Designated" schools received the same status as schools in the public system and many of their benefits. As will be discussed in chapter 7, in the 1930s, this change in policy would shape the course of the demand to bow at Shinto shrines.

The colonial government's engagement of the missionary community continued even after the initial wave of demonstrations subsided. For example, the GGK dispatched high-ranking officials to attend and speak at the Annual Meetings of the Federal Council of Protestant Evangelical Missions throughout the 1920s. In 1921, Mizuno Rentarō, who held the second-highest post in the colonial bureaucracy, addressed the council. He opened by stating that his trips through the countryside had impressed upon him the critical need missionaries met by providing for the moral uplift of the Korean people, stressing that missionaries and colonial officials were coworkers and that the work of missionaries was a great aid to the efforts of the GGK. With regard to the abuses perpetrated by colonial officials, he admitted that "mistakes and blunders" had been committed, and he thanked the missionaries for pointing out obvious faults. But he also noted that many allegations were based on unsubstantiated hearsay, and he mildly rebuked those in the missionary community who had made claims "based upon sheer misunderstanding or upon stories maliciously fabricated." Mizuno contended that further dissemination abroad of propaganda concerning alleged Japanese abuses was unwarranted and threatened peace on the peninsula. Concluding his address, he once again urged cooperation: "In this spirit of sincerity, Ladies and Gentlemen, we of the Government are open to your [missionary] approach, and you will ever find us ready to lend a willing ear to you so that no shadow of distrust may darken your relations with the authorities."[77] In short, Mizuno and the Government-General returned to the language of partnership when engaging the missionaries.

Chapter 6

Ecclesiastical Extraterritoriality

Missionary Power, Ecclesiastical Autonomy, and Church Schisms

In the first decades of the twentieth century, tales of churches bursting at the seams with Koreans flocking to hear the gospel and the tremendous spirituality of the Great Revival of 1907 convinced the Western world that Korea was one of the great successes of Christianity's spread in Asia. The missionaries to Korea took pride in the country's strong Christian population and emphasized the strength of their partnerships with Korean churches, arguing that the reason for this spectacular growth was their demand, from the very start of their work in the field, that Koreans take control of all aspects of the church. The Presbyterians, in particular, who held the largest share of Korean believers, credited their success to their "wise" use of policies like the Nevius Method. In reality, as we have seen, the conversion strategy of the Nevius Method meant that missionaries continued to occupy positions of dominance, as Koreans had to perform acts of obedience and demonstrate their "faith." Even after the rise of a group of committed and apparently sincere Korean Christian leaders, missionaries remained in the country and continued to direct Korean Christianity's development. By the 1920s, the issue of native control threatened the relationships between missionaries and the churches they had helped form and grow.

William Clark, who had arrived in Korea in 1909, wrote that despite their best intentions, missionaries were like other individuals in that they had trouble relinquishing the power of leadership.[1] Specifically, he likened the missionaries' reluctance to cede power to Koreans to the United States' refusal to grant independence to the

Philippines, despite repeated promises. In other words, whether intentionally or not, Clark characterized the missionary endeavor as a form of imperialism. Certainly, the power wielded by missionaries was less political than religious: they oversaw a network of Christian churches on the Korean Peninsula. At the same time, just as Western nations demanded that countries like China, Japan, and Korea establish modern systems of governance and participate in the global nation-state political economy, so too did Protestant missionaries want Koreans to establish ecclesiastical bodies and participate in a supposedly universal and global system of Protestant churches. In theory, these churches were equal; in reality, the missionaries' superior access to resources and domination of theological legitimacy meant that Korean Christians were limited in strongly advocating for the right to act as independent and fully autonomous leaders of the church on the peninsula. Some Koreans worked alongside missionaries, even though disgruntled about this inequality. Others attempted to break free of foreign control by creating independent churches.

Ecclesiastical Extraterritoriality: A Strong Strategic Alliance?

In 1922, Charles Allen Clark published a brief article for the *Korea Mission Field* titled "The Korean Presbyterian Church and the Missionaries." Responding to a set of questions sent by the International Missionary Council to mission boards around the world asking about the level of "self-determination" of native churches, Clark boasted that the Presbyterian missions in Korea had already attained the objective of establishing a self-governing church.[2] Referring to the Nevius Method, he asserted that from nearly the very beginning, the missionaries to Korea had sought to give Koreans autonomy. To prove his assertion of local independence, he pointed to the establishment of an independent Korean presbytery in 1907, which theoretically gave full ecclesiastical control to Koreans, and to the revision of the Korean Presbyterian Church's constitution in 1919. The 1907 constitution had granted membership to ordained Western missionaries and permitted them to attend General Assembly meetings and vote; it also specified that missionaries would remain a part of the presbytery until two-thirds of them voted to withdraw. Clark emphasized that during the 1910s, the missionaries repeatedly inquired whether the Korean presbytery wished missionaries to withdraw. The Korean leadership had refused. Moreover, at the missionaries' behest, the revised 1919 constitution included additional clauses that granted power to the General Assembly to oversee the work of member missionaries and, if necessary, censure or expel them. Clark concluded, thus, that the Korean Presbyterian Church exercised full independence but that it also understood the universality of Christianity. Apparently, the missionary-Korean alliance was strong.

On the surface, Clark's assessment that control of the church rested in the hands of Koreans appeared accurate. In fact, one veteran missionary who had served in India cited Korean churches as ideal examples of "self-supporting, self-governing, and self-propagating" institutions.[3] However, the establishment of an independent Korean presbytery in 1907 created an odd system of overlapping spheres of power that kept Korean Christians from true independence. In the first place, according to the rules of the new presbytery, missionaries could serve at any church that lacked a Korean minister. Because the first class of graduates from the seminary in P'yŏngyang in 1907 numbered only seven, in practice missionaries continued to run most churches, administer baptism, and provide pastoral care. Moreover, missionaries influenced the selection and cultivation of Korean Christian pastors. For instance, graduates of the P'yŏngyang seminary often worked in tandem with a missionary, the two forming a co-pastorate. William Swallen noted that this practice "provide[ed] opportunity to test the strength and wisdom of the new pastor and at the same time enable[d] him [the Korean pastor] occasionally to secure the much needed help of the missionary."[4] Swallen was not alone in his assumption that the abilities of Korean ministers needed testing and development. Several years later, Rodger Winn contended against those who wanted to allow Korean pastors to take full control of a congregation immediately after graduating from the seminary. On the one hand, he argued reasonably that running a church would be a challenge for any newly ordained pastor—Korean or otherwise. On the other hand, Winn indicated his belief that continued missionary oversight of the Korean Presbyterian Church was required. By being tactful in offering suggestions to their Korean partners, he said, missionaries could prolong their exertion of "real power over these Churches and make our [missionaries'] influence to count for the spiritual good and vital advancement of the Church."[5]

But another way missionaries maintained their power in the field was through what might be called "ecclesiastical extraterritoriality."[6] Extraterritoriality refers to the principle that citizens of foreign nations fall outside the jurisdictional control of domestic governments. Its use has often been seen as epitomizing the essential inequality of the various treaties that countries like Korea were forced to sign with Western powers during the nineteenth century.[7] Certainly, critics of missionaries have argued that these foreigners manipulated extraterritoriality to evade consequences for evangelizing where Christianity was banned.[8] But in "ecclesiastical extraterritoriality," missionaries exercised power over Korean church institutions without being subject to their jurisdictional control.

Missionaries effectively penetrated the Korean Presbyterian Church's sphere of influence, while Koreans possessed little direct power over the missionaries' sphere. Most obviously, because a number of ordained missionaries retained the right to speak and to vote during General Assembly meetings, they could shape the decisions made by native leaders.[9] In contrast, no Korean sat with voting privileges at the annual meetings of the joint Presbyterian missions of Korea. Since Korean Presbyterians lacked the power to directly affect the various enterprises run by the missionaries, the Korean General Assembly's right to censure and expel missionaries was a limited provision.[10] Even if expelled, missionaries could still operate on the peninsula through their respective mission societies. Stated differently, though claiming that Korean Presbyterians were fully independent, Clark reported that when censuring or expelling missionaries, the General Assembly could only prevent them from engaging in work directly controlled by the Korean Presbyterian Church. In making this point, Clark noted that missionaries were "not wholly under their [Korean Presbyterians] jurisdiction."[11] Furthermore, expelling missionaries from the General Assembly could pose a danger to Korean churches. Though the Nevius Method called for native believers to be self-governing and financially self-sufficient, the missionaries owned a network of large-scale social institutions, from hospitals and orphanages to private schools. These institutions constituted valuable resources for Korean Protestant communities. Thus, Korean leaders needed to exercise care lest they jeopardize their access to these properties.

An examination of the Korean Presbyterian Church's mission work in Shandong, China, sheds light on the significance of the special treatment missionaries received as outsiders who exercised power over Korean churches while remaining beyond their control. Though the Korean Presbyterian Church had engaged in mission work since 1907, its endeavors were directed at Koreans. In 1912, the leadership discussed plans to evangelize to the Chinese in China—a key moment in the presbytery's history. This plan required careful negotiation because of the potential conflicts with missionary groups already established in the field. Western Presbyterian missionaries stationed in Korea contacted their colleagues in China, who agreed to give Koreans oversight of the district of Laiyang, located in Shandong Province.[12] After a rough beginning, the Korean missionaries soon cultivated a vibrant church community. From 1915 to 1920, the church grew from a mere forty members to over five hundred.[13] The Korean Christian leaders' undertaking of a foreign mission represented a declaration of their maturation from a group dependent on Western missionaries to one now capable of supporting its own "mission church" in a foreign land. Stated differently, the Korean Presbyterian Church attempted to signify its equality with Western churches by entering into the business of foreign missions. Its success on this point, however, was mixed. On the one hand, Western missionaries working in China publicly announced their admiration of the effectiveness of Korean missionaries in Shandong. On the other hand, this admiration bordered on astonishment. One observer noted with surprise that "the Korean Church has sufficient Christian vitality to begin to take part in the problem of reaching the unevangelized portions of the world."[14] By expressing wonder at the Koreans' "sufficient vitality," the observer indicated a belief that these efforts were signs of a still maturing (not yet fully mature) Christianity in Korea.

More problematic than any veiled sense of superiority, however, was that Korean church leaders had to agree to several conditions stipulated by their foreign counterparts in China before the latter agreed to their presence in the same territory. In particular, Korean missionaries had to become full members of the local (Chinese) presbytery overseeing whatever region the Koreans were assigned.[15] This demand stood in stark contrast to the status of Western missionaries in Korea.[16] When the Korean General Assembly started to revise its 1919 constitution, it proposed a provision requiring missionaries to sever their memberships in their home presbyteries and transfer their memberships to Korea, which would have placed missionaries more firmly under the authority of the Korean Presbyterian Church.

However, according to Charles Clark, when the Australian Presbyterians responded that their church bylaws prohibited this move, the other Presbyterian mission societies likewise refused, and the Korean General Assembly relented.[17] Evidently the rules for Korean and Westerners were not the same. While Western mission organizations engaged in evangelism in Korean territory without effective oversight by Korean ecclesiastical institutions, Korean missionaries in China had no "extraterritoriality" privileges. Instead, they were subjected to the jurisdictional control of a Chinese presbytery. The presence of Korean missionaries in China only reinforced the inequality of the Korean-Western Christian alliance.

A United Methodist Church of Korea

An effort on the part of Koreans to create a single united Methodist Church for Korea revealed that Methodist missionaries, like their Presbyterian counterparts, wielded outsized influence over Christianity in Korea. To begin with, whereas the four Presbyterian missions—the Northern and Southern Presbyterians, the Canadian Presbyterians, and the Australian Presbyterians—had moved to form a united Korean Presbyterian Church by 1907, union for Korean Methodism would have to wait an additional two decades. The two main Methodist organizations of the United States, the Methodist Episcopal Church (Northern Methodists) and the Methodist Episcopal Church, South (Southern Methodists)—the latter formed in 1845, when it split from the main body over the issue of slavery—operated separate missions in Korea. In 1927, Korean Methodist leaders petitioned to create a united Methodist church in Korea. This request sent shockwaves through the two Methodist missionary communities. Union represented a clear break with the "mother" churches of the United States, still divided long after the end of the Civil War, and the request so stunned American Methodists that some questioned whether it revealed latent antiforeign sentiments among the Koreans.

J. S. Ryang [Yang Chu-sam], who would eventually serve as the first chairperson of the united Korean Methodist Church, penned an article for the *Korea Mission Field* in September 1927 to explain the aims of the Korean Methodists and to assuage the missionaries' fears. Throughout the article, Ryang negotiated a fine line between claiming membership in a universal Christian community and asserting the right of Koreans to take control. He opened by explaining that he represented the "mind of the Korean people called Methodists." In other words, he claimed solidarity with the world Christian community by emphasizing that this decision was undertaken by Methodists who happened to be Korean. While appreciating the sacrifices of the missionaries who had transported this religion to the peninsula, Ryang stated that the "Golden Age" of Christianity lay not in the past but in the future. To reach that Golden Age, Koreans needed to take control, for the simple reason that Korean Christians were better equipped—culturally, socially, and linguistically—to reach their unconverted compatriots. Ryang took pains, however, to dispel the notion that this move represented an attack on missionaries. He argued that the relationship between Korean Methodists and missionaries would "be the same as it has ever been"; at the same time, he stressed that they had separate roles and criticized the continued division of Methodism as a vestige of the unique cultural and sociopolitical context of the United States. Because Koreans were a homogeneous ethnic group, he implied, they should not be forced to adhere to a division rooted in the particular history of the United States or to wait until their American partners resolved their differences and reunited.[18]

From 1927 to 1930, Methodist leaders met to hammer out a new constitution, and in December 1930, the first meeting of the united Korean Methodist Church was held. However, the institution was still tied to its US counterparts both financially and structurally. The Methodist missions were important sources of financial support, as they owned most, if not all, of the major structures—from hospitals to schools—through which the Korean Methodist churches operated. Even in his 1927 article explaining the rationale for establishing a united Korean Methodist Church, Ryang had stressed that this institution would require the organizational and financial assistance from both the Northern and Southern Methodist Churches of the United States. Moreover, in his first report after the united Korean Methodist Church was established, Ryang noted that the loss of aid from the two mission boards had been a huge financial burden. He stated that the average monthly salary for Korean pastors was only $20.77 and that many communities met in houses rather than church buildings. Though these congregations supposedly met "joyously" and without complaint, many other communities urgently required some type of church structure but lacked the financial resources to build one. Thus, Ryang submitted a request for the Methodist churches of the United States to provide approximately 70 percent of the financial needs of the churches in Korea.[19]

The structure of the new Methodist union in Korea indicated that much as in the Korean Presbyterian Church, missionaries continued to fill positions of influence in this Korean institution. On the one hand, Koreans could send representatives to the general conferences of both the Northern Methodist and Southern Methodist Churches to "give information, and to render assistance *on legislation relating to the Korean Methodist Church* and to world brotherhood."[20] On the other hand, this right to participate did not include full voting privileges. In contrast, ordained Methodist missionaries to Korea were permitted to hold both membership and voting rights in the Korean Methodist Church while maintaining their membership in their home churches. In addition, missionaries holding membership in the Korean Methodist Church could participate in committees that determined who would run local churches.[21] In these manners, Methodist missionaries, like their Presbyterian counterparts, could influence the Korean church, while Korean leaders were unable to regulate the missionary endeavor.

Methodist Schism and Challenging Missionary Discipline

In describing the relationship between missionaries and Korean Christians, Charles Clark stressed they worked with "no line drawn between them" because of the "cordiality" of their working relationship.[22] Yet by the time Clark penned these comments in 1922, some efforts by groups of Korean Christians to break from foreign control and create independent churches had already shaken the mission societies in Korea, both Presbyterian and Methodist. One of the first major schisms occurred immediately after the Great Revival of 1907, within the Methodist church of P'yŏngyang. Mattie Noble, who arrived with her husband, William Noble, in 1892, kept a journal in which she recorded her impressions of Korea, her experiences with Koreans, and issues facing the church. Her diary provides a detailed account of the rift that opened in July 1907.

The root of the dispute was a conflict between Douglas Follwell, a Methodist medical missionary, and a local Korean Christian. The latter had recently purchased land adjacent to property owned by Follwell and started to build a house. Follwell, believing that the foundations of the house extended over the property line, requested that his Korean neighbor cease building. When this request was ignored, Follwell attempted, unsuccessfully, to persuade the Korean Christian to sell him the land. Finally, before heading to Seoul to attend to some matters, Follwell again instructed his neighbor to stop building over the property line. When Follwell returned, he found that the foundation had been completed in total disregard of his demand. Follwell then requested that the local magistrate determine the proper boundary and ensure, if Follwell's claim was correct, that the neighbor keep his house contained to his allotted plot. The magistrate subsequently summoned this Korean Christian for questioning.

Needless to say, this man and his friends were displeased with the turn of events. Things came to a head at a Sunday service. Mattie recorded what transpired at church:

> no sooner had the service begun than a commotion arose on the men's side. There was shouting and weeping behind the center partition, and threatening. We ladies at first thought it was a crazy man, but when the commotion continued and they were not put out, but Arthur [William Noble] tried to carry out the service by singing, we concluded it was something more serious than a crazy man's presence. We soon learned that it was a number of men trying to break up the service, and to get Arthur to publicly proclaim Dr. Follwell a wicked man. They were trying to get up a sentence against Dr. Follwell by a public mob clamour.[23]

At that time, in consideration of Korean social norms requiring the separation of men and women, a curtain was drawn down the center of the church. William Noble's attempt to settle the situation through singing failed when one of the men ran over to the women's side, shouting "stop singing, stop worshipping" and claiming that sin had entered the church and needed to be expelled before worship could continue. The sudden appearance of this man on the women's side, shouting and, one can imagine, waving his arms furiously, apparently startled a number of the women, and many made haste to exit. Even after a semblance of order was restored, some of the men continued to voice their displeasure while Noble attempted to lead the congregation in prayer. Order was not fully restored until Yun Ch'i-ho, a prominent Korean Christian of the elite class, who was in attendance to translate for a special guest speaker, stood up and "shamed" the congregation into silence.[24]

At issue here was Follwell's recourse to the local magistrate. Church bylaws stated that disputes between members should be decided by a church trial. The reasoning was that Christians should resolve their differences through the church rather than submitting to a worldly authority. Many Korean Christians, who had been drilled repeatedly on church laws and were expected to abide by them, were incensed by Follwell's failure to follow the established rules. And though they sat patiently through the remainder of the Sunday service, their anger did not dissipate. Immediately after the service, they insisted that Noble condemn Follwell. When he refused, stating that he needed time to look into the matter, they decided to leave the church.

While Mattie Noble did not record the number of people who walked out, apparently not a few decided to become "secessionists." Even those who stayed appeared to harbor resentment against Follwell. For about two weeks, the situation appeared bleak. Yi Ŭn-sŭng, the Korean pastor attached to the Methodist church in P'yŏngyang, attempted to act as an intermediary between the missionaries and the leaders of the group that had left. In addition, Korean Christians from both sides met with each other informally to discuss how to resolve the impasse. Eventually, the leaders of those who had left agreed to meet with Douglas Follwell and William Noble on a Saturday night. The two missionaries pleaded with the Korean Christians to return. Follwell also offered an apology, saying that he was wrong not to have first sought a church trial. However, Follwell and Noble left the meeting without any assurances of reconciliation. In fact, they sensed that their continued presence would cause more unrest. After the departure of the missionaries, the "secessionists" continued to debate the next step. In the end, they decided on reconciliation, and on the following Sunday morning it seemed that peace had been restored, as all but three of those who had left the church returned.[25]

William Noble argued that one of the factors that contributed to the schism was the sudden, massive influx of converts, which prevented missionaries from sufficiently indoctrinating them in church laws.[26] Far from believing that Koreans were ready to be granted independence, he believed that continued oversight and assurances that converts were endowed with a full measure of Christian maturity were still needed. The departure of these Christians did not, however, indicate a poor grasp of church law. Rather, it was by virtue of their knowledge of Methodist regulations that they demanded that

Follwell be reprimanded, if not harshly punished, for his failure to bring his land dispute with his Korean Christian neighbor to trial before the church. Noble's congregation wanted Follwell, a missionary, to be held to the same standards that all Korean Christians needed to respect. In claiming equality with the missionaries, those Korean Methodists who left the church expressed their refusal to be treated as inferior.

This episode demonstrates that many Korean Christians were prepared to challenge the missionaries' authority. They believed in the righteousness of their cause and were unafraid to press their claims. Why, then, did they ultimately choose to return? One likely reason for their decision was the lack of a pastor or church leader. Mattie Noble recorded that those who had left the church originally attempted to recruit Yi to lead their new group. Yi had been in Seoul when the commotion over Follwell's actions first erupted. Mattie Noble expressed some anxiety over how Yi would react after he returned and whether he would leave with the secessionists or remain "true to his Church and the missionaries."[27] In the end, Yi stood steadfastly by the missionaries and urged those who had left to reenter the fold.[28] Without a pastor, the schism attempt quickly fizzled. For groups to truly break free of missionary control, the legitimacy of a pastor was required.

Ch'oe Chung-jin's Challenge of the Nevius Method

Attempts to break free of missionary control occurred within the Presbyterian community also. Though the establishment of an independent Korean presbytery failed to erase the influence of missionaries, this institution possessed the right to ordain pastors. With the ordination of the first set of Korean pastors in 1907, Presbyterian missionaries no longer held a monopoly over baptism or the determination of Christian orthodoxy. Within three years, a Korean Presbyterian pastor, Ch'oe Chung-jin, would initiate an independent church movement.

Ch'oe was born in Chŏngŭp County, North Chŏlla Province, in 1870. After a brief time in the Catholic Church, from roughly 1896 to 1897, Ch'oe met Lewis B. Tate, who had arrived in the mission field in 1892 and pioneered the Southern Presbyterian Mission's work in North Chŏlla. Under Tate's guidance and instruction, Ch'oe converted to Protestantism and soon became one of the Southern

Presbyterians' most effective workers.[29] Tate entrusted Ch'oe with more and more responsibility and eventually came to describe Ch'oe's passion for evangelism as on a par with the Apostle Paul's. As a result of this vigor, in 1904 Ch'oe joined two other Koreans from North and South Chŏlla to become part of the first group of Koreans from the region to attend the Presbyterian seminary in P'yŏngyang. In 1909, Ch'oe graduated as a member of the third class of seminary graduates and was ordained. The Korean Presbyterian Church then dispatched him back to his home region to work with John Nisbet.

Ch'oe was not in his position long before he caused controversy. In early January 1910, Ch'oe sent a letter to the North Chŏlla sub-presbytery with five demands.[30] Particularly striking, he called for a relaxation of the requirements for conversion and baptism, he petitioned for his area of responsibility to be expanded, and he requested that he be given a house to allow him to conduct his work without too much hardship.[31] The sub-presbytery crafted a response letter to him on January 7, 1910. After rejecting each of Ch'oe's five demands, the letter proceeded to state that because these requests contravened Presbyterian methods and church regulations, Ch'oe needed to appear in front of the sub-presbytery on January 25 to give an explanation.[32]

On January 10, Ch'oe Chung-jin responded by announcing his intention to break free from the Korean presbytery and form an independent church. As news of his decision spread across North Chŏlla, debates arose in the various churches of the province about whether to join Ch'oe.[33] In the end, Ch'oe's movement fizzled, due largely to his alleged mismanagement of funds. In 1912, the colonial government convicted him of financial corruption and sentenced him to two years in prison. After his release in 1914, he pleaded for forgiveness before the Chŏlla presbytery, which had been established in 1911, and was accepted back into the fold. But, perhaps unable to deal with his diminished role in the church, he left again, joining Japanese Christian missionaries who were attempting to make inroads in North Chŏlla.[34]

Not surprisingly, Western missionaries were quick to denounce Ch'oe as having succumbed to greed and pride.[35] A closer examination of Ch'oe's challenge, however, offers important insights into the unequal power dynamic between missionaries and Korean Christians. To begin with, Ch'oe's five requests, in some way, all critiqued the Nevius Method. As we have seen, the purpose of the Nevius Method was to ensure correct belief by constantly testing potential converts for outward signs of sincerity. But this method made conversion both difficult and costly, and it meant that missionaries, and later Korean church leaders, could compel potential converts to abide by a legalistic code of behavior. In fact, Ch'oe referred to the members of the sub-presbytery as Pharisees—the Jewish order Jesus had condemned for its formalistic adherence to Jewish law while missing the law's spirit and intention.[36] Ch'oe's call for the abolishment of these rigorous standards challenged the burden that the Nevius Method's emphasis on outward demonstration of changed lives and the rote memorization of Christian dogma placed on many Korean Christians.

Ch'oe's demand for a house represented a reversion to the pre–Nevius Method approach wherein new churches and Korean Christian workers relied on outside funding rather than being financially self-sufficient. Considering also his later conviction for financial fraud and corruption, Ch'oe appears to have been fixated on money. Still, his demand also represented a call for equality. First, missionaries received healthy allowances from their home mission boards for the purchase and upkeep of homes. To cite one example, in 1902, Luther McCutcheon joined the Southern Presbyterian Mission. In 1904, he received a sum of $2,050 to purchase a house—a figure more than four times his salary of $500.[37] Houses were expensive and beyond the means of missionaries; a housing stipend was viewed as a necessity. In fact, during the first meeting of the Korean Presbyterian Church in 1907, when the Evangelistic Association Committee put forth a motion to send a Korean missionary and two evangelists to Cheju Island,[38] the committee recommended that in addition to a salary, the presbytery supply funds to defray travel costs and provide housing.[39] As this motion indicates, many Korean Christians believed that housing and other expenses related to work in the field should be covered. For a former missionary assistant like Ch'oe, the request that the presbytery provide housing would not have seemed unreasonable, given that missionaries, both Korean and foreign, received such provisions. Having risen to the status of a minister, which was a rank at least equal to that of the missionaries (many of whom were not ordained), Ch'oe believed he was entitled to the same benefits.

In addition, the salary disparity between missionaries and Korean workers was vast. For example, in 1908, Presbyterian missionaries stationed in the provinces of North and South Chŏlla earned salaries ranging from $600 to $1,150, depending on the size of their families. The salary for missionary helpers in the same region ranged from $72 to $90.[40] While missionaries recognized the difference in pay, they worried that giving helpers a higher salary would attract "rice Christians," who sought conversion simply for the sake of employment. Regardless, the pay differential must have been a source of friction. Along these lines, Ch'oe's request to expand his territory may have been connected to the issue of financial stability. While we do not know his motivation for asking for control over counties such as Puan, Koch'ang, and Mujang, we do know that the addition of these counties to Ch'oe's charge would have given him control over much of the southwestern portion of North Chŏlla. If Ch'oe was concerned with his salary, increasing the territory and, more importantly, the population under his watch would have made a significant difference. More Koreans to evangelize meant more potential church members, and more church members meant access to greater financial wealth.

The request for additional territory might also have been driven by the power dynamic between missionaries and Korean Christians. When the Korean Presbyterian Church gave Ch'oe Chung-jin his initial charge over the churches in Chŏngŭp and T'aein, it made Ch'oe a partner with John Nisbet. In theory, missionaries worked under the auspices of the Korean Presbyterian Church, and thus Ch'oe and Nisbet were at the very least of the same status and on equal terms. The reality was more complex. Before becoming a pastor, Ch'oe had worked under the authority of Western missionaries; Ch'oe's ordination as a pastor did not change this past. Furthermore, the Southern Presbyterian Mission had nominated Ch'oe for theological training, and it even paid part of his expenses related to his schooling.[41] As Ch'oe neared graduation, the Southern Presbyterian Mission petitioned the Korean Presbyterian Church to dispatch Ch'oe to the Chŏnju station to work with Nisbet in the position of an "evangelist." In sum, it was the Southern Presbyterian missionaries who sent Ch'oe to the seminary, provided financial assistance, and ensured that he would be stationed in Chŏnju to work with a Western missionary. Although Nisbet may have attempted to treat Ch'oe as an equal, the facts of Ch'oe's training, ordination, and appointment in the field would have placed him below Nisbet in status and power.

For their part, the missionaries felt deeply betrayed by Ch'oe's actions. This feeling may have been why the letter sent to Ch'oe on January 7 used the Korean term *pae*—which is used in words denoting betrayal—five times. Tate, who had been on furlough in the United States during the initial period of Ch'oe's schism, was particularly shocked. He returned in early 1910 to find that the work he had left in the care of Nisbet and Ch'oe had been severely damaged. Tate labored frantically to win back the churches that had left as part of Ch'oe's movement. But the shame of knowing that the man he had converted and to whom he had entrusted so much power had, only moments after receiving ordination, betrayed him enervated Tate and damaged his standing in the missionary community. Not only did Ch'oe's schism reflect poorly on Tate's ability to judge character and measure a Korean's sincerity; it was also a direct attack on Tate: in requesting control over Puan, Koch'ang, and Mujang, Ch'oe asked for much of the territory under Tate's watch. Effectively, he was asking for the removal of Tate from the field. This stinging rebuke of Tate was a clear indication of the tension between missionaries and Korean church leaders.

Yi Man-jip and Korean Christian Independence

Ch'oe Chung-jin was only the first of several Korean Presbyterian leaders who sought to break free of the Korean Presbyterian Church, which was still heavily influenced by Western missionaries.[42] Perhaps the greatest challenge to missionary power, and one that ultimately required the state's intervention, took place in Taegu, North Kyŏngsang Province. As noted in chapter 2, the Northern Presbyterians established the Taegu station in 1896. In 1900, James Adams converted Yi Man-jip. Like Ch'oe Chung-jin, Yi demonstrated both great intelligence and zeal for his new faith, and he quickly rose in the membership ranks. He later served as Henry M. Bruen's helper and became a favorite of Walter Erdman, who in 1912 advocated sending Yi to the Presbyterian seminary in P'yŏngyang. After receiving his ordination in July 1917, Yi returned to Taegu and served as a pastor at Namsan Church. He was shortly thereafter transferred to serve as a co-pastor with Erdman at Namsŏngjŏng Church, the first Presbyterian church established in Taegu, in January 1918.

Demonstrating both a desire to work with youth and an interest in the social, if not the political, well-being of the Korean nation, Yi took on a leading role in establishing a branch of the YMCA in Taegu in September 1918. He became a leader of the March First

Movement in Taegu the following year and was sent to prison for two years by the Japanese colonial government. When on his release Yi returned to his post at Namsŏngjŏng, he met with opposition from a segment of his congregation. The opposition stemmed from a generation gap between the younger, progressive majority and the older, conservative minority of the congregation.[43] Throughout the 1920s, in line with theological discussions taking place around the globe at the time, a growing movement took root within institutions such as the YMCA and among Korean Christian leaders such as Yi Man-jip, Sin Hŭng-u (Hugh Cynn), Pae Min-su, and many others to ensure that religion and Christian spirituality was manifested in practice in the lives of individuals. Stated differently, Christianity should address real social conditions.[44]

The socially engaged and active theology of Yi Man-jip enjoyed tremendous support from his congregation in Taegu. However, many Korean Presbyterians and missionaries were theologically conservative and suspected that support of the social gospel indicated an acceptance of liberal theology.[45] The tensions between the more socially focused and more theologically centered groups in the church came to a head in early 1923. At the annual meeting of the North Kyŏngsang presbytery in January, about fifty members of Yi's church petitioned for his dismissal. The presbytery denied the request on the grounds that sufficient cause had not been presented; however, the effort to remove Yi raised concerns, and William Blair, who was chairing the meeting, ordered the formation of a committee, to be led by Henry Bruen and Kim Yŏng-ok, to investigate what was occurring at Namsŏngjŏng.[46] On March 1, 1923, a special session of the presbytery was convened to hear a report concerning this matter. Kim Yŏng-ok announced that from January 8 to 10, the committee had met with both those seeking Yi Man-jip's dismissal and the leadership of Namsŏngjŏng Church. No amicable resolution of their dispute could be reached.[47] When Bruen then approached Yi to discuss the friction, not only did they reach an impasse, but Yi indicated that both Namsŏngjŏng and Namsan would leave the Northern Kyŏngsang presbytery and join the Kyŏngsŏng (Seoul) presbytery. After Kim finished his report, a motion was passed to convene another special session of the presbytery to prevent Yi's attempt to switch the membership of Taegu's two main churches. On March 6, 1923, the presbytery suspended Yi Man-jip and Pak Yŏng-jo, the pastor of Namsan Church.

Rather than quietly retreating, Yi and Pak responded on March 18 by declaring their withdrawal from the presbytery and from missionary control. At a meeting attended by nearly five hundred congregants of Namsŏngjŏng Church, roughly four hundred voted to declare independence.[48] Yi also drew up a "declaration of independence," had around three thousand copies printed, and on March 26 distributed them widely to churches and other Christian groups throughout the peninsula. In his declaration, he announced that the Taegu churches could no longer abide unrighteousness and thus had chosen to break free of the North Kyŏngsang presbytery, which he claimed was under the control of missionaries.[49] For this action, the North Kyŏngsang presbytery expelled Yi and Pak in April 1923.

Though the initial dispute between Yi and his opponents may have originated over differences in theology, Yi's movement focused on issues of control and independence from outside influence. The root of Yi's schism was twofold. Most obviously, Yi had been a leader of the March First demonstrations of 1919. It is likely that his not being able to achieve Korean political independence made the issue of religious independence a more sensitive topic. More subtly but no less importantly, as with Ch'oe Chung-jin's attempted schism, Yi's complaint was connected to the Nevius Method—which had long emphasized that churches should be self-governing. As noted above, only a minority of church members had complained of Yi Man-jip's leadership. The majority supported Yi. That a minority could prompt the missionaries and the North Kyŏngsang presbytery to "investigate" and potentially censure him was appalling to Yi. In issuing the declaration of independence, Yi and his supporters were declaring the right of local churches to be truly self-governing, free from outside interference—especially from *foreign* missionaries.

Significantly, from Blair's oversight of the presbytery to Bruen's leadership of the investigation, missionaries were clearly influential in the administration of Christianity in Taegu. The reality of the missionaries' power in the region came to light following Yi's declaration. During several months of extreme tension, the congregations of Taegu's two main churches fractured into those who wanted to remain with the presbytery and those who followed Yi. Yi and his supporters outnumbered those who wished to stay and thus were able to physically occupy Namsŏngjŏng and Namsan. In addition, they presented a lawsuit to take control not only of the churches but also of the land on which the churches sat. Though the governor of North Kyŏngsang Province ordered that Namsan be returned to the missionaries, he permitted Yi the continued use of Namsŏngjŏng. Of this situation, Martha Bruen cynically remarked that the Japanese colonial officials were "protecting the thieves" and preventing the "lawful owners" from controlling the church. She went so far as to snicker that the Japanese government vigilantly patrolled the northern border of Korea to ensure that communist elements could not enter the country yet "allow[ed] and protect[ed] a small crowd of utterly lawless men to stage a 'red show.'"[50]

The judicial system's ruling that the missionaries could not remove Yi from Namsŏngjŏng stemmed from confusion over who owned the church. While Bruen was listed as the founder *(sŏllipcha)* of Namsan Church, a Korean, Hong Sŭng-han, was listed as the founder of Namsŏngjŏng. In August 1908, a typhoon had severely damaged the original building at Namsŏngjŏng. The congregation raised the funds to erect a new church and therefore gained a stake in the church building.[51] Thus, when the Japanese colonial government issued the "Religious Propagation Ordinance (1915)," which required that each church appoint a founder, the pastor of the church was named "founder."[52] The missionaries did not fully understand at the time, however, the special privileges and power that this individual held in the Japanese legal system. Charles Clark remarked to the Board of Foreign Missions of the Presbyterian Church in the USA that when the Government-General first required churches to appoint a founder, the missionaries had assumed that it was merely a "convenient device" for the colonial government to contact a leader when it needed "official information regarding the churches." Now confronted with Yi's schism, Clark lamented that "the Sullipja [founder] is supreme in control of the organization. His appointees as pastor are the ones recognized, not those approved by the Presbytery. His word as to the property is final, not the word of the General Assembly."[53] The schism in Taegu revealed that control of church property depended not on who held deeds of ownership or on the directives of the Presbyterian General Assembly but on who held the position of founder—a position that ultimately drew its power from the state.

When the local presbytery discovered that it could not depose Yi and take control of the church without authorization from the founder, it quickly wrote to Hong Sŭng-han, who, after appointing Yi Man-jip as head pastor, had departed to serve as a missionary to

China in 1917. Hong provided his official seal, and the North Kyŏngsang presbytery applied to the state to have Yi removed as head pastor. But Yi responded by filing another lawsuit to have Hong removed as founder on the grounds that he had left in 1917 and that the church in fact belonged to the congregation as a trust. Thus, the congregation should possess the right to appoint a new founder.

In November 1923, the district court of North Kyŏngsang Province ruled in favor of the North Kyŏngsang presbytery. The judge based his ruling on an interpretation of the church community being a "trust" that diverged from the one espoused by Yi. The ruling held that though Namsŏngjŏng lacked legal status as a trust, in practice the position of founder and the church community existed like a trust. But because a portion of the community still desired to meet according to the original conditions under which the church was established, Yi and his group had no right to break free. Moreover, by declaring independence, Yi had clearly left the presbytery and thus forfeited any right to appoint a new founder.

Yi and his group maintained control over the church while they continued to appeal, and the courts refrained from ordering them to give up that control. According to Cleland McAfee, this was because of a supposed Japanese custom of compensating those evicted from private spaces even if they possessed no right to those spaces.[54] While the missionaries at first balked at the idea of providing compensation, as the conflict grew longer, they became willing to offer something. Yi and his group demanded partial ownership of the land. The missionaries refused.

When the schism had first occurred, the missionaries had been confident in their claim because they owned the land on which the church building stood. Much to their dismay, their ownership came into question over the course of the protracted legal struggle. Under the initial district court decision, the judge had ruled that the church had to be administered according to the original conditions of its founding. Initially, the missionaries praised this decision. However, it also had implications for their property rights. The land was included as a part of the functional trust of the church community, and thus the missionaries could not simply use the property as they wished. They quickly realized that though they held the deeds to the land, any attempt to sell it or transfer ownership to another party might lead to a new round of litigation. Further complicating the matter, the missionaries learned that during the Japanese colonial government's land survey of the 1910s, the official owner of the land had been listed as "Yesu Kyo Dang" (Jesus Church), not James Adams or the Board of Foreign Missions of the Presbyterian Church in the USA. When the Land Bureau had published its findings, the missionaries had had a ninety-day window to make corrections, after which the findings of the survey became official. Unaware of this requirement at the time, the missionaries had raised no objections. During the litigation, Yi had used the title "Yesu Kyo Dang" for his "new" congregation.[55] For all these reasons, the validity of the Northern Presbyterians' claim to the land was in question.

Because of the number of legal issues over ownership and the reluctance of Japanese officials to simply evict Yi, the struggle over control of Namsŏngjŏng continued until October 1931, when the courts finally ordered that officials restore the building to the original tenants.[56] Yi and his followers vacated the church. By this time, however, Yi's movement had gained enough momentum to continue. With over eight hundred members, he established the Chosŏn Yesugyo Pongsan Kyohoe.

Refusal to Leave

The 1920s witnessed a number of conflicts within the Korean Christian, in particular Presbyterian, community. A common explanation for these conflicts holds that a younger generation of Korean Protestant leaders, theologically educated abroad and more accepting of liberal theology, were critical of missionaries and an older generation of Korean leaders, who stood in solidarity with their Western colleagues.[57] This line of interpretation, however, underplays the tensions that existed between Korean Protestants and missionaries over the issue of the inequality of the relations between these two groups. Indeed, the attempted schism within the Methodist church of P'yŏngyang took place among the first generation of Korean converts and missionaries. Moreover, both Ch'oe and Yi received their theological training within the missionary-run Presbyterian seminary of P'yŏngyang. The common thread running through all three of these schisms was neither generational nor theological training but rather a chafing at the inequality of the relationships between Koreans and missionaries.

For their part, the missionaries viewed repeated attempts by Korean leaders to break free of foreign control as signs not of perhaps justifiable discontentment but of spiritual weakness within the churches. In other words, their efforts to assert independence provided further justification for a continued foreign presence. Indeed, William Hunt described the weaknesses of the Korean church leadership as stemming not from ignorance of scriptural truth but from a "lack of faith" and a "false spirit of independence." For example, Hunt argued that Korean leaders complained excessively about their low salaries and their constant reliance on "begging" or "borrowing" to survive; though he was sympathetic to them, he held that they needed to trust in God's grace to provide for their material needs. Hunt suggested that in place of faith and trust, Korean Christian leaders harbored antiforeign sentiments.[58]

Yi Man-jip's attempted schism raised the stakes. Here the missionaries' primary concern lay not with Yi's spirit of rebellion but with whether the colonial state would recognize church governance. According to the bylaws of the Korean Presbyterian Church, the presbytery had control over the property and the right to appoint and dismiss pastors. Yi challenged the authority of church law by appealing to civil law. In justifying their repeated requests for funding from the Board of Foreign Missions of the Presbyterian Church in the USA to prosecute this case, the missionaries noted that it would set a precedent. Would civil authorities recognize and respect church law? Or would civil law supersede church law? Though missionaries rejoiced at the courts' final decision, Yi Man-jip's case revealed the authority of the colonial state to intervene in a "religious" debate.

By the early 1930s, the stage had been set for an eruption of controversy between missionaries, Korean Christians, and colonial officials. Moving forward, it is important to keep in mind that many Korean Christian leaders had become disenchanted with the language of partnership espoused by the missionaries. One of the most visible forms of this discontent was the establishment of the Positive Religious Band (Chŏkgŭk sinang tan), by Sin Hŭng-u (Hugh Cynn), a contemporary of Yi Man-jip. Sin was the former general secretary of the YMCA in Korea and had, during the 1920s, promoted the need for Korean cultural and social reform. By 1932, however, Sin had become more critical of the applicability of "Western" democracy for Korea's situation and the continued power wielded by foreign missionaries. Instead, he sought to create a form of Christianity controlled by Koreans and that spoke to the practical conditions in the country.[59] Inspired by the Positive Christianity movement in Nazi

Germany, Sin organized the Positive Religious Band.[60] Most missionaries dismissed Sin's organization. Some viewed it as another sign for the need to monitor the development of Christianity in Korea. Others viewed this movement as a sign of the dangers of "modernism." Very few missionaries, if any, understood it as being rooted in the frustration that many Korean Christian leaders felt over the unequal relations between Western and Korean churches.

Chapter 7

Ties Severed

Shinto Shrines and the Expulsion of Missionaries

From the moment Protestant missionaries first stepped onto the Korean Peninsula, one of their stated objectives had been the creation of strong and independent Korean churches. Yet even after the establishment of native ecclesiastical institutions and the development of a cohort of theologically trained and ordained Korean pastors, missionaries remained in the country and exerted influence. As explored in chapter 6, Korean Christian leaders attempted multiple times to assert their equality with, if not independence from, missionaries. But Korean Christians were not the only group that confronted the issue of the continued presence and power of these foreigners. The colonial government was also concerned with how to handle missionaries, albeit with the different goal of regulating Christianity on the peninsula. The March First demonstrations of 1919 were a reminder that religion could serve as a node for protest against the state and that missionaries often disseminated unfavorable portrayals of colonial rule to the international public.

The decline of missionary influence in Korea was ultimately caused by pressure from both the colonial government and the Korean Christian community during the 1930s. The immediate catalyst precipitating this decline was the Government-General of Korea's (GGK) renewed efforts to have all Koreans attend State Shinto ceremonies.[1] State Shinto had been a problematic facet of Japanese society, and by extension the Japanese empire, for Christians since the Meiji Period (1868–1912).[2] Helen Hardacre and others have long noted that during the second half of the nineteenth century, the early architects of "modern" Japan marshalled a (re)invented Shintoism to construct a new Japanese nation.[3] Before the nineteenth century, Shintoism, as a system of belief practiced in Japan, was intertwined with Buddhism. However, starting in the early nineteenth century, a group of scholars from the domain of Mito became increasingly concerned about the encroachment of Western nations and, in particular, their use of Christianity and conversion to undermine the rule of local leaders by assimilating at least a part of the native population.[4] In response, Mito scholars called for the purification of Japanese customs and identified Shinto as the native religion of Japan. Their prescription influenced the early Meiji Restorationists, who first sought to disassociate Shinto practices from Buddhism and based their newly established imperial system on a reconstructed form of State Shinto. Yet, as Trent Maxey has elucidated, the attempt to base the Meiji state on a "sacred" system of shrines produced a number of sectarian conflicts in Japan and protests from Western nations.[5] In response, government officials continuously redefined the newly adopted category of "religion" (Jp.: *shūkyō*) to distinguish State Shinto—upon which imperial authority was based—as a secular, yet still sacred, system separate from religion and religious beliefs. This "nonreligious" form of Shinto was the version the GGK would require Koreans, regardless of personal faith or beliefs, to observe.

One of Maxey's observations has been that "religious policy" within Japan did not develop in a linear manner but was disjointed and evolved over time, in response to specific problems and stimuli. The same was true as the Japanese empire expanded beyond the Japanese metropole; regulations on religion were often unevenly applied in its colonies. Stated differently, religious policy was not first fully developed in Japan and then exported to and imposed on colonial territories.[6] Instead, the GGK's directives on Shintoism in Korea were often a response to conditions within the country and reflected tensions in the ways officials, practitioners, and society as a whole understood this religion.

Presbyterian Communities in Korea: Modernism, Fundamentalism, and Dissension

Of the major denominations operating in Korea, the narrative of straightforward Christian resistance to Shintoism is applicable only to the Presbyterians, which on the whole initially opposed shrine ceremonies. The colonial government's order to bow at shrines exacerbated theological controversies that swirled both within Korea and in the United States at the time. Starting in the early 1930s, many Presbyterian leaders observed with concern that some members were becoming enamored with modernism, which included liberal theology and the social gospel.[7] For example, in 1934 the Korean Sunday School Association (Chosŏn Chuil Hakkyo Yŏnhaphoe) published an article questioning the inerrancy of the Bible. Though the article was published anonymously, it was known that a Korean Presbyterian pastor had written this piece. Thus, in 1935 the General Assembly of the Presbyterian Church decided to issue a clear statement in condemnation of any who questioned the accuracy of the Bible.[8]

The other challenge, related to the first, confronting the Korean Presbyterian Church was the threat of a schism. In 1932, the General Assembly approved the formation of a new presbytery for Kyŏnggi Province. Until this time, all the churches in the region had belonged to the Kyŏngsŏng (Seoul) presbytery. The creation of the new presbytery was a recognition of significant differences between churches located in Seoul, an urban area that leaned toward a more modernist interpretation of Protestantism, and churches in the countryside. Even with this action, however, tensions lingered among the churches of Seoul, and in 1933 six churches in the city petitioned the General Assembly to join the Kyŏnggi presbytery. The General Assembly denied the request, but concerned with the conflict in Seoul, it appointed a special commission to mediate between the competing factions and to take the steps necessary to bring about harmony. The commission failed to resolve the conflict and instead presented a report chastising several leaders on both sides of the dispute.[9] In reaction, representatives from the Kyŏngsŏng presbytery lodged a formal protest at the General Assembly's annual meeting, held in September 1934, arguing that the commission had unconstitutionally served as a judicial committee, dictating how a presbytery—which was supposed to have full institutional autonomy—should conduct its internal activities.[10] Kyŏngsŏng demanded that the commission rescind its report and challenged the authority of the General Assembly. It was joined in protest by other presbyteries located in the southern half of the peninsula.

The Korean Presbyterian Church was in danger of splitting along a north-south line, and the Presbyterian missionaries moved to hold a special "retreat" in the spring of 1935 to avert a schism.

Though schism was avoided, the missionaries recognized that tensions still remained and feared for the overall health of churches located in the southern half of the country.[11] In explaining the root of animosity, Stanley Soltau—a missionary with the Northern Presbyterians—argued that the conflict reflected anger over the changed fortunes of the northern and southern halves of the peninsula.[12] For most of the Chosŏn Dynasty (1392–1910), those from the southern provinces dominated elite positions in the bureaucracy. They monopolized sociopolitical power and tended to look down on those from the northern regions of the peninsula.[13] However, the uneven growth of Christianity, with most converts coming from the provinces of North and South P'yŏngan and Hwanghae (in 1932, roughly 55 percent of all Korean Presbyterians were from one of these three provinces, while only 4.5 percent were from the Seoul region),[14] meant that the northern provinces dominated positions of power in the General Assembly and exerted tremendous influence in defining orthodoxy on the peninsula. Describing this situation, Soltau argued that those who resided in the "north" held the "decadent south" in disdain. In return, southerners had a severe "inferiority complex" and were prone to think northerners were constantly attempting to slight them.[15] Whether regional discrimination was truly driving the Korean Presbyterian Church toward schism or whether it was simply a convenient rallying cry for the disaffected members of the Kyŏngsŏng presbytery is unclear. Regardless, tensions simmered between Christians centered in the northwestern part of the peninsula and those in Seoul.

The turmoil surrounding the Kyŏngsŏng presbytery was particularly worrisome to missionaries and the Board of Foreign Missions of the Presbyterian Church in the USA (BFMPCUSA; Home Board). First, the debate over modernism in Korea during the 1920s and 1930s was tied to contemporary currents in the United States. Sparked by Harry Fosdick's provocative 1922 sermon "Shall the Fundamentalist Win?," the debates that would become known for pitting modernism against fundamentalism dominated religious life in America during this period.[16] Because of a perceived shift in the Presbyterian community toward liberalism, John Gresham Machen, a professor at the PCUSA's flagship seminary in Princeton, New Jersey, left his position in 1929 to establish a new institution, Westminster Theological Seminary. Eventually, the modernism-versus-fundamentalism divide spread to affect foreign missions. Suspicious that the BFMPCUSA secretly harbored a modernist tendency and was willing to accommodate foreign religions, Machen formed a separate agency, the Independent Board for Presbyterian Foreign Missions, in 1933—the same year that the six Seoul churches petitioned to transfer their membership to the Kyŏnggi presbytery.[17] In response, the General Assembly of the PCUSA declared that this newly established institution violated its constitution and ordered the ordained pastors working for the Independent Board to cease. For many PCUSA members, this demand was an unconstitutional exertion of ecclesiastical power. In contrast, those who supported the actions of the General Assembly noted its right to prevent members from working at any agency that claimed to be operating as part of the Presbyterian faith in the United States.[18] In the end, the General Assembly defrocked Machen in 1935. Machen responded by establishing the Orthodox Presbyterian Church in June 1936.

In sum, Korean Presbyterians and missionaries confronted a debate over liberal theology, dealt with the threat of schisms both in Korea and in the United States, pondered the constitutional limits of the General Assembly, and questioned whether the BFMPCUSA was guilty of harboring modernist tendencies during the same period in which the GGK was ratcheting up pressure on all groups in Korea to participate in State Shinto ceremonies. For at least some Presbyterians, firmly rejecting Shintoism represented more than maintaining the integrity of individual faith. It also meant protecting Christianity from a slide toward modernism and, in the case of missionaries, protecting the mission's right to decide on issues free from undue—and unconstitutional—intervention from the Home Board.

P'yŏngyang and the Refusal to Bow at Shrines

For at least the first two decades of the colonial period, the GGK had been largely unsuccessful in convincing Koreans to participate voluntarily in Shinto ceremonies as a part of its effort to assimilate Koreans into the empire.[19] But starting in the early 1930s, officials enforced attendance with growing resolve. This move coincided with an increased militarization of the Japanese empire. After the Mukden Incident (1931) in Manchuria and the establishment of the Japanese puppet state, Manchukuo, the position of Korea in the Japanese colonial empire shifted. Japanese leaders came increasingly to believe that the transformation and assimilation of Koreans into loyal Japanese subjects were crucial for Japan's expansion on the Asian continent.[20]

One key prong in the colonial government's plan to assimilate Koreans into the empire was having all school children bow at shrine ceremonies.[21] This order would set the stage for conflict with the major mission societies operating in Korea, as education constituted a significant aspect of their work.[22] In 1932, Governor-General Ugaki Kazushige ordered mandatory attendance at shrine ceremonies for all schools.[23] Throughout the year, officials across the peninsula summoned students to bow at shrines. However, compliance from students attending the missionaries' private schools varied, as local officials were often willing to compromise with missionaries. Yet, the change in the GGK's desire to enforce attendance for all students was clear. Reporting on an early conflict regarding this new direction, the US consul-general to Korea, John K. Davis, noted that Japanese officials had met with leaders of the mission societies in P'yŏngyang in November 1932. The cause was the refusal of the principals of the various missionary-run private schools to send their students to bow at government-mandated State Shinto ceremonies in September of that year. Davis reported to his superiors that the governor of South P'yŏngan Province insisted that the missionaries sign a document declaring they would comply with future orders to send students to shrines if so required. Eventually, the missionaries agreed to sign it, but only if the governor added a provision that they were so obligated only for "ceremonies that have no religious significance—in which no religious element is involved." Though the crisis had apparently passed, Davis concluded that this incident had "greater significance than appears on the surface and represents an effort on the part of an element among the military . . . whereby all Christian schools might be coerced into participating in Shinto."[24] His assessment was prophetic.

By the summer of 1935, the Protestant missionary community anticipated that the GGK would again demand that students participate in State Shinto ceremonies.[25] In preparation, the Northern Presbyterians made the issue of how to respond to requests to bow at shrines the major topic of discussion at their annual meeting.[26] They passed a resolution calling on its executive committee to meet with the GGK to lay out its concerns regarding State Shinto and, if compromises could not be reached, to go no further than agree to having students attend, but not fully participate in, ceremonies.[27]

In early October 1935, the GGK ordered schools in Seoul to go to the Imperial Shrine.[28] The Presbyterian missionaries protested, and the Executive Committee of the Northern Presbyterian Mission passed a three-point resolution. They would first ask that their students be exempted. If this was refused, they would ask that their students be permitted to perform alternative acts of patriotism. If this was refused, mission schools would send students only on the basis of accepting the colonial government's insistence that bowing at shrines held no religious meaning. Nevertheless, even in this case, the Northern Presbyterian missionaries would consider attendance as a provisional compromise and would seek further meetings with colonial officials to address the attendance at Shinto shrines.[29] The colonial government denied the Northern Presbyterian Mission's first two requests, and, though under protest, the principals of the Chungsin (Chŏngsin) Girls School and Kyungsin (Kyŏngsin) Boys School (John D. Wells' Boys Academy) sent their students to participate.[30]

The episode in Seoul did not lead to a major conflict because of the Seoul station's decision to comply with the government's order. One month later, on the morning of November 14, 1935, the principals of the middle schools of South P'yŏngan Province gathered for a meeting called by Governor Yasatake. When the principals and their assistants arrived, they were informed that cars were waiting outside to transport them to and from the local shrine.[31] At this point, George McCune, who oversaw Soongsil (Sungsil) Boys' Academy and Union Christian College, and his assistant; Velma Snook's assistant, who attended on behalf of Soongeui (Sungŭi) Girls' Academy; and Hei Man Lee, who represented the Seventh Day Adventists' Ŭimyŏng Academy in Sunan, and his assistant refused to enter the cars. After those who agreed to participate in the shrine ceremonies returned, Yasatake summoned to his office the five who had remained behind and insisted that they immediately go to and bow at the shrine. McCune and the others inquired about the meaning of the ceremonies; Yasatake allegedly replied that the Japanese people believed that the spirit of Amaterasu, sun goddess and mythic founder of the Imperial House of Japan, and the spirit of the Japanese emperor were present at the services. The five responded that this was a religious ceremony and thus they could not in good conscience participate. The governor, in turn, inquired whether their objections were based on personal convictions or on their status as school principals. McCune and the others asked for more time before giving a formal answer. Their hesitation in giving an immediate reply was because they suspected their responses would have repercussions on their work in secular education. This fear was not unfounded. For example, in July 1935, the Northern Presbyterians discussed how refusal to bow at shrines might result in the loss of licenses to operate at their annual meeting. In addition, when the Executive Committee of the Northern Presbyterian Mission approached the Educational Department, in October 1935, to discuss the matter of sending students to shrines, officials indicated that the GGK viewed principals of all schools as "government officials and agents . . . subject to the Government's orders."[32]

Yasatake agreed to give the principals until December 20 to respond. On December 9, George McCune, Harry Rhodes, and James Holdcroft met with Watanabe Toyohiko, director of the Educational Department of the GGK, in Seoul to discuss the matter. Watanabe opened the meeting by remarking how regrettable it was that of all the denominations, only the Presbyterians had refused to accept the GGK's explanation that these ceremonies were nonreligious in nature.[33] He then attempted to assuage the missionaries' concerns by encouraging them to publish in their various church periodicals the news that the GGK had officially and publicly announced that no religious elements were contained in the shrine ceremonies that schools were required to attend. In response, the missionaries requested that Watanabe issue a formal statement that there were no "spirits" present at the ceremonies. Watanabe refused, though he suggested that the statement that State Shinto had no religious significance should logically address the issue of spirits.[34]

On December 13, McCune submitted to Yasatake his refusal to participate in shrine ceremonies on the grounds that such events were religious, because, according to the governor's own admission, spirits were present.[35] Perhaps viewing this refusal as an attempt by the Northern Presbyterians to obtain proof that the GGK in fact understood State Shinto to be a religious affair and thus a violation of the document signed earlier in November 1932, Yasatake returned the letter, stating that McCune had misunderstood him. Specifically, Yasatake claimed that he had never stated that there were "spiritual" elements in shrine ceremonies.[36] Then, on the morning of December 31, officials met with McCune. In McCune's presence, Watanabe Toyohiko read a formal "warning." This warning first laid out that the Japanese government adhered to the principle of separation of church and state and supported the free practice of religion. It continued by stating that the Northern Presbyterians had misconceptions regarding bowing at shrines. The warning repeated that State Shinto ceremonies were nonreligious—a point that the other mission societies and schools were now coming to realize. Expressing regret that the Northern Presbyterians refused to accept repeated explanations given by the GGK, the "warning" chastised McCune and the Northern Presbyterians for confusing education and religion. The purpose of schools was not to teach religion but to provide national education. For this reason, in setting up schools, the missionaries had entered into the realm of the state. In short, education was a national or a public concern. Regardless of individual beliefs, principals at private schools, thus, had an obligation to follow state directives and policies. Private schools were not exempt from national directives on education. The warning concluded by demanding that McCune quickly comply and have his students attend shrine ceremonies.[37]

In early 1936, Governor Yasatake summoned not only George McCune but also Samuel A. Moffett to appear before him to submit an official response. McCune informed the governor that he would not observe shrine ceremonies. He explained that on the one hand, as a Christian he believed in being loyal to government authorities, and as a principal of the school he had offered repeated assurances that he would "pay the highest honor and respect to His Imperial Majesty, The Emperor, to the Imperial House and to the Exalted Personages whose memory the state so rightly cherishes."[38] On the other hand, while acknowledging the GGK's claims that State Shinto was not religious in nature, McCune bluntly stated that these statements had "failed" to erase his "conscientious objections" or his suspicion that religious elements imbued these ceremonies. With this response in hand, Yasatake removed McCune from his position as principal of Soongsil Boys Academy and forwarded a recommendation to the governor-general that McCune also be removed from the presidency of Union Christian College. Per this recommendation, McCune was stripped of his presidency on January 20.

The Presbyterian missionaries in P'yŏngyang decided to wait and see whether colonial officials would continue to order that students, faculty, and school administrators participate in shrine ceremonies before making a final decision regarding their next steps. Many took a pessimistic view of the situation and turned to the BFMPCUSA for assistance. As early as October 1935, the Executive Committee had urged it to take a definitive and strong stance on State Shinto, arguing that this would strengthen the bargaining position of the missionaries in Korea.[39] In March 1936, the Executive Committee renewed this plea, painting a dreary picture of colonial officials' commitment to enforcing obeisance at shrines.[40] In the past, missionaries had been able to reach acceptable compromises with local officials. However, now the central government had ordered that teachers and students, without exception, participate.

Indicating the firmness of its stance, the GGK forbade missionaries to discuss the issue at meetings on the grounds that any discussion was an act of sedition. Moreover, in April 1936, the government officially declared that Shintoism was the foundation of the Japanese empire and that all must fulfill their patriotic duty to observe shrine ceremonies.[41] In anticipation of being forced to attend shrine ceremonies once the new school year commenced, the Presbyterian missionaries in P'yŏngyang made plans to stop taking new students at their secular educational institutions. In addition, at their annual meeting in July 1936, they decided to close their schools in P'yŏngyang if colonial officials continued to insist on shrine attendance.[42] In September, the Home Board approved this decision. The conflict the missionaries were preparing for came in October 1936, when the governor of South P'yŏngan Province once again required all schools to appear at the shrine. Shortly thereafter, the Northern Presbyterians working in P'yŏngyang moved to shut down their schools.

Whose Schools?

After the confrontation in P'yŏngyang, both foreign and Korean Christian communities throughout the peninsula had to decide how schools should handle forced participation in shrine ceremonies. Most denominations and groups accepted the colonial government's assertion that State Shinto was secular. For instance, the Methodist missionaries in Korea officially adopted the stance that attendance at shrines was an act of patriotism with no religious significance.[43] In taking this position, they noted that keeping schools open would provide opportunities not only to teach students about Christianity but also to instruct them in the differences between State and non-State Shinto. Though they may have been skeptical of the colonial government's official explanation, the Methodists held that full withdrawal from the realm of secular education would remove many young Koreans' only chance to be exposed to Christianity and to a Christian perspective on issues like Shintoism.

In contrast, the Presbyterians' refusal to participate in shrine ceremonies required them to consider what to do with their educational institutions. Both Northern and Southern Presbyterians had invested a great deal of resources into building and running schools. The two mission societies quickly discovered that divesting themselves of these institutions would be a complex affair and would bring to the fore the question of who actually owned them.

In explaining its refusal to send students to bow at shrines in response to the governor of South P'yŏngan Province's order, the Executive Committee of the Northern Presbyterian Mission argued that the Korean Presbyterian Church was both unified in its opposition to Shintoism and prepared to suffer for its faith.[44] Those against participation argued that because of this strong objection from Korean Christians, they had realized that the mission would lose all moral authority if it permitted students to bow. Reporting to the Home Board on the Executive Committee's decision, for example, James Holdcroft wrote that the GGK had nearly convinced them that there was "no solid reason" their students should not participate.[45] The actions of more vocal and conservative forces within the Korean Presbyterian Church apparently gave momentum to those within the mission who staunchly opposed Shinto ceremonies.[46] Bolstered, if not feeling compelled, by the actions of the Korean Christian community and perhaps seeing themselves as acting on behalf of all Christians throughout the Japanese empire, the Northern Presbyterians decided to oppose the colonial government's order to send their students to shrines.[47]

Though McCune and his supporters argued that the Korean Presbyterians were united in their opposition to State Shinto ceremonies, there were differences of opinion on whether bowing was truly a form of idolatry. Moreover, when confronted with the prospect of having their schools closed, many Korean Christians reacted in protest. For example, in July and August 1937, a number of prominent Korean Protestants—from pastors to elders and principals to teachers—submitted to the Northern Presbyterian Mission petitions stating that they did not believe Shinto was "religious" and requesting that the Northern Presbyterians continue their work in secular education. Of note, the elders of Sorae also submitted petitions calling for the missionaries to keep their schools open.[48]

Korean opposition to shuttering schools was widespread, and missionaries turned to their home boards for assistance. For example, the Southern Presbyterian missionaries were in step with their Northern colleagues in opposing the command for obeisance at shrines. But when the Southern Presbyterians in Korea made the decision in November 1936 to shutter their schools, local protests from Koreans prompted the missionaries to seek guidance from their Home Board. In December 1936, they requested that Charles Darby Fulton, executive secretary of the Southern Presbyterians' Foreign Mission Board, come quickly to Korea to render assistance. After inspecting conditions in the country, Fulton argued that most Korean Christians shared with missionaries a belief that Shintoism was a form of idolatry but would opt to have their children educated regardless of the spiritual compromises they might be making. With this assessment in hand, the Southern Presbyterians decided to close their schools gradually. No new students would be accepted, and the schools would close once the remaining students had graduated. However, if the GGK continued to insist on participation in shrine ceremonies, then missionaries were to immediately close their schools.[49] On September 6, 1937, the governor of South Chŏlla Province again ordered all students to bow at shrine ceremonies. The Southern Presbyterians declared the following day that all their schools were closed, effective immediately.

The Southern Presbyterians shut down their schools with relative ease compared to the Northern Presbyterians, who faced more resistance from local officials, opposition from Korean Christians, and turmoil both within the mission and between the mission and the Home Board.

To return to the case of P'yŏngyang, after the second order issued by the governor of South P'yŏngan for all schools to attend shrine ceremonies in October 1936, the missionaries moved to close their schools. But they confronted a series of legal obstacles. First, because of failing health and pressure from colonial officials, Moffett retired and left Korea in October 1936. Velma Snook left the same month. Both Moffett and Snook held the position of founder *(sŏllipcha)* for the Northern Presbyterians' schools in P'yŏngyang, and, legally, only the founder possessed the power to close a school. Thus, the Northern Presbyterians could not shut down or make any fundamental changes to the administration of these institutions. The missionaries submitted applications for the approval of new founders in the spring of 1937, but, as Ralph Reiner reported, colonial officials were slow to process these applications.[50]

Even with new founders, the missionaries ran into an additional roadblock. In July 1937, the GGK revised the private school regulations. Arguing that private schools were "permanent institutions" of the state, serving the public interest, the revised regulations specified that these schools required government approval not only to open but also to close. The P'yŏngyang station found local officials to be slow in granting this approval. Apparently, one reason for the colonial government's refusal to permit the closure of these institutions in P'yŏngyang was the social unrest such an action might incur, as Korean students had already protested in early 1936, after rumors emerged that Moffett would shut down Union Christian College.[51]

A great deal of anxiety and anger existed within P'yŏngyang as discussions of what the Northern Presbyterians would do with their educational institutions percolated in society. Local officials needed a ready plan to mitigate the potential for unrest if these schools closed. Officials in P'yŏngyang called Edward Miller, Ralph Reiner, and Charles Bernheisel to the provincial office in January 1938 and explained that they would not forward the proposal to close the Northern Presbyterians' schools to their superiors unless the missionaries agreed to lend some of their buildings to the government. P'yŏngyang lacked the infrastructure to immediately absorb the soon-to-be-displaced students, and officials desired to use some of the mission school buildings on a temporary basis, at least until new structures could be erected. The P'yŏngyang missionaries quickly contacted the Executive Committee, which agreed that a loan of three buildings should be made pending Home Board approval. After receiving this approval, the Northern Presbyterians loaned the buildings to the colonial authorities. In turn, officials of South P'yŏngan Province formally forwarded the request to shut down the schools to the central government.[52]

Beginning with the initial decision by the Northern Presbyterians to close their schools in P'yŏngyang, missionaries throughout Korea also confronted opposition from current students, alumni, and Korean Christian leaders, who, claiming these educational institutions were vital parts of local communities, asserted their "right" to have them transferred to local control if the missionaries wished to depart.[53] In P'yŏngyang, in 1936, for example, almost as soon as news of the desire of the Northern Presbyterians to shutter their schools became public knowledge, local church leaders came forward and petitioned to have them pass over to their control. The Northern

Presbyterians were hesitant, believing that any individual or group who would take control of the schools would be required by the GGK to agree to shrine ceremonies. They sought the guidance of the Home Board but received the response that the responsibility for dealing with this problem rested on the shoulders of the missionaries in Korea. Pressured by local demand, the Executive Committee agreed to give Korean leaders time to find potential buyers for the schools, and indeed multiple parties vigorously attempted to purchase them.[54] But both those stationed in Korea and the Home Board rejected these initial offers, believing that the prospective buyers would be unable to maintain the Christian character of the schools.[55]

In the end, the rhetoric of working in partnership with Korean Christians and the missionaries' own insistence that Koreans eventually take control of the church put into place the conditions necessary for many schools to be transferred to native ownership. The prime example concerned Keisung (Kyesŏng) Academy of Taegu. This institution had been established in January 1906 through the efforts of James Adams and Yi Man-jip. By the 1930s, Keisung was a prominent fixture in Taegu's educational market, and entering the institution was a competitive process. Local Koreans responded in anger to the missionaries' announcement of school closure. They had expected transfer of property to their control. Instead, the Presbyterian missionaries had unilaterally decided to close their schools and sell the properties.[56] In protesting the decision to shut down these institutions, Harold Henderson emphasized that neither students nor teachers viewed Shinto shrine obeisance as religious, and he held that shutting down these schools would unnecessarily deprive the missionaries of an important tool of evangelism.[57]

But the fate of Keisung would be determined by the language of its own constitution, which had been rewritten during the 1920s in the aftermath of the March First Movement. As a part of its Cultural Rule measures, the colonial government adjusted its education policy, allowing mission schools to receive "designation," which effectively would place them on par with schools in the public system. To receive designation, schools needed to conform to government standards, which included improving the level of instruction, upgrading facilities, and increasing endowments. In turn, schools had to compose new constitutions that outlined these changes.[58] Reflecting the oft-repeated ideal that Koreans should eventually take full control of Christianity on the peninsula, the new constitution for Keisung stated that it was a joint institution overseen by the Northern Presbyterians and the local presbytery and that, in this spirit, if one party or the other decided to cease work at the school, its administration would transfer wholly to the remaining party as long as the Christian character of the institution remained intact.[59] As a result of this provision, the missionaries discovered that their decision to withdraw from Keisung required the transfer of the institution to the presbytery, which claimed its right to oversee the school.[60] Thus, starting in March 1939, Korean Christians took official control.[61]

Keisung was not an exception. The Northern Presbyterians soon learned that other educational institutions had included similar clauses in their constitutions.[62] In Sŏnch'ŏn, in North P'yŏngan Province, for example, the local missionaries stated that the constitution for their educational institutions contained a clause giving the local presbytery the right to take over the schools if the Northern Presbyterians chose to withdraw.[63] In speaking of the transfer, Henry Lampe maintained that the local presbytery represented not a "new" organization but rather a "continuing" body, which would seek to maintain the schools now that the Northern Presbyterians had decided to exit secular education.[64] Importantly, in all these cases, the missionaries who supported the transfer of control emphasized that Korean Christians administered these schools in partnership and on an equal basis with the Northern Presbyterians.[65]

Whose Conscience?

The inability to exit secular education cleanly was not simply externally imposed by the GGK but was also driven by infighting within the Northern Presbyterian Mission. Horace H. Underwood, Harold Henderson, and those who called for the transfer of schools to local control complained that the Northern Presbyterian Mission's decision to withdraw from secular education was motivated primarily by the concerns of the P'yŏngyang station. Because of its dominance in numbers—in terms of both Korean Christians and missionaries—this station was able to push an agenda regardless of other opinions.[66] Indeed, just as had happened with the Kyŏngsŏng and Kyŏnggi presbyteries, missionaries located in the southern part of the peninsula, and in particular in Seoul and Taegu, complained of the dominance of their colleagues to the north throughout the debates on what to do with their educational institutions.[67] On the whole, the Presbyterian missionaries stationed in P'yŏngyang were unbending in their opposition to the observance of Shinto ceremonies, while those stationed in Seoul and Taegu were more willing to accede to the GGK's orders, if doing so would permit the continuance of Christian influences in secular education. The "southern" missionaries, though in the minority, were vocal in their beliefs.[68] As early as July 1936, at the annual meeting for the Northern Presbyterian Mission, Horace Underwood and others forwarded a motion to close schools only on a case-by-case basis. In other words, the motion protested a blanket withdrawal from education and sought to give each school the flexibility to first seek alternative solutions. Though the motion was defeated, Underwood and others of his viewpoint pressed forward to ensure that the Presbyterians' educational work would continue.

The Seoul and Taegu station missionaries' objection to the rigidity of their colleagues from the north was partly motivated by the implication that those who permitted shrine attendance were somehow not Christian. Viewed differently, at the heart of the struggle between those who opposed and those who permitted bowing at Shinto shrines was judgment of the "conscience," or internal belief, of others.[69] Since at least the adoption of the Nevius Method, Presbyterian missionaries had observed the actions of converts to assess true or sincere belief. McCune had declared that the Japanese government had failed to overcome his personal "conscientious objections" that even State Shinto contained religious elements. He and his supporters, however, extended their "personal" beliefs to levy a judgment regarding how all Christians should approach Shinto rituals. Now even the faith of missionaries was to be judged according to certain specific actions. A "true Christian," in short, did not bow at shrines. In criticizing those who would hand control of schools to Koreans, James Holdcroft stated that Horace Underwood, Edwin Koons, and Harold Henderson were "not and never have been the spiritual leaders of the Mission."[70]

In contrast, those who believed that a Christian could bow at shrines complained of having their "conscience" and faith judged by others.[71] They opposed using the conscience of one or even many Christians to evaluate all Christians.[72] Viewed broadly, this position was a challenge of the Nevius Method, which had first been promoted by Horace G. Underwood. Ironically, his son, Horace H. Underwood, offered the clearest reasoning why actions alone were not reliable to judge the private beliefs of others.[73] Instead, missionaries also needed to consider statements and explanations. He articulated this argument to his colleague William Swallen. Underwood stated that he might assume that Swallen was praying if he saw Swallen with his head bowed and eyes closed. However, if Swallen spoke to the contrary, then Underwood would have no choice but to accept this statement. In a similar fashion, Underwood argued that if the colonial government claimed that bowing at shrines held no religious significance, then he had no choice but to accept this explanation. In addition, Underwood also observed that individuals perform certain acts of courtesy daily and that bowing in Japanese society was a form of respect. He cited an example of when he attended the funeral service of Bishop Gustav Mutel. As a sign of respect, he bowed his head, but he argued that his act was certainly not an act of worship or an indication that he adhered to Roman Catholicism. Because Underwood was satisfied that State Shinto was nonreligious and did not view his own participation as holding religious significance, his bowing at shrine ceremonies posed no conflict with his faith.[74] He therefore felt no hesitation in handing control of schools over to those who believed that State Shinto was only a patriotic exercise. Likewise, in writing to the Home Board, influential leaders in the United States, and his friends, Underwood emphasized that the GGK had consistently claimed that State Shinto contained no religious elements and that many Korean Christians accepted these claims at face value. In other words, for Underwood, the question of bowing was one of personal conscience, which varied from individual to individual.

The conflict within the Northern Presbyterian Mission community over actions and "conscience of belief" was exacerbated by measures taken by the BFMPCUSA.[75] At least some of the more conservative-minded missionaries in Korea suspected that the Home Board secretly harbored modernist tendencies. Nevertheless, confronting the colonial government, the Executive Committee of the Northern Presbyterian Mission turned to the Home Board for support. The Executive Committee's fears that the Home Board would be unsupportive were temporarily allayed in September 1936, when it endorsed the committee's decision to withdraw from secular education if the GGK continued to insist that mission schools participate in shrine ceremonies.[76] Suddenly, however, in February 1937, the Home Board sent the Executive Committee instructions to wait for the arrival of Charles T. Leber and Joseph L. Dodds, two secretaries from the BFMPCUSA, before making any final decisions regarding the closure of schools.[77]

Leber and Dodd's directives were to inspect the conditions in Korea and make a recommendation regarding how to proceed. In mid-April 1937, they submitted their report to the BFMPCUSA, remarking on the visible tensions as the various mission stations quarreled over what to do with their institutions. While P'yŏngyang was largely united in seeking to close its schools, both Seoul and Taegu seemed adamant about seeking alternative solutions. Leber and Dodds noted that Korean Christians also seemed divided in their opinions. Though many appeared to consider Shinto obeisance a form of idolatry, they also strove to keep their schools open at any cost. The report recommended that the Home Board instruct the Executive Committee to inform all parties, including the GGK and the groups seeking to take control of the schools, that only the BFMPCUSA had the power to dispose of property. As noted above, the Executive Committee had in fact made this request in March 1936, only to be told that the responsibility and authority rested with the missionaries in the field. But only a year later, Leber and Dodd recommended that the Home Board reverse course. In addition, until a final decision had been made regarding the schools, the P'yŏngyang station was to maintain the current policy of refusing to take new students for the next school year to impress upon the GGK that the Northern Presbyterians' threat to withdraw from secular education was not idle.[78]

By putting the final decision in the hands of the Home Board, Leber and Dodds reasoned, pressure on the missionary community would be attenuated. They believed that their proposals would support the efforts of the Northern Presbyterians. The hope was that as the Home Board moved to address the problem of educational work in Korea, missionaries, the GGK, and Korean Christians would be able to work out a mutually satisfactory compromise. However, the Executive Committee found these proposals to be counterproductive, as the Executive Committee remarked that the very sending of the Leber and Dodds commission weakened the hand of the Northern Presbyterians. The Home Board appeared to waver in its insistence that secular education cease.[79] Furthermore, the longer the Home Board delayed its decision about closing schools, the more aggravated the Executive Committee became, and the more anxiety and animosity built up among Korean Christians and missionaries. On the one hand, many Koreans hoped all the more that transfer would become a reality; on the other, the potential for violent reaction if the transfer failed to occur grew as time passed.[80]

The Home Board continued to issue directives that seemed, to the Executive Committee, to countermand the order to withdraw from secular education. The tide appeared to turn in March 1938, when the Home Board requested that the Northern Presbyterians again vote to see whether they had any changes in opinions. Subsequently, in September 1938, the Home Board issued a series of "troubling" recommendations.[81] First, noting that several institutions, such as Keisung, were to be transferred to "church groups" or "Christian boards of trustees," the Home Board requested that the Northern Presbyterians assist these organizations in taking over these institutions. Furthermore, the Home Board also urged the Executive Committee to permit missionaries to work at these institutions, if only unofficially and on a temporary basis. Then, in contradiction to a proposal to immediately withdraw from secular education administered in union with other mission societies, such as Chōsen Christian College, the Home Board remarked that a final decision on this matter should be made at a later date. Finally, the Home Board urged the Executive Committee to seek a transfer of ownership of Chungsin Women's Academy to local control.

Many Presbyterian missionaries in Korea responded to the September 1938 orders with disgust. One missionary wrote to the Home Board, "My first reactions after reading the letter was one of anger, then resentment, and then one of pity."[82] Charles Allen Clark echoed these sentiments: "We all feel outraged and betrayed and anticipate sorrows upon sorrows here."[83] Their anger was connected to the contemporaneous debates in the United States over the rise of modernism in Christianity. Indeed, as news of the Shinto issue in Korea became publicized in America, a number of private citizens had written the BFMPCUSA to complain. One individual, a self-identified "Presbyterian and fundamentalist," declared that the church could not participate in shrine ceremonies and still be Christian.[84] Those opposed to handing over schools to Korean leaders argued that the Home Board had been misled by the petitions received from Korean Christians and the letters and reports from missionaries like Underwood. Confident of their assessment that State Shinto was a form of idolatry and pointing to the oppression of the colonial state, these missionaries chafed at the Home Board's sudden change in policy and resisted.

The Executive Committee's anger was not limited to theological concerns or personal conscience. It complained that the Home Board had acted unconstitutionally.[85] The committee urged the Home Board to reconsider its change in policy on administrative grounds.[86] The Home Board did not relent, and it made several attempts to explain its position and assert its "supreme authority" over all decisions made in the mission field. In the end, the internal debates within the Presbyterian community led a group of missionaries—including William Chisholm and James Holdcroft—to tender their resignations and join Machen's Independent Board of Presbyterian Foreign Missions. Informing his friends of this decision, Chisholm reported he was pleased to be joining a mission society that desired "to maintain a clear testimony in this land [Korea] to the existence of the One only, the Living and True God."[87]

The 1938 General Assembly Meeting of the Korean Presbyterian Church

One reason colonial officials remained stubborn in insisting that all schools, without exception and regardless of faith, participate in shrine ceremonies was that the loyalty of Christians remained suspect. Just as many missionaries doubted the GGK's claims that State Shinto was devoid of religious significance, so too did Japanese officials doubt the missionaries' claim to respect government authorities. When confronted with a choice between being loyal to one's religion and being loyal to the state, many chose their religion. William Swallen summed up his position on this conflict by writing: "I have always taught that the Bible teaches obedience to the powers that be. But when the nation's laws cross God's law, His clear expressed Word—never."[88] Many Korean Christians, likewise, were willing to choose their faith over their citizenship.

After the outbreak of the Asia-Pacific War in July 1937, the Japanese imperative to transform Koreans into loyal subjects became even more pressing. Toward this end, in 1938 the GGK announced that it would pursue the assimilation of Koreans in three sectors: education, participation, and unity.[89] As a part of this direction, colonial officials took steps to ensure that the Korean Presbyterian Church would approve shrine attendance for its members. First, the GGK forced local presbyteries to accept its characterization of State Shinto as nonreligious before the annual meeting of the General Assembly was held in September 1938. The North P'yŏngan presbytery complied in February, and shortly thereafter the other presbyteries of Korea followed suit. Next, the GGK screened members of each presbytery and sought to ensure that the presbyteries would only send delegates who would approve shrine obeisance to the annual gathering.

On the opening day of the meeting, the missionaries arrived at the hall and found a "cordon of police" surrounding the building to prevent entry by anyone who was not a delegate. More plainclothes police were scattered throughout the hall, as were a number of high-ranking government officials. Right before the close of the first session, a motion to vote on the issue of shrine participation was put to the floor. Japanese officials had previously informed missionaries that they would not be permitted to speak or vote on this issue. Ignoring the warning, one missionary rose and demanded the right to speak. The moderator responded that missionaries would not be recognized. For the next several minutes, one missionary after another rose in protest. Despite these protests, a vote of "yea" was presented, and the motion to approve shrine participation passed without a vote for "nay" ever being taken.

The 1938 General Assembly marked a turning point in the relationship between Presbyterian missionaries and the Korean Presbyterian Church, at least on the institutional and formal level. In subsequent meetings, the Korean Presbyterian Church continued to assert its independence from Western control. The General Assembly announced in 1939 and 1940 that it would participate in the "total national force movement" and align itself more closely with Japanese Christianity. During these meetings, Korean Christian leaders declared a commitment to eradicating their reliance on "Europe and America" and gaining control over schools, Bible institutes, and all of the other institutions in Korea that missionaries controlled. They further affirmed a commitment to the "radical reforms" of the constitution, rituals, and evangelistic principles of the Korean Presbyterian Church. Furthermore, the 1939 and 1940 annual meetings of the General Assembly required not only school staff and students but all members of the church to attend Shinto shrine ceremonies. Indeed, in December 1939, the General Assembly issued a "warning" to all member churches that failure to perform Shinto obeisance would "not only scorn the decision of the General Assembly" but also be "a regretful act that is in opposition to the will of the Lord."[90]

Charles Clark and others had long stressed the independence of the Korean General Assembly, yet they had maintained their membership in this ecclesiastical institution and wielded power on the peninsula.[91] At least some Korean Christian leaders were disgruntled over the missionaries' continued presence in the country, control over schools, and refusal to permit schools to participate in shrine obeisance. For instance, to protest the closure of schools, Cho Sŭng-hak wrote a letter to the BFMPCUSA. Though he was president of the Korean Student Federation of North America, he stressed that he was writing in a private capacity. After stating that most Korean Christians viewed shrine ceremonies as no more religious than saluting the "stripes and stars" or "placing florals before the tombs on Decoration Day," Cho complained that the Home Board should "give some attention to Korean Christians when they try to tell you the fact and subtract somewhat what your missionaries tell you. Dr. McCune has done a great damage to the Korean Church in the end."[92] Other Korean Christians were less restrained in voicing their displeasure. Archibald G. Fletcher reported in the spring of 1938 that even more than Japanese officials, "Koreans, Christian as well as unchristian, are bitter in their denunciation of the American Missionaries and are agitating that the Westerners be driven out."[93]

In sum, there was a breakdown in the relationship between missionaries and Korean Christians. Indeed, many missionaries viewed the 1938 General Assembly's decision to participate in shrine ceremonies with dismay, if not disgust. One missionary declared with disdain that Korean pastors had been "careless and shallow" in permitting the 1938 vote.[94] Another missionary announced that he had chosen to ignore the General Assembly's decision to approve of shrine obeisance on the grounds that it was unconstitutional.[95] Many others severed their connections with the Korean Presbyterian Church.[96] Stripped of their work in schools and churches, missionaries increasingly found it difficult to justify their presence on the peninsula. This difficulty was only heightened when, in 1939, Clark received a notice from the governor of South P'yŏngan that the seminary and Bible institutes could not open unless they received government permits. Because the missionaries understood that receiving permits required an agreement to participate in shrine ceremonies, they decided to close the seminary and Bible institutes.[97] Literally lacking work to do, missionaries started to leave Korea. Though some continued to operate in the country, every year their influence and numbers decreased.

By 1940, Douglas B. Avison opened his annual report by remarking that regardless of occupation, these were the "finishing days for the white man in Korea." Many missionaries made the decision to return home "for reasons other than old age or sickness," and no replacements were dispatched.[98] The slow departure of missionaries out of the country became a mass exodus in October 1940, when the US State Department advised its citizens to leave Japanese territory. By December 1941, on the eve of the bombing of Pearl Harbor, only a handful of missionaries remained in Korea. The colonial government placed the remaining missionaries from non-Axis countries either under house arrest or interred them in makeshift prisons. By the spring of 1942, the US State Department had negotiated with the Japanese government an agreement to repatriate its remaining citizens in Korea. On June 1, 1942, they left Korea. With this, the Japanese colonial government completed the severing of the missionaries' direct ties to Korean churches and their presence on the Korean Peninsula.

This is not to say, however, that Korean Christian institutions were free. Instead, in line with the Japanese empire's larger discourse on the Greater East Asia Co-Prosperity Sphere, colonial officials continued to coerce Korean Christian leaders to sever their connections to a universal or Western Christian community in favor of a Christian church that fell under the aegis of Japan. In this manner, colonial officials attempted to remove the ambiguity of Korean Christians' religious and national identity by establishing a single church that paid allegiance to the Japanese empire. The colonial government used coercive force on those who opposed or resisted.

Conclusion

Communities Reimagined

In late September 1942, nearly ten months after the attack on Pearl Harbor, August Karl Reischauer, a longtime missionary to Japan, shared his personal observations and thoughts with the Board of Foreign Missions of the Presbyterian Church in the USA (BFMPC-USA) regarding the shrine controversy that had shaken the Christian community in Korea. He argued that Japan existed under a "divine blur." Though the Japanese constitution guaranteed freedom of religion, the same document characterized the state as "divinely constituted." Thus, despite claims that bowing at state ceremonies was merely a patriotic act, subjects who pledged loyalty to the imperial house were paying homage to an institution shrouded in sacred imagery. Most Japanese Christians had accepted the government's claims that State Shinto was secular in nature, but a great deal of anxiety remained, because this "blur" could resolve into focus if an increasingly autocratic government chose to favor a more religious interpretation.[1] Indeed, Reischauer and his colleagues had earlier asserted that during the 1930s, State Shinto rituals were veering from secular to religious. Missionaries in Korea shared this viewpoint. William P. Parker commented that when the Government-General of Korea (GGK) previously required schools to bow at shrines, "nothing objectionable" appeared to take place in the presence of Christians. By 1936, however, the priests who officiated these rituals claimed that the "spirits of the dead" would descend from heaven during the ceremonies.[2] Because of this, many Presbyterian missionaries in Korea felt that the GGK, regardless of its official stance, viewed State Shinto as religious. Whereas missionaries had previously been able to rationalize Japan's ancient stories as myth, the state was now forcing acceptance of these stories about the sun goddess as truth.[3] As the "blur" that shrouded shrine ceremonies came into focus, so too were Christian actors forced to declare clearly their communal allegiances, which led to conflict.

As a concept, the "divine blur" is useful for more than merely explaining the varied understandings of and responses to State Shintoism. It also captures how these relationships between missionaries and Korean Christians and between missionaries and government officials formed, fractured, and realigned within the ambiguities that emerged as Christian actors in Korea struggled to balance their multiple communal identities. For example, rather than casting themselves clearly and consistently as "Christians," "Americans," "Koreans," or "Japanese subjects," individuals expediently shifted between identities in response to the demands of the situation. But the potential for conflict was ever present, as clashes arose when actors were required to choose one communal association over another. From Chejungwŏn to the mission-run private schools, the question of whether these spaces were "religious" or "secular" and the question of who owned these spaces sparked controversies. In the case of Chejungwŏn, these questions caused a decade of strife within the Northern Presbyterian Mission. In the case of the GGK's 1915 revised ordinances on private schools, these questions fractured efforts at ecumenical cooperation between the mission societies in Korea. In the case of the demand to bow at shrines, these questions created rifts in the relationships both between missionaries and Korean Christians and among the missionaries themselves. Individuals like James Holdcroft doubted the spirituality of colleagues like Horace H. Underwood, who were willing to have students bow at shrines in obedience to the state. Others, disgusted with the actions of Underwood and his supporters, ultimately chose to sever their association with the BFMPCUSA.

Dae Young Ryu, a prominent scholar of Korean Christianity, has argued that for missionaries, bowing at shrines was primarily a theological issue. In contrast, for Koreans this demand carried a national or patriotic element. But the struggle over Shinto rituals and the control of mission schools cannot be properly understood as a national or political conflict between Korean Christians and the Japanese colonial regime. Nor was it simply a theological clash. Indeed, even

Ryu noted that some missionaries, such as Harold Henderson, took a "minority" position and sided with Koreans.[4] Though Henderson may have been in the "minority," his decision indicates that the missionaries' understanding of and responses to Shintoism varied; these responses cut across the binaries of foreign missionary/Korean Christian and theological/national in part because of the language of communal partnership. George McCune, James Holdcroft, and those who opposed State Shinto believed that they stood in theological unity with Korean Christians, who were supposedly united in viewing shrine ceremonies as a form of idolatry. They held that colonial violence was causing Koreans to violate their consciences by bowing at shrines. But Harold Henderson, Horace Underwood, and others also maintained that they stood in solidarity with Korean Christians, who purportedly believed that they could in good faith attend State Shinto ceremonies. These missionaries held that they did not have the right to determine the practice of Christianity in Korea—this was a national or political issue that should be decided by the Korean Christian community.[5]

The colonial government's political demand that Koreans, regardless of faith, bow at shrines fractured attempts at Christian community in Korea on multiple levels. As a part of their withdrawal from secular education (discussed in chapter 7), the Northern Presbyterians also withdrew from the various types of "union" work that they shared with other denominations. As the largest mission society in Korea, their sudden departure left the remaining bodies short of both funding and staff. Even within the Northern Presbyterian Mission, missionaries fought among themselves and with their home boards about the issue of how to respond to the command to bow. One issue in these debates was whether to respect the ecclesiastical autonomy of the Korean Presbyterian Church and, by extension, whether Koreans should control Christian-affiliated programs. The question was whether missionaries should respect, if not support, the decisions made by the Korean Christian community—even if those decisions were made under duress.

Significantly, regardless of the side the missionaries took in this debate, they enjoyed a privileged status in Korea; unlike their Korean "partners," missionaries could simply leave the country and return home. In contrast, Korean children at both public and private schools would have to bow at shrines or bear the weight of the oppressive colonial judicial system.[6] Confronted with this situation, many

Korean students decided to comply with the command to attend State Shinto ceremonies. Rather than support them, the Northern and Southern Presbyterian missionaries chose to leave, forcing Korean churches to confront the colonial government alone.

Post-1945 Return

The command to bow at shrines, the declaration by Korean churches that State Shinto was a nonreligious affair, and the increased governmental pressure on Korean churches to both sever and denounce their ties with the international community created an awkward situation for the mission societies that sought to return to Korea after World War II. The members of these societies were unsure how they would be received by Korean Christians. Indeed, from 1943 to 1945, the major Protestant mission societies of the United States met repeatedly to discuss whether and how to reenter the Korea field. The first major meeting of the Northern Presbyterians took place in 1943. Horace Underwood, William Blair, Archibald Fletcher, Harold Voelkel, and others expressed confidence that the United States would eventually emerge victorious and that Koreans would welcome missionaries back. Curiously, these participants appeared oblivious to the signs indicating that many Korean Christian leaders sought to be independent of foreign control and were critical of missionary influence. Only one observer—who was not a missionary to Korea—questioned whether there was a contradiction between a nation "striving for full political independence" and the persistence of various mission boards in maintaining control of finances and ecclesiastical extraterritoriality. In response, Voelkel bluntly retorted that Koreans had "always" controlled their own churches and that there had "never" been ecclesiastical extraterritoriality in any form in Korea.[7]

Rather than reflecting on their methods and attitudes, the missionaries blamed the failings of Korean churches. Blair, for one, lamented that the missionaries' multiple efforts at ecumenism had slowly eroded in "proportion to Korean assumption of leadership." Perhaps because of this critical view of Korean Christian leadership, Blair suggested that the initial period of the missionaries' return to Korea after the war would be marked by "confusion" and "serious conflict" as opposed to cooperation. He warned that in restarting their work and attempting to regain ownership of their property and their social institutions, missionaries needed to act cautiously.

Specifically, he urged the Home Board to refrain from interfering in the Korea field and sparking controversy. Instead, Blair recommended that missionaries in Korea be given the power to exercise good judgment and discuss matters of strategy "in due time and in wise ways."[8]

"In due time and in wise ways" concerned the steps missionaries should take to regain control of church property and institutions, such as schools, and restart their work in Korea. The premise in this phrase was that the resumption of their work would be difficult both because of uncertainty regarding how Koreans might respond to the return of the missionaries and because of the dissension that had roiled the various mission societies during the 1930s. Indeed, in 1943, the Congregational Board of Missions advised that "only missionaries who were not definitely warped by the experiences of the last few years" should return to Korea.[9] But "in due time" became largely moot with the emergence of "in due course." In November 1943, the leaders of the Allied Powers met in Cairo, Egypt. They agreed, among other things, that Korea should be freed from Japanese colonial rule. However, on the assumption that Korea had been a colony for so long that it would be unprepared for self-rule, they decided that Korea would fall under a period of trusteeship and receive full independence "in due course." After Japan's surrender to the Allied Powers, on August 15, 1945, the United States government suddenly became concerned that the Soviet Union, which had entered the Asia-Pacific theater the previous week per a prior agreement with the United States, would occupy the entirety of the Korean Peninsula. The US State Department floated to its Soviet counterpart the proposal, which was accepted, that the country should be temporarily divided at the 38th parallel, with the Soviets overseeing the area north and the United States overseeing the area south of the parallel.

The division of the peninsula and the establishment of the US Army Military Government in Korea (USAMGIK) set up advantageous conditions for the missionaries planning to return to the country. To begin, the Cold War context meant that the USAMGIK was extremely concerned about rooting out leftist elements. To this end, it sought to assess the "psychological" mindset of Korean actors to determine who was truly a leftist and who was supportive of democracy and the United States.[10] A major impediment to this project was a lack of experts on Korea. It was because of this lack that former missionaries and even the children of missionaries came to occupy positions of influence in the military government. In this manner, the issues of property ownership and missionary influence in Korea, at least south of the 38th parallel, were quickly resolved. Regarding property, the USAMGIK determined the ownership and administration of large-scale social institutions like schools and hospitals. Missionaries quickly reoccupied positions of leadership in these institutions or even regained control of the institutions entirely. Likewise, since the missionaries were trusted by the USAMGIK, they had access to political influence. Especially because many of the Korean churches' resources were located north of the 38th parallel, missionary support and connections were valuable assets to Korean church leaders.

Missionaries, then, found themselves "welcomed" by Korean churches after liberation in 1945. Though many Korean churches certainly looked forward to reestablishing lost ties to missionaries in a spirit of Christian community, the practical issue of assistance should not be ignored. In fact, the first missionaries to Korea often reported that local Christian leaders expressed dismay that support from the United States was too slow and too scant.[11] Furthermore, the old pattern of hierarchical and unequal relations between missionaries and Korean Christian leaders resurfaced in the postwar period. For instance, in 1949, Helen Kim—a well-known Korean Methodist and the president of Ewha Womans University—traveled to the United States. During her time in the country, she spoke to an interdenominational group of mission board leaders. While stating that Koreans welcomed the support of missionaries, she criticized the resurfacing of "old forms of mission relationships." In particular, she observed that missionaries tended to make major decisions in the field without consulting or receiving input from Korean Christian leaders.[12] As Helen Kim's critique suggests, Harry Voelkel's assertion that Koreans were in full control of the church and that no form of ecclesiastical extraterritoriality existed in Korea was false.

Resurrected and Reimagined for the (South) Korean Nation

The realities of the missionaries' historical presence in Korea are complex. As this book has shown, the missionaries constantly negotiated competing communal demands. At times they broke laws to advance their religious work; at others, they worked in the service of the Korean nation. After World War II, they returned to Korea, and the problematic pattern of relations between missionaries, Korean Christians, and political powers resurfaced.

The missionaries and their actions are not frozen in the past but rather are continually reinterpreted in the present. One recent example concerns a struggle to claim ownership of Yanghwajin Foreign Missionary Cemetery and transform it into a place of commemoration. As noted in chapter 2, this cemetery was established after the death of John Heron, in 1890, and it became the final resting place of many of the first wave of Protestant missionaries to the country. From roughly 1956 to 2007, Seoul Union Church, a predominantly expatriate congregation, oversaw the administration and care of the cemetery. However, it did not own the land on which the cemetery was situated. Indeed, because of laws barring foreign ownership of land, the church itself lacked a permanent home—a point that would become a significant part of the Yanghwajin saga.

In 1981, the various Protestant denominations in South Korea established the Organization for the Celebration of the Hundredth Anniversary of the Korean Church (Han'guk kidokkyo 100 chunyŏn chedan; HKCC). The purpose was to prepare for the anniversary of the inception of the Protestant missionary movement in Korea. In 1985, after a series of negotiations between Horace Underwood, a member of Seoul Union, and Han Kyŏng-jik—the head pastor of the powerful Yŏngnak Presbyterian Church of Seoul and chairman of the committee—formal administration of Yanghwajin was transferred from Seoul Union to the HKCC.[13] As part of the agreement, Seoul Union moved into a memorial chapel, which the committee built to stand next to the cemetery, and this expatriate community continued to care for Yanghwajin.

Seoul Union moved into the chapel believing it had found its permanent home. But in 2005, the HKCC requested that the newly established Hundredth Anniversary Memorial Church (HAMC) be permitted to share the chapel. Seoul Union agreed. Almost immediately, tensions surfaced. In the summer of 2007, the predominantly Korean congregation of the HAMC attempted to wrest control of the ownership and maintenance of the cemetery from Seoul Union.[14] In July 2007, the head pastor of the HAMC, Yi Chae-ch'ŏl, gave a sermon justifying the church's claim to the cemetery. Pointing to the early history of Christianity, he crafted a careful argument that both criticized his Western counterparts and emphasized their common purpose. Yi opened with the observation that while the apostles Peter and John had played an important initial role in spreading the gospel to the "heathen" Gentiles, they quickly turned from their obligations in Samaria. Thus, God transferred the "candlestick" of responsibility from these first followers of Jesus to Paul.[15] Yi then recounted the history of Protestantism in Korea, from the baptism of Koreans on the Manchurian side of the Yalu River in 1879 to the present day. Noting that the first generation of missionaries to Korea played important roles in spreading this religion and in Korean history more generally, he argued that the more recent expatriate community had failed to care for Yanghwajin. He criticized Seoul Union Church not only for neglecting the cemetery and allowing it to fall into disrepair (he even asserted that the foreign community had been illicitly selling gravesites) but also for its disdainful treatment of Korean Christians. In particular, he lamented that Koreans had unequal access to buildings and other facilities on the cemetery grounds.

However, in a rhetorical move reminiscent of many other instances of the language of partnership, Yi followed his criticism of Seoul Union Church by emphasizing the common membership of all Christians in a universal heavenly kingdom, stating that they should work in harmony. Returning to his scriptural frame, Yi suggested that the root of the conflict was the refusal of Seoul Union to recognize that by "the will of God" the mantle of responsibility over Yanghwajin had transferred to the HAMC. In much the same way that the first apostles had accepted that the mantle of responsibility for preaching to the Gentiles had been transferred to Paul, Yi argued, Seoul Union Church and others needed to "willingly" recognize that the mantle of responsibility for caring for Yanghwajin now rested on the shoulders of the HAMC. He concluded with a prayer suggesting that if both the HAMC and Seoul Union recognized and maintained their "right positions" and the "right order," then a "beautiful relationship of faith embracing each other in the Lord" could be restored.[16] Ultimately, neither congregation was willing to relinquish control of Yanghwajin, and both sued for ownership of the cemetery. In 2013, the South Korean judicial system ruled in favor of the HAMC.[17]

There are many layers to the HAMC's efforts to seize control over Yanghwajin and then to cultivate a particular narrative of the history of Protestantism in Korea through this cemetery. In regard to the latter effort, Elizabeth Underwood has argued that the HAMC has sought to transform Yanghwajin into a sacred site and to create a certain interpretation of the missionaries' historical significance in Korea. What prompted this attempt was a series of contemporary instabilities and challenges to Christianity within South Korea. In response, many Korean Protestant churches have reemphasized the roles Christianity played during the twentieth century in advancing nationalism and modernizing the country.[18] In this vein, the HAMC has sought to "sacralize" and "sanitize" missionaries in order to scrub away associations with imperialism and emphasize instead how they served the modernization of Korea.

The attempt to tie Yanghwajin and Christianity more generally to the history of the formation of the modern South Korean nation is evident in the stories told at this cemetery, which has become a site of religious tourism well known within Korean Christian circles and promoted by the South Korean government's official tourism website. Churches, Christian organizations, and others visit Yanghwajin in groups numbering from the tens to the hundreds. Most visitors to Yanghwajin join one of the free tours conducted in Korean, English, Japanese, or Chinese. These visitors are first shown a short video explaining the missionaries' service in Korea and illustrating how Christianity served as a conduit for modern knowledge and technology. They then take the guided tour and finally visit a special exhibition hall that displays items once owned by the first generation of Protestant missionaries to the country.

Yanghwajin suggests a commitment to the universality of Christianity. To begin, the HAMC has insisted that this cemetery is the "most sacred land of Korean Protestantism."[19] Indeed, the HAMC has claimed that Yanghwajin is the "legacy of the Korean Church and landmark of the Protestant faith" and that "its identity grounded on Christianity [must] be made even more clear."[20] Yet though the HAMC outwardly venerates Western missionaries, its primary goal is to define the place of Christianity in *Korean* history. For example, during tours of the cemetery, guides include a visit to Ernest Bethel's tombstone. Bethel was a British reporter with the *Daily Chronicle* who first traveled to Korea in 1904. He chose to remain in the country, and in the same year, he established the newspaper *Taehan Maeil Sinbo*. After the Protectorate Treaty of 1905 with Japan, Japanese officials moved to censor and suppress Korean-language newspapers. However, because of Bethel's ownership of *Taehan Maeil Sinbo*, this publication was largely exempted, and the paper became a thorn in the side of the Japanese administration in Korea. Bethel died in 1909 and was buried at Yanghwajin. What is interesting in Bethel's case is that he was not a missionary. He first arrived in Korea as a journalist; he was not affiliated—officially or unofficially—with a missionary agency, nor did he explicitly support Christianity. Yet a visit to Bethel's tombstone figures prominently in most, if not all, HAMC tours of Yanghwajin Foreign Missionary Cemetery. Put simply, the HAMC's fixation on Bethel undermines its own argument that the cemetery is primarily aimed at commemorating the sacrifices of missionaries.

Even when describing missionaries, the HAMC paints an idealized picture of their history in order to cast them as having worked for the Korean nation. Considering the multiple criticisms levied by Korean Christian leaders such as Han Sŏk-chin, Ch'oe Chung-jin, and Yi Man-jip to the effect that Western missionaries had overstayed their welcome, it is ironic that the long service of individuals like Horace G. Underwood and Samuel A. Moffett in Korea is now seen as a sign of their devotion to the country, rather than of imperialism or even of their Christian faith.[21] But history, at least selectively interpreted, provides the necessary facts. For example, guided tours of the cemetery always stop at the tombstone of Homer Hulbert. To many Koreans, Hulbert is best known for his role in helping Emperor Kojong dispatch a secret delegation to The Hague Peace Conference of 1907 to announce to the world that Japan had illegally forced Korea to sign the Protectorate Treaty. For his role, the resident-general had Hulbert deported in 1907. He returned to Korea in 1949 and died in the country after contracting pneumonia. The HAMC website describes Hulbert as "a man who loved Korea more than Koreans."[22] Tour guides invariably highlight the epitaph on Hulbert's tombstone: "I'd rather be buried in Korea than in Westminster Abbey." The HAMC praises Hulbert for his devotion not to his faith but to Korea; he supposedly overcame his "national" or "foreign" origins in the service of God and died for the Korean nation. In a sense, he became Korean.

The stories told at the cemetery do more than simply "sacralize" and "sanitize" missionaries, as suggested by Elizabeth Underwood; they cast these *foreign* missionaries as Korean. These Westerners supposedly acted like Koreans on behalf of Korea; their devotion to the country is literally exhibited by their burial in the cemetery—their bodies have nourished the soil of the Korean Peninsula. This narrative line, however, oversimplifies history by evaluating these actors primarily in terms of how they advanced the cause of the Korean nation-state. The history of Christianity's spread to and development in Korea involves more than simply the acculturation of this religion to Korea or the missionaries' devotion to the country. It also includes the negotiation of membership in a universal Christian community, a community that purportedly transcends national boundaries. Balancing competing religious and political identities produces conflicts and instabilities. Attention to this detail not only opens the study of Christianity in countries like South Korea to new avenues of interpretation; it also sheds light on how this religion is practiced and understood in the present day.

Notes

Notes on Romanization and Terms

Korean terms are Romanized using McCune-Reischauer. The only exceptions are for terms and names with well-known alternative spellings (e.g., Seoul). Japanese terms are Romanized using Revised Hepburn, and Chinese terms Pinyin.

Introduction: Protestant Partners?

1. Only three years previously, Charles Clark and the Presbyterian mission community had responded to a questionnaire sent by the IMC querying the level of self-determination of Koreans in leading the administration of Christianity in the country. The missionaries boasted that Korean churches were self-governing. In a similar vein, Bishop Herbert Welch of the Methodist Church argued that Koreans were in full control of the administration and governance of Methodism in Korea. See Charles A. Clark, "The Korean Presbyterian Church and the Missionaries," *The Korea Mission Field* 17, no. 9 (September 1922): 191–194; and Bishop Herbert Welch, "Korean Methodist Episcopal Church and the Missionaries," *The Korea Mission Field* 17, no. 9 (September 1922): 194–197. Hereafter this source will be abbreviated as *KMF.*

2. Charles Clark would later argue that the success of Korean Protestantism was rooted in the adoption of the Nevius Method. The Nevius Method will be discussed in chapter 3. See Charles Allen Clark, *The Korean Church and the Nevius Method* (New York: Fleming H. Revell Co., 1930).

3. Han'guk Kidokkyo Yŏksa Yŏn'guso, ed., *Han'guk kidokkyo ŭi yŏksa II* (Seoul: Han'guk Kidokkyo Yŏksa Yŏn'guso, 1990), 173–174. Hereafter this source will appear as *HKY II.*

4. Starting in the 1960s, Protestantism experienced rapid growth in South Korea. Since the early 2000s, the rate of its growth has stagnated. But success or vitality is not measured only in numbers of converts. South Korean churches are highly active in missionary work, and the South Korean experience has stood as an example for other church communities in Asia to study or emulate. Indeed, the status of Protestantism in the country has been such that Paul Freston, a scholar of Brazil, characterized South Korea as a "regional Protestant

superpower." Timothy S. Lee echoed this sentiment. See Paul Freston, *Evangelicals and Politics in Asia, Africa, and Latin America* (Cambridge: Cambridge University Press, 2001); and Timothy S. Lee, "What Should Christians Do about a Shaman-Progenitor?" *Church History* 78, no. 1 (March 2009): 66.

5. In its 2017 annual survey, the Korea World Missions Association (Han'guk Segye Sŏn'gyo Hyŏbŭihoe) reported that 27,436 South Koreans had participated in foreign missions to 170 different countries. An English summary of the report can be accessed at http://kwma.or.kr/cm_notice/3401. The full Korean report can also be downloaded.

6. On the use of Christianity for political purposes, see Timothy S. Lee, "A Political Factor in the Rise of Protestantism in Korea," *Church History* 69, no. 1 (March 2000): 116–142; Wi Jo Kang, *Christ and Caesar in Modern Korea* (Albany: State University of New York Press, 1997); Kyong-man Hong, "Formation of Korean Protestantism and Its Political Nature," *Korea Journal* 23, no. 12 (December 1983): 18–29; and Yun Kyŏng-no, *105 in sagŏn kwa sinminhoe yŏn'gu* (Seoul: Ilchisa, 1990). On inculturating Christianity to align with Korea's social and cultural norms, see Sung Deuk Oak, *The Making of Korean Christianity* (Waco, TX: Baylor University Press, 2015); David Chung, *Syncretism* (Albany: State University of New York Press, 2001); and Yi Tŏk-chu, *T'och'akhwa wa minjok undong yŏn'gu* (Seoul: Han'guk Kidokkyo Yŏn'guso, 2018).

7. Agency is a theoretically thorny issue, as the meaning of the term has been contested. Mustafa Emirbayer and Ann Mische have noted that agency has been described and associated with terms like "self-hood, motivation, will, purposiveness, intentionality, choice, initiative, freedom, and creativity." The common theme in these various terms is the notion that individuals make choices of their own volition. But this concept is complicated by the attendant notion of structure, which shapes, or for some scholars determines, the decisions individuals make. See Mustafa Emirbayer and Ann Mische, "What Is Agency," *American Journal of Sociology* 103, no. 4 (January 1998): 962–1023. For an insightful and clear analysis of the relationship between structure and agency, see William Sewell Jr., *Logics of History* (Chicago: University of Chicago Press, 2005), 124–151.

8. One area of tension in the study of Korean "Christianity" is the uneven treatment given to Catholicism and Protestantism. Often, when scholars use the term "Christianity," they are narrowly referring to Protestantism, excluding other branches of this religion, especially Roman Catholicism. I am sensitive to this issue and believe that Roman Catholicism, in particular, constitutes an important part of the "Christian" experience in South Korea today. However, though this work focuses on Protestantism, I use the more general term "Christianity" throughout this book. The primary reason is that missionaries, Korean Christians, and government officials all used the terms "Christian" and "Christianity." In converting, Korean Protestants believed they were converting to "Christianity" as opposed to Protestantism. The centralized structure of the Catholic Church and the existence of the Vatican as a sovereign state call for a separate analytical treatment. However, I suggest that at

least some of the observations made in this work regarding the difficulties in balancing competing communal demands are applicable to the history of Catholicism in Korea. When necessary because of specific issues of theology, structure, or practice, I have used the more precise terms "Catholicism" and "Protestantism."

9. The story that the first missionaries to Korea were Korean can be found in textbooks and heard in church sermons. One relatively recent account appeared in *Christianity Today* in February 2018. See Kirsteen Kim and Hoon Ko, "Who Brought Christianity to Korea? Koreans Did," *Christianity Today,* February 2018, https://www.christianitytoday.com/history/2018/february/korean-christianity.html.

10. Specialists in the history of Christianity, in particular world Christianity, and missions are generally more nuanced in their approaches to missionaries. In part understanding that the criticism of (cultural) imperialism, when applied to missionaries, strips native believers of agency, scholars such as Andrew Walls, Brian Stanley, and Lamin Sanneh have explored the ways missionaries—though full of flaws and with mixed motivations—engaged societies. Moreover, even though missionaries often viewed converts through a hierarchical or racist lens, there was room to "translate" (to use Walls's metaphor) Christianity into local contexts. However, even with these insights by scholars of world Christianity and missions, missionaries continue to be tied to imperialism in academic and even popular circles. For instance, Ryan Dunch has noted that the linking of missionaries to (cultural) imperialism is not restricted to academia but is prevalent in popular discourse. As an example, he cited Barbara Kingsolver's *The Poisonwood Bible* (New York: HarperCollins, 1998). On world Christianity, see Andrew F. Walls, *The Cross-Cultural Process in Christian History* (Maryknoll, NY: Orbis, 2002); Brian Stanley, *The Bible and the Flag* (Nottingham: SPCK, 1990); and Lamin Sanneh, *Translating the Message* (Maryknoll, NY: Orbis, 2009). For a critique of cultural imperialism as a paradigm and the common portrayal of missionaries as cultural imperialists, see Ryan Dunch, "Beyond Cultural Imperialism," *History and Theory* 41, no. 3 (October 2002): 301–325.

11. Jean and John Comaroff have argued that the roles of missionaries in the colonial machinery were "indeterminate," as missionaries consistently maintained that they adhered to the principle of separation of church and state and respected local authority. However, their very presence in mission fields often altered the ways local societies viewed the world, changing (if only subtly) the social and cultural practices upon which local authority rested. In this manner, missionaries destabilized political systems. See Jean Comaroff and John Comaroff, *Of Revelation and Revolution* (Chicago: University of Chicago Press, 1991).

12. William Hutchinson, *Errand to the World* (Chicago: University of Chicago Press, 1987).

13. For a succinct summary of Japanese colonial scholarship on Korean history, see Yi Man-yŏl, "Ilche kwanhakcha tŭl ŭi singmin sagwan," in *Han'guk ŭi yŏksa insik II,* ed. Yi U-sŏng and Kang Man-gil (Seoul: Ch'angjak kwa pip'yŏng sa, 1993).

14. For an insightful examination of the importance of history in the effort to articulate a "Korean" sovereignty, see Henry H. Em, *The Great Enterprise* (Durham, NC: Duke University Press, 2013).

15. With the appearance of Yi Ki-baek's influential *Kuksa sillon*, in 1961, South Korean historians began to write "new" Korean histories that highlighted the creative agency of Koreans to lead "internally" driven historical transformations of the nation. See Yi Ki-baek, *Kuksa sillon* (Seoul: T'aesŏngsa, 1961). See also Kang Man-gil, *Chosŏn hugi sangŏp chabon ŭi paldal* (Seoul: Koryŏ Taehakkyo Munkwa Taehak, 1970); and Kim Yong-sŏp, *Chosŏn hugi nonghak ŭi paldal* (Seoul: Han'guk Munhwa Yŏn'guso, 1970).

16. Jai-keun Choi, *The Korean Church under Japanese Colonialism* (Seoul: Jimoondang, 2007), 22–23.

17. Describing the intellectual climate of the 1960s, 1970s, and 1980s, Namhee Lee has argued that many South Korean student dissidents felt a profound "crisis of historical subjectivity." They believed that Koreans had been stripped of their agency to direct their own national history. Instead, the country was subjected to outside forces—whether colonialism, Cold War politics, or capitalism. Thus, the question of how to regain historical subjectivity and agency was of critical importance to these intellectuals. I argue that a similar set of concerns existed for Korean Christian leaders. But this particular subset of Korean intellectuals confronted the additional problem of adhering to a foreign religion. See Namhee Lee, *Making of the Minjung* (Ithaca, NY: Cornell University Press, 2007), 2–8.

18. Criticism of missionaries for their imperialistic attitudes and activities has been surprisingly rare in the field of Korean Christianity. One of the few scholars to provide insightful critiques of missionaries for their complex ties to imperial powers is Dae Young Ryu, who has written extensively on this issue. For two representative English-language pieces, see Dae Young Ryu, "The Origin and Characteristics of Evangelical Protestantism in Korea at the Turn of the Twentieth Century," *Church History* 77, no. 2 (June 2008): 371–98; and Dae Young Ryu, "Treaties, Extraterritorial Rights, and American Protestant Missions in Late Joseon Korea," *Korea Journal* 43, no. 1 (Spring 2003): 174–203.

19. As stated in note 18, in general, the field of Korean Christianity, and in particular Protestantism, has been reserved in criticizing missionaries for being imperialists. However, to argue that Korean Protestant scholars have not been concerned with the specter of imperialism is incorrect. Korean Protestant scholars have long understood the problems the association between missionaries and imperialism poses for their own efforts to cast this religion as an integral part of the Korean nation. But even in pointing to the missionaries' imperialistic attitudes, scholars have emphasized that the main imperial power in Korea was Japan. For example, Min Kyŏng-bae, who originated the "national church" (*minjok kyohoe*) paradigm when examining the history of Korean Christianity, argued that Korea was unique in that the colonial power was Japan and not a

Western nation. He maintained that this was a significant factor in Koreans' turn to Christianity: the religion was not negatively associated with colonialism in Korea. On a general level, I agree with this assessment. However, the fact that Japan was the colonizing power in Korea does not mean that Korean Christian leaders were not troubled by their unequal relations with missionaries. Indeed, a subtext of the Han-Moffett conflict concerned control of church governance. See Min Kyŏng-bae, *Han'guk ŭi kidokkyohoe sa* (Seoul: Taehan Kidokkyo Sŏhoe, 1972), 18–24.

20. A. W. Wasson, "Observation on the Mott Conference," *KMF* 21, no. 2 (February 1926): 31–32.

21. Benedict Anderson, *Imagined Communities,* rev. ed. (London: Verso, 2006), 6–7.

22. Robert Speer was specifically contrasting Protestants' valuing of national diversity to the approach of Roman Catholicism, which he argued attempted to impose its ecclesiastical authority and practices around the globe. See Robert E. Speer, *Christianity and the Nations* (New York: Fleming H. Revell, 1910), 66–67, 113.

23. Numerous scholars have examined the supposed intersection of religion and nationalism. For a classic examination of whether the United States was founded as a "Christian nation" that over time became increasingly secular, see Robert Handy, *A Christian America* (New York: Oxford University Press, 1971). For a powerful critique of Handy and the argument that the United States was founded on the principle of freedom of religion, see David Sehat, *The Myth of American Religious Freedom* (New York: Oxford University Press, 2010).

24. Prasenjit Duara has observed that the uniqueness of nationalism is not the articulation of a "new" form of identity or consciousness. Instead, he has argued that its uniqueness lies in "the world system of nation-states," which views the nation-state as the only "legitimate expression of sovereignty." See Prasenjit Duara, *Rescuing History from the Nation* (Chicago: University of Chicago Press, 1995), 8.

25. The first Protestant missionary to China arrived in 1807, and the first to Japan arrived in 1859. In all three countries in East Asia, Catholicism predated the arrival of Protestantism. The years cited here for the first Protestant missionary refer to the arrival of the first *resident* missionary and not the first "Protestant" who sought to evangelize to Koreans either in passing or on the borders of the country.

26. Dana L. Robert, *Christian Mission* (Malden, MA: Wiley-Blackwell, 2009), 60.

27. David Hollinger, *Protestants Abroad* (Princeton, NJ: Princeton University Press, 2017), 1–23.

28. Brian Stanley has noted that the planners of the World Missionary Conference confronted multiple controversial issues. One major point of contention concerned ecclesiastical autonomy. The various church leaders sought to

ensure that there would be no resolution or motion regarding church polity or doctrine that could potentially threaten the ecclesiastical authority of individual churches or societies. See Brian Stanley, *The World Missionary Conference, Edinburgh, 1910* (Grand Rapids, MI: William B. Eerdmans, 2009), 36, 38–41.

29. Comity was practiced, in varying degrees, in other mission fields from the late nineteenth century onward. As a relatively late mission field, however, Korea saw comity practiced nearly from the arrival of the first generation of Protestant missionaries in the country. For a detailed examination of comity agreements in Korea, see Chang Uk Byun, "Comity Agreements between Missions in Koreas from 1884 to 1910," (PhD diss., Princeton Theological Seminary, 2003).

30. Within the Protestant tradition, this work primarily examines four mainline Protestant denominations from the United States. The official names of these denominations were the Presbyterian Church in the United States of America (Northern Presbyterians), the Presbyterian Church in the United States (Southern Presbyterians), the Methodist Episcopal Church (Northern Methodists), and the Methodist Episcopal Church, South (Southern Methodists). The existence of northern and southern branches of both Presbyterianism and Methodism in the United States at the time was a legacy of secession and the Civil War.

31. Anderson, *Imagined Communities,* 7.

32. Sung Deuk Oak has argued that the creation of "Korean Christianity" was the result of a "creative combination of the principle of Christian universality (vertical transcendence) and that of inculturation (horizontal adaptation)." Missing from this assessment, however, is an exploration of the concrete social or political structures through which "Christian universality" and "inculturation" were put into practice. Put differently, this work neither denies nor rejects the notion of "vertical transcendence," or rather the idea that individuals and religious communities engage in an other-worldly relationship. Instead, I argue that even vertically oriented communities are connected horizontally to other religious, social, or political groups. In this manner, "vertical transcendence" exists on a horizontal plane (to use Oak's metaphor). In his study, Oak chose to emphasize the amicable ways that missionaries and Korean Christians worked together. In contrast, this work sheds light on points of both cooperation and conflict as multiple horizontal communities overlapped in Korea. See Oak, *The Making of Korean Christianity,* 316.

33. I suggest that this situation evokes Andre Schmid's observation that Korean nationalist reformers during the colonial period found themselves in a logical bind. Before colonization, many had looked to Japan as a source of inspiration and information about modern knowledge and technology. After colonization, many Japanese officials argued that they shared with Koreans the common goal of "uplifting" Korea and thus should work in partnership with them. Korean intellectuals were in a rhetorically weak position to argue against their Japanese counterparts. See Andre Schmid, *Korea between Empires, 1895–1919* (New York: Columbia University Press, 2002), 4–9.

34. In the opening editorial of the September 1922 edition of the *KMF,* the editors lamented the racist rhetoric that had led to the outbreak of World War I. They argued that Christians, in contrast, believed in simply "*ONE* race": "the *HUMAN* race." Aside from the fact that in practice Christians and Christianity were often racist, the call for "racial equality," as if all Christians belonged to "one race," could also be a form of coercion; it sought to erase the "differences" (in this case) between Korean and Western Christians and undermined arguments that the former were entitled to have full control of the church in Korea. If all Christians were "equal," then on what grounds should missionaries leave Korea? Should not missionaries remain and work alongside Koreans in a united effort to spread the kingdom of heaven? See "Editorial: Will the Church Function Today?" *KMF* 17, no. 9 (September 1922): 189–190.

35. Kyung Moon Hwang, *Rationalizing Korea* (Berkeley: University of California Press, 2016), 146–167.

36. Gauri Viswanathan, *Outside the Fold* (Princeton, NJ: Princeton University Press, 1998).

37. Yumi Moon has examined how Koreans, during the late nineteenth and first half of the twentieth century, sought to protect local autonomy in the face of state making, even if this meant aligning with foreign forces. Resistance to the centralization of power included, in the case of Hwanghae Province, the adoption of Catholicism. Chapter 4 of this work will examine the place of these Korean Catholics in the social dynamics in this province. See Yumi Moon, *Populist Collaborators* (Ithaca, NY: Cornell University Press, 2013), 50–58.

38. For a study of the silk letter, see Franklin Rausch, "Wicked Officials and Virtuous Martyrs," *Kyohoe sa yŏn'gu* 32 (July 2009): 5–30. See also Franklin Rausch, "Like Birds and Beasts," *Acta Koreana* 15, no. 1 (June 2012): 43–71. For an insightful examination of Catholicism and the anti-Catholic movement, see Donald Baker and Franklin Rausch, *Catholics and Anti-Catholicism in Chosŏn Korea* (Honolulu: University of Hawai'i Press, 2017).

39. The biases that Protestant missionaries in Korea held against Catholicism reflected broader sentiments in the Protestant communities of the United States. For example, Philip Hamburger has shown that during the mid–nineteenth century, American Protestants marshaled the doctrine of separation of church and state to ostracize Catholics. Arguing that all Catholics followed the dictates of the pope first and thus posed a threat to American democracy, leaders of the mainstream Protestant community moved to exclude Catholics from the political sphere. See Philip Hamburger, *Separation of Church and State* (Cambridge, MA: Harvard University Press, 2004), 193–194, 228, 247–250, 302–308.

Chapter 1: Tangled Relations

1. The term *kapsin* refers to the year, 1884, in which the coup occurred. A major counting system used in Asia before the twentieth century is known as the sexagenary cycle. This counting system combined what are known as the ten

Heavenly Stems and twelve Earthly Branches in a set order and combination to mark the numbers one to sixty. The sexagenary system was often used in Asia to mark the year in which events occurred or commenced.

2. Horace N. Allen to F. F. Ellinwood, February 4, 1885, Korea—Letters and Correspondences, Board of Foreign Missions of the Presbyterian Church of the USA, Microfilm, Reel 174, PHS. The Presbyterian Historical Society has microfilmed letters and reports from the various mission fields of the Board of Foreign Missions of the Presbyterian Church in the USA (BFMPCUSA) from the years 1833 to 1911. This series will be abbreviated KLC—BFMPCUSA.

3. Fred Harrington, *God, Mammon, and the Japanese* (Madison: University of Wisconsin Press, 1944), 6.

4. Everett N. Hunt, *Protestant Pioneers in Korea* (Maryknoll, NY: Orbis, 1990), 16; Martha Huntley, *Caring, Growing, Changing* (New York: Friendship, 1984), 30–33.

5. Dae Young Ryu, "Understanding Early American Missionaries in Korea (1884–1910)," *Archives de sciences sociales des religions* 46, no. 113 (January–March 2001): 94–95.

6. *Manual for the Missionary Candidates of the American Board of Commissioners for Foreign Missions* (1880), 67.

7. Presbyterian Church in the USA, ed., *Manual of the Board of Foreign Missions of the Presbyterian Church in the U.S.A.* (New York: [s.n.], 1889).

8. Horace G. Underwood to F. F. Ellinwood, December 27, 1886, KLC—BFMPCUSA, Roll 174, PHS.

9. Samuel A. Moffett to F. F. Ellinwood, July 24, 1890, KLC—BFMPCUSA, Roll 179, PHS.

10. Samuel A. Moffett to F. F. Ellinwood, July 2, 1891, KLC—BFMPCUSA, Roll 179, PHS.

11. Horace N. Allen to F. F. Ellinwood, September 2, 1885, KLC—BFMPCUSA, Roll 174, PHS.

12. Samuel A. Moffett to F. F. Ellinwood, March 18, 1890, KLC—BFMPCUSA, Roll 179, PHS.

13. Daniel M. Davies, "Henry G. Appenzeller," *Methodist History* 30, no. 4 (July 1992): 201. Some accounts state that George Foulk, who was head of the US legation, was the individual who warned the Appenzellers and Horace Underwood of the political unrest in Korea and advised a temporary return to Japan. In contrast, citing Henry G. Appenzeller's diary, Davies's study identifies Captain McGlensy of the USS *Ossipee* as having presented this warning and advice.

14. Dae Young Ryu has argued that the missionaries were overly sensitive about the issue of danger on the peninsula. As proof, he states that the number of incidents of violence against Americans were quite few. While this is true, he underestimates the impact of the Kapsin Coup and the history of anti-Catholic campaigns. Moreover, he also downplays incidents such as an attack on Horace G. Underwood and his wife while they were traveling through the northern

provinces. Clearly missionaries confronted dangerous situations. See Dae Young Ryu, "Treaties, Extraterritorial Rights, and American Protestant Missions in Late Joseon Korea," *Korea Journal* 43, no. 1 (Spring 2003): 174–203.

15. Horace N. Allen to F. F. Ellinwood, February 12, 1886, KLC—BFMP-CUSA, Roll 174, PHS.

16. John Heron to F. F. Ellinwood, September 11, 1887, KLC—BFMP-CUSA, Roll 174, PHS.

17. Horace G. Underwood, "Report to the Board of Foreign Missions of the Presbyterian Church of America," September 17, 1886, KLC—BFMPCUSA, Reel 174, PHS.

18. Underwood, "Report to the Board of Foreign Missions."

19. John Heron to F. F. Ellinwood, August 27, 1886; Horace G. Underwood to F. F. Ellinwood, September 17, 1886, KLC—BFMPCUSA, Roll 174, PHS.

20. John Heron to F. F. Ellinwood, January 24, 1887, KLC—BFMPCUSA, Roll 174, PHS.

21. John Heron to F. F. Ellinwood, August 27, 1886, KLC—BFMPCUSA, Roll 174, PHS. Heron would later suggest that Horace Allen was in fact "abusing" hospital funds. See John Heron to F. F. Ellinwood, September 11, 1886, KLC—BFMPCUSA, Roll 174, PHS.

22. Horace N. Allen to F. F. Ellinwood, April 25, 1887; John Heron to F. F. Ellinwood, May 1, 1887, KLC—BFMPCUSA, Roll 174, PHS.

23. Horace G. Underwood to the Board of Foreign Missions of the Presbyterian Church of America, September 17, 1886, KLC—BFMPCUSA, Roll 174, PHS.

24. Horace N. Allen to F. F. Ellinwood, January 17, 1887, KLC—BFMP-CUSA, Roll 174, PHS.

25. John Heron to Board of Foreign Missions of the Presbyterian Church of America, September 11, 1886; Horace G. Underwood to Board of Foreign Missions of the Presbyterian Church of America, September 17, 1886, KLC—BFMPCUSA, Roll 174, PHS.

26. Horace G. Underwood to Presbyterian Mission to Korea, January 1887, KLC—BFMPCUSA, Roll 174, PHS.

27. Horace G. Underwood to F. F. Ellinwood, January 22, 1887, KLC—BFMPCUSA, Roll 174, PHS.

28. "Action of the Board," March 7, 1887, KLC—BFMPCUSA, Roll 174, PHS.

29. Han'guk Kidokkyo Yŏksa Yŏn'guso, ed., *Annual Report of the Board of Foreign Missions of the Methodist Episcopal Church: Korea Mission, 1884–1943* (Seoul: Han'guk Kidokkyo Yŏksa Yŏn'guso, 2001), 18. Hereafter this source will appear as *ARBFMMEC*.

30. The term "Taewŏn'gun" was an honorific title given to the father of the ruling king in the Chosŏn bureaucracy.

31. James B. Palais, *Politics and Policy in Traditional Korea* (Cambridge, MA: Harvard University Press, 1975), 23.

32. Ryu, "Treaties, Extraterritorial Rights, and American Protestant Missions," 184–194.

33. Horace N. Allen to F. F. Ellinwood, October 8, 1884, KLC—BFMPCUSA, Roll 174, PHS.

34. Allen to Ellinwood, February 4, 1885.

35. Annie J. Ellers to F. F. Ellinwood, August 18, 1886, KLC—BFMPCUSA, Reel 174/175, PHS.

36. For an attempt to recast Kojong as a strong, reform-minded ruler, see Yi T'aejin, *Kojong sidae ŭi chae chomyŏng* (Seoul: T'aehaksa, 2000).

37. Do-hyung Kim, "Introduction: The Nature of Reform in the Taehan Empire," in *Reform and Modernity in the Taehan Empire,* ed. Dong-no Kim, John B. Duncan, and Do-hyung Kim (Seoul: Jimoondang, 2006), 9–14.

38. *Kojong sillok,* 19/8/5 (lunar calendar date). This edict was recorded in the fifth day of the eighth month of the nineteenth year of Kojong's reign.

39. *Hansŏng sunbo,* October 31, 1883, November 10, 1883.

40. *Hansŏng sunbo,* June 13, 1884.

41. When reporting to Francis Ellinwood on his first introduction to Kojong, in October 1884, Horace Allen stated that Lucius Foote informed him that in private Kojong had expressed a willingness to allow missionaries to establish schools. Kojong was aware that missionaries were seeking entry into Korea. However, he may not have been sure of Allen's status as a missionary. In contrast, in June 1885, Allen reported that Kojong knew he was a missionary. See Horace N. Allen to F. F. Ellinwood, June 1885, KLC—BFMPCUSA, Roll 174, PHS.

42. Robert Maclay's account of his journey to Seoul was published in 1896 in at least two sources. See Robert S. Maclay, "Korea's Permit to Christianity," *Missionary Review of the World* 19, no. 9 (April 1896): 287–296; and Robert S. Maclay, "A Fortnight in Seoul, Korea, in 1884," *Gospel in All Lands* (August 1896): 354–360.

43. Horace G. Underwood to Horace N. Allen, January 27, 1887, KLC—BFMPCUSA, Roll 174, PHS.

44. Sonja Kim, "The Search for Health," in *Reform and Modernity in the Taehan Empire,* ed. Kim Dong-no, John B. Duncan, and Kim Do-hyung (Seoul: Jimoondang, 2006), 304.

45. "Man'guk wisaeng hoe," *Hansŏng sunbo,* May 9, 1884.

46. *Ku Han'guk oegyo munsŏ,* vol. 10, comp. and ed. Koryŏ Taehak Asea Munje Yŏn'guso (Seoul: Koryŏdae Minjok Munhwa Yŏn'guso, 1991), 112–113. Hereafter this source will be abbreviated *KHOM* followed by volume number and page number.

47. Yunjae Park has observed that by 1884 at least some Koreans desired to cultivate Western medicine but lacked access to Western medicine and knowledge. Allen's request came, thus, at an opportune time. The establishment of Chejungwŏn, in other words, cannot be viewed as simply the response of a

"grateful" Kojong, who after the Kapsin Coup came to realize the value of Western medicine. See Yunjae Park, "Between Mission and Medicine," in *Encountering Modernity,* ed. Albert L. Park and David K. Yoo (Honolulu: University of Hawai'i Press, 2014), 141–142.

48. John Heron to F. F. Ellinwood, February 12, 1886, KLC—BFMPCUSA, Reel 174, PHS.

49. Horace N. Allen to F. F. Ellinwood, June 3, 1886, and June 20, 1886, KLC—BFMPCUSA, Roll 174, PHS.

50. Horace N. Allen to F. F. Ellinwood, April 25, 1887, KLC—BFMPCUSA, Roll 174, PHS.

51. John Heron to F. F. Ellinwood, May 14, 1886, KLC—BFMPCUSA, Roll 174, PHS.

52. Horace Allen, for example, detailed one situation in which Kojong had given horses as a gift to the hospital. Scranton, who was working temporarily at the hospital, attempted to take one of the horses when he left. Allen refused, stating that the horses were his because he oversaw the hospital and that Scranton's claim to the horse had ended with the termination of his service at the hospital. See Horace N. Allen to F. F. Ellinwood, July 4, 1885, KLC—BFMPCUSA, Roll 174, PHS.

53. Henry Hyunsuk Kim, "Horace N. Allen," *Journal for the Sociological Integration of Religion and Society* 3, no. 1 (2013): 1–21.

54. Huntley, *Caring, Growing, Changing,* 30.

55. Horace N. Allen to F. F. Ellinwood, March 25, 1887, KLC—BFMPCUSA, Roll 174, PHS.

56. Horace Underwood had made several such sojourns, since the Korean government granted Westerners the right to travel with valid documents outside treaty ports and Seoul.

57. John Heron to F. F. Ellinwood, March 25, 1889, KLC—BFMPCUSA, Roll 175, PHS.

58. John Heron to F. F. Ellinwood, March 29, 1889, KLC—BFMPCUSA, Roll 175, PHS.

59. John Heron to F. F. Ellinwood, May 2, 1889, KLC—BFMPCUSA, Roll 175, PHS.

60. John Heron to F. F. Ellinwood, May 12, 1889, March 25, 1889, and July 11, 1889, KLC—BFMPCUSA, Roll 175, PHS.

61. Daniel Gifford to F. F. Ellinwood, December 31, 1889; Horace G. Underwood to F. F. Ellinwood, August 5, 1889, KLC—BFMPCUSA, Roll 175, PHS.

62. John Heron to F. F. Ellinwood, December 30, 1889, KLC—BFMPCUSA, Roll 175, PHS.

63. Lillias Underwood to F. F. Ellinwood, March 8, 1889; Horace G. Underwood to F. F. Ellinwood, August 5, 1889, KLC—BFMPCUSA, Roll 175, PHS.

64. Lillias Underwood to F. F Ellinwood, November 22, 1889, KLC—BFMPCUSA, Roll 175, PHS.

65. John Heron to F. F. Ellinwood, January 8, 1888, KLC—BFMPCUSA, Roll 175, PHS.

66. John Heron to F. F. Ellinwood, September 4, 1889, KLC—BFMPCUSA, Roll 175, PHS.

67. Lillias Underwood to F. F Ellinwood, July 30, 1890, KLC—BFMPCUSA, Roll 175, PHS.

68. Horace G. Underwood to F. F. Ellinwood, August 4, 1890, KLC—BFMPCUSA, Roll 175, PHS.

69. Horace G. Underwood to the Board of Foreign Missions of the Presbyterian Church, August 11, 1890; Horace N. Allen to F. F. Ellinwood, August 8, 1890, KLC—BFMPCUSA, Reel 176, PHS.

70. Horace Underwood reported to Francis Ellinwood that he had encouraged Horace Allen to remain a missionary when Allen first broached the issue of accepting the position of secretary of the US legation. Now that Allen had accepted the position, Underwood argued that Allen should "sever his connection" with the BFMPCUSA. See Underwood to F. F. Ellinwood, August 4.

71. Horace N. Allen to F. F. Ellinwood, August 13, 1890, KLC—BFMPCUSA, Roll 175, PHS.

72. Cadwallader C. Vinton to F. F. Ellinwood, July 3, 1891, KLC—BFMPCUSA, Roll 176, PHS.

73. Cadwallader C. Vinton to F. F. Ellinwood, May 20, 1891, KLC—BFMPCUSA, Roll 176, PHS.

74. Horace N. Allen to F. F. Ellinwood, May 13, 1891, KLC—BFMPCUSA, Roll 176, PHS.

75. Augustine Heard to William M. Baird, July 31 and August 1, 1891, KLC—BFMPCUSA, Roll 176, PHS.

76. Cadwallader C. Vinton to F. F. Ellinwood, August 27, 1891, KLC—BFMPCUSA, Roll 176, PHS.

77. William Baird to F. F. Ellinwood, December 29, 1893, KLC—BFMPCUSA, Roll 177, PHS.

78. *KHOM* 11, 27–28.

79. Cadwallader C. Vinton to F. F. Ellinwood, July 3, 1891, KLC—BFMPCUSA, Roll 176, PHS.

80. Oliver Avison to F. F. Ellinwood, September 27, 1894, KLC—BFMPCUSA, Roll 178, PHS.

81. Avison to Ellinwood, September 27, 1894.

82. Horace N. Allen to F. F. Ellinwood, April 3, 1885, KLC—BFMPCUSA, Roll 174, PHS.

83. For example, in a letter to Francis Ellinwood, Cadwallader Vinton wrote: "You speak of my relations to the king. I have no relations to him." See Cadwallader C. Vinton to F. F. Ellinwood, September 16, 1892, KLC—BFMPCUSA, Roll 176, PHS.

Chapter 2: Creating Separation

1. Donald Clark has detailed how missionaries to Korea established communities and lived in the country during the first half of the twentieth century. His work serves as an important reminder that while missionaries were certainly motivated by religious ideals, they were also simply people who confronted the challenge of living in a foreign country. See Donald Clark, *Living Dangerously in Korea* (Norwalk, CT: EastBridge, 2003), 5–26.

2. For an overview of the establishment of Yanghwajin Foreign Missionary Cemetery, see Kim Sŭng-t'ae, *Hanmal Ilche kangjŏm ki sŏn'gyosa yŏn'gu* (Seoul: Han'guk Kidokkyo Yŏksa Yŏn'guso, 2006), 12–25.

3. Yumi Moon, *Populist Collborators* (Ithaca, NY: Cornell University Press, 2013), 39–43.

4. For an examination of the strategies that Korean reformers used to "demote" China and assert Korea's equality with all nations, see Andre Schmid, *Korea between Empires* (New York: Columbia University Press, 2002), 55–100.

5. Schmid, *Korea between Empires,* 73.

6. Kenneth Wells, *New God, New Nation* (Honolulu: University of Hawai'i Press, 1990), 59–60.

7. For a short study on the *Christian News*, see Ok Sŏng-dŭk, *Ch'ŏt sagŏn ŭro pon ch'odae Han'guk kyohoe sa* (Seoul: Chitda, 2016), 222–226.

8. "Chisik ira," *Kŭrisŭdo sinmun,* April 1, 1897.

9. Lillias Underwood, *Underwood of Korea* (Seoul: Yonsei University Press, 1983), 164.

10. Schmid, *Korea between Empires,* 73.

11. *HKY II,* 247–258.

12. A useful reminder of the realities of international relations is Dong Wang's observation that in most, if not all, international treaty agreements there is a clear expression of power and inequality. See Dong Wang, *China's Unequal Treaties* (Plymouth: Lexington, 2008).

13. Henry Loomis to F. F. Ellinwood, August 9, 1884, KLC—BFMPCUSA, Roll 174, PHS.

14. Missionaries to other countries made similar appeals. For example, in 1896, a group of missionaries in China wrote the Chinese emperor to highlight the many benefits that Christianity offered the country. Among these benefits was the cultivation of loyal subjects. See W. Muirhead, W. Ashmore, J. S. Burdon, et al., "Memorial to the Chinese Emperor on Christian Missions," *Chinese Recorder* 27, no. 4 (April 1896): 180. The original was written in Chinese and presented to *Zongli yamen* by J. Wherry and Timothy Richard on November 14, 1895. Hereafter, the *Chinese Recorder* will be abbreviated as *CR*.

15. Horace G. Underwood, "Evangelistic Report for Year Ending Oct. 31st, 1896," KLC—BFMPCUSA, Roll 180, PHS.

16. James Hevia and Lydia Liu have demonstrated that during the nineteenth century, China and Western nations competed over which system of international relations would govern their interactions. Treaty laws, extraterritoriality, and the translation of Chinese terms all helped Westerners advance their vision of promoting a modern society and "teaching" China how supposedly civilized countries acted. I suggest that a similar process took place in Korea. See James Hevia, *English Lessons* (Durham, NC: Duke University Press, 2003); and Lydia Liu, *The Clash of Empires* (Cambridge, MA: Harvard University Press, 2004).

17. R. Bin Wong has argued that in the West, modern citizenship was the product of a long contest between citizens and their governments over the relative merits of their respective claims. Implicit in these conflicts was a belief in the existence of an objective third-party judge who could weigh the evidence and rule on which side possessed a superior claim. In reality, such an observer was either absent or weak. In contrast, in Korea, the US legation was both a visible and powerful third-party judge. See R. Bin Wong, "Citizenship in Chinese History," in *Extending Citizenship, Reconfiguring States,* ed. Michael Hanagan and Charles Tilly (Oxford: Rowman & Littlefield, 1999), 97–98.

18. *KHOM* 10, 221.

19. *KHOM* 10, 396–397. In making this point, Hugh Dinsmore stated that neither he nor Hulbert desired to possess property that had been fraudulently sold. However, Dinsmore indicated that Hulbert was entitled to due process and perhaps even compensation.

20. "Minutes of Mission Meeting," October 21, 1890, KLC—BFMPCUSA, Roll 176, PHS.

21. Augustine Heard to William M. Baird, August 1, 1891, KLC—BFMPCUSA, Roll 176, PHS.

22. *KHOM* 10, 570–572.

23. *KHOM* 10, 570–572.

24. Heard to Baird, August 1, 1891.

25. For William Baird's response to Heard, see William Baird to Augustine Heard, July 29, 1891, KLC—BFMPCUSA, Roll 176, PHS.

26. Heard to Baird, August 1, 1891.

27. Horace N. Allen to F. F. Ellinwood, July 31, 1891, KLC—BFMPCUSA, Roll 176, PHS.

28. Following the terminology used by the first generation of Protestant missionaries for this event, scholars of Korean Christianity have referred to this event as a persecution. However, as the present analysis will reveal, the P'yŏngyang Persecution was not a religious persecution. The governor of the province in fact had just cause for arresting those Koreans who helped missionaries reside illegally in the city.

29. For a detailed but brief accounting on this event, see Ok, *Ch'ŏt Sagŏn ŭro*, 287–299.

30. Samuel A. Moffett to F. F. Ellinwood, September 15, 1890, KLC—BFMPCUSA, Roll 179, PHS.

31. Samuel A. Moffett to F. F. Ellinwood, March 17 and September 6, 1892, KLC—BFMPCUSA, Roll 179, PHS. Some advocated first establishing a station at Ŭiju because it seemed as though establishing a station at P'yŏngyang was, at the time, impossible. See Samuel A. Moffett to F. F. Ellinwood, October 20, 1890, KLC—BFMPCUSA, Roll 179, PHS.

32. William Baird to F. F. Ellinwood, October 6, 1891, KLC—BFMPCUSA, Roll 176, PHS.

33. Dae Young Ryu has suggested that the purchase of property in the name of a Korean Christian was a tactic the missionaries to Korea borrowed from their colleagues in Japan. However, in writing to Francis Ellinwood, William Baird did not reference the activities of other missionaries in Japan. Instead, he emphasized the tactics that were being used by other foreign actors, in particular Catholic missionaries, operating on the peninsula. Viewed differently, by at least 1890, the Northern Presbyterians debated whether to establish a station in Pusan or P'yŏngyang. Horace Underwood advocated for the latter. Regarding the problem of the city not being an "open port," he observed that Japanese were residing in the city. He thus believed that missionaries should be able to do the same. Underwood's statement indicates that missionaries in Korea understood that foreigners were residing outside of "open ports" but were uncertain how this was being accomplished. Though their colleagues in Japan may have purchased property in the name of a of Japanese convert, Underwood and his fellow workers did not cite this as a tactic to reside outside of "open ports." See Horace G. Underwood to F. F. Ellinwood, August 4, 1890, KLC—BFMPCUSA, Roll 175, PHS. See also, Dae Young Ryu, "Treaties, Extraterritorial Rights, and American Protestant Missions in Late Joseon Korea," *Korea Journal* 43, no. 1 (Spring 2003): 197.

34. William Swallen disagreed with this attempt to purchase property secretly. He preferred to stay in the treaty ports and train native Koreans to evangelize in the interior. Despite personal misgivings, however, he accompanied Samuel Moffett and Graham Lee in their efforts to secure a house. He reported that they exercised caution to prevent local Koreans from learning of their involvement in the purchase. William Swallen to F. F. Ellinwood, May 22, 1893, KLC—BFMPCUSA, Roll 177, PHS.

35. Rosetta Sherwood Hall, *The Life of Rev. William James Hall, M.D.* (New York: Press of Eaton and Mains, 1897), 123, 254–255.

36. Hall, *The Life of Rev. William James Hall,* 273–274.

37. Daniel Gifford to F. F. Ellinwood, May 12, 1894, KLC—BFMPCUSA, Roll 178, PHS.

38. Daniel Gifford to F. F. Ellinwood, May 17, 1894, KLC—BFMPCUSA, Roll 178, PHS.

39. Gifford to Ellinwood, May 17, 1894.

40. "Copy of Letter from Samuel A. Moffett to John Sills," May 25, 1894, KLC—BFMPCUSA, Roll 179, PHS. Moffett submitted a copy of this letter to F. F. Ellinwood with another letter explaining the current situation in P'yŏngyang on August 27, 1894.

41. "Copy of Letter from Samuel A. Moffett to John Sills," May 25, 1894.

42. "Copy of Letter from Samuel A. Moffett to John Sills," May 25, 1894. See also Samuel A. Moffett to F. F. Ellinwood, August 27, 1894, KLC—BFMPCUSA, Roll 179, PHS.

43. Daniel Gifford to F. F. Ellinwood, August 13, 1894, KLC—BFMPCUSA, Roll 178, PHS.

44. Kuksa p'yŏnch'an wiwŏnhoe ed., *Kaksa tŭngnok*, vol. 25 (Seoul: Kuksa p'yŏnch'an wiwŏnhoe, 1981–), 266–267, 282–283, 336–338. Hereafter this source will be abbreviated *KSTN* followed by the volume number and page number.

45. Horace N. Allen, who was in charge of the legation at the time, grumbled about the number of complaints he received from missionaries and the difficulties in responding to all of them. See Horace N. Allen to F. F. Ellinwood, March 6, 1901; and Horace N. Allen to Norman Whittermore, August 15, 1901, KLC—BFMPCUSA, Roll 280, PHS.

46. William Baird, "Report on the Opening of Taigoo," 1896, KLC—BFMPCUSA, Roll 180, PHS.

47. James E. Adams to F. F. Ellinwood, December 11, 1896, KLC—BFMPCUSA, Roll 178, PHS.

48. *KSTN* 15, 615–616.

49. *KHOM* 11, 783–786.

50. *KHOM* 12, 56–64. The governor believed that the tiles were for a church. Thus, the governor punished Kim for the illicit spread and practice of Christianity. In contrast, the missionaries claimed that the tiles were for a residence. This claim is questionable, however. In June 1900, just a few months before the purchase of the tiles, the Taegu Station received funding to build a "chapel." See James E. Adams to F. F. Ellinwood, June 12, 1900, KLC—BFMPCUSA, Roll 179, PHS.

51. *KHOM* 11, 784; *KHOM* 17, 57.

52. *KHOM* 12, 58.

Chapter 3: The Conversion Conundrum

1. William N. Blair, a missionary to Korea, titled his work on the history of Presbyterian missions in Korea *Gold in Korea*. See William N. Blair, *Gold in Korea* (Topeka, KS: H. M. Ives and Sons, 1947).

2. Robert E. Speer, *Report on the Mission in Korea of the Presbyterian Board of Foreign Missions* (New York: Board of Foreign Missions of the Presbyterian Church in the USA, 1897), 5.

3. Speer, *Report on the Mission in Korea,* 7.

4. Speer, *Report on the Mission in Korea,* 9.

5. F. F. Ellinwood to the Korea Mission, December 17, 1890, KLC—BFMPCUSA, Roll 223, PHS.

6. John Nevius, "Principles and Methods Applicable to Station Work, Letter II," *CR* 16, no. 11 (December 1885): 461–462.

7. Jessie Gregory Lutz, *Opening China* (Grand Rapids, MI: William B. Eerdmans, 2008), 237–239.

8. *ARBFMMEC,* 18.

9. *ARBFMMEC,* 63.

10. Michel Foucault has observed that Christian pastors and priests confront the dilemma of balancing the salvation of one and the potential cost of the salvation of all. Simply put, the leaders of the church are responsible for *each* lost soul and thus must permit even those with "evil intent" or impure motives to convert in the hopes of reforming their souls. However, this action introduces a dangerous element into the congregation and threatens the overall health of the church. Thus, priests and pastors are also, paradoxically, supposed to expel dangerous individuals. I suggest that the debate over rice Christians is an example of this dilemma. See Michel Foucault, *Security, Territory, Population* (New York: Palgrave Macmillan, 2007), 168–170.

11. Speer, *Report on the Mission in Korea,* 30.

12. [N.A.], "How Shall We Best Meet the Difficulties Which Arise in Our Work from the Self-Seeking Which Characterizes the Chinese People?" *CR* 14, no. 5 (September–October 1883): 366–379; H. D. Porter, "What Ought to Be the Policy of Missionaries in Regard to the Ordination of Native Pastors," *CR* 17, no. 5 (May 1886): 178–186; Henry Blodget, "May Native Agents Be Supported by Foreign Funds?" *CR* 17, no. 12 (December 1886): 446–453; Gilbert Reid, "The Principle of Self-Support and Benevolence," *CR* 18, no. 9 (September 1887): 346–351.

13. Samuel Moore to the Foreign Missionary Board of the Presbyterian Church of the U.S.A., February 27, 1894, KLC—BFMPCUSA, Roll 178, PHS.

14. Dae Young Ryu has argued that American missionaries to Korea were largely evangelical and followed a "puritan-type" of morality. Thus, they required converts to abide by a strict moral code of behavior. While agreeing with the broad outlines of Ryu's argument, here I argue that the missionaries' concern with assessing "true" belief caused them to search for signs of insincerity. See Dae Young Ryu, "The Origin and Characteristics of Evangelical Protestantism in Korea at the Turn of the Twentieth Century," *Church History* 77, no. 2 (June 2008): 378–382.

15. Han'guk Kyohoesa Yŏn'guso, ed., *Sŏul kyogu yŏnbo I (1878–1903)* (Seoul: Ch'ŏnjugyo Myŏngdong Kyohoe, 1984), 143.

16. Han'guk Kyohoesa Yŏn'guso, ed., *Sŏul kyogu yŏnbo I (1878–1903),* 304. Chapter 4 demonstrates, however, that despite Wilhelm's claims of not becoming involved in political affairs, he often intervened in political issues on behalf of Korean Catholics.

17. Han'guk Kyohoesa Yŏn'guso, ed., *Sŏul kyogu yŏnbo I (1878–1903)*, 299.

18. *ARBFMMEC*, 77.

19. John Nevius, "Principles and Methods Applicable to Station Work, Letter I," *CR* 16, no. 10 (November 1885): 421–424.

20. For missionary-focused studies of the Nevius Method, see George Paik, *History of Protestant Missions in Korea, 1832–1910* (P'yŏngyang: Union Christian College Press, 1929), 405–413; and Charles Allen, *The Korean Church and the Nevius Method* (New York: Fleming H. Revell Co., 1930). See also Pak Yong-gyu, "Han'guk kyohoe sŏn'gyo chŏngch'aek ŭrosŏ ŭi Nebiusŭ pangbŏp," *Sinhak chinam* (Fall 2002): 57–83. For a discussion of how the Nevius Method promoted anti-intellectualism and the advancement of denominationalism, see Sŏ Kwang-sŏn, *Han'guk kidokkyo ŭi sae insik* (Seoul: Taehan Kidokkyo Ch'ulp'ansa, 1985); and Song Kil-sŏp, *Han'guk sinhak sasang sa* (Seoul: Taehan Kidokkyo Ch'ulp'ansa, 1987).

21. Nevius, "Principles and Methods . . . Letter II."

22. Within these groups there were further gradations. In particular, for full church members, there was a difference between those who were, for example, lay members and those who were leaders. John Nevius, "Methods of Mission Work, Letter IV," *CR* 17, no. 2 (February 1886): 57–64.

23. Nevius, "Methods of Mission Work, Letter IV."

24. The issue of the Lord's Supper was of particular importance because it distinguished not only Protestants from Catholics but also one Protestant denomination from another. Theological debates concerning sacramental issues like baptism and the Lord's Supper often became the basis of church divisions. As a result, the demonstration of a proper understanding of these concepts was important. This was especially the case in Hwanghae, where the Catholics were particularly strong.

25. Eugene Bell to Parents, January 31, 1897, in Han'guk Kyohoesa Munhŏn Yŏn'guwŏn, ed., *Personal Reports of the Southern Presbyterian Missionaries in Korea*, vol. 4 (Seoul: Han'guk kyohoesa munhŏn yŏn'guwŏn, 1993).

26. Michel Foucault has argued that modern governments exert power or control over populations through surveillance, normalized judgement, and examination. Through these processes, governments discipline and transform individuals into "loyal" subjects or citizens. A similar process was underway in the system of observation and conversion established by missionaries in Korea. See Michel Foucault, *Discipline and Punish* (New York: Vintage, 1995).

27. Nevius, "Methods of Mission Work, Letter IV," 60.

28. Nevius stated that in his experience in Shandong, about 80 percent of his cases dealt with minor things like "neglect of Christian duties, commencing with giving up Bible study, disregard of the Sabbath, and neglect of public worship." See John Nevius, "Methods of Mission Work, Letter V," *CR* 17, no. 3 (March 1886): 107–109.

29. Clark, *The Korean Church and the Nevius Method,* 113.

30. Scholars have rightly observed that missionaries transported antiquated notions of gender relations in countries like Korea and China. Thus, the argument that missionaries "liberated" women or championed women's rights must be, at the very least, properly contextualized in regards to broader discourses on women's rights taking place in Western countries at the time and the sense of concern many Christian leaders held in regards to the "breakdown" of the family. See Jane Hunter, *The Gospel of Gentility* (New Haven, CT: Yale University Press, 1989); Hyaeweol Choi, "The Missionary Home as a Pulpit: Domestic Paradoxes in Early Twentieth-Century Korea," in *Diving Domesticities,* ed. Hyaeweol Choi and Margaret Jolly (Canberra: Australian National University Press, 2014); and Hyaeweol Choi, *Gender and Mission Encounters in Korea* (Berkeley: University of California Press, 2009).

31. Lillias Underwood, *Underwood of Korea* (New York: Fleming H. Revell, Co., 1918), 160–161.

32. Roy E. Shearer, *Wildfire* (Grand Rapids, MI: W. B. Eerdmans, 1966).

33. Horace G. Underwood to F. F. Ellinwood, September 8, 1899, KLC—BFMPCUSA, Roll 179, PHS; Blanche Lee to F. F. Ellinwood, May 31, 1898, KLC—BFMPCUSA, Roll 178, PHS.

34. Missionary remarks concerning the changed nature of Korean Christians are too numerous to cite in full. Examples include Samuel A. Moffett, "Evangelistic Report, 1894," and "Evangelistic Work in Eui Ju and the North," October 1895, KLC—BFMPCUSA, Roll 179, PHS. See also Georgina E. Whiting, "The Korean Mission Reports," 1898; William Baird, "Evangelistic Report, Pyengyang, 1898"; and Katherine Wambold, "Report, Korea," July 14, 1902, KLC—BFMPCUSA, Roll 180, PHS. See also Margaret Best to F. F. Ellinwood, February 24, 1900; and Lillias Underwood, "Report of Medical and Evangelical Work by Mrs. Underwood for 1900" KLC—BFMPCUSA, Roll 181, PHS.

35. William Davis Reynolds, "The Native Ministry," *Korean Repository* 3 (May 1896): 199.

36. Samuel A. Moffett to Robert LeRoy Haslup, June 29, 1896, KLC—BFMPCUSA, Roll 178, PHS.

37. Michel Foucault has discussed how pastors used the power of sacraments and rituals to regulate and shape the hearts and minds of their "flock." He views this as a source of modern-day governance. See Foucault, *Security, Territory, Population,* 135–157.

38. Lillias Underwood to F. F. Ellinwood, June 8, 1893, KLC—BFMPCUSA, Roll 177, PHS. See also Underwood, *Underwood of Korea,* 127.

39. Horace G. Underwood, "The 'Today' from Korea," *Missionary Review of the World* 6, no. 11 (November 1893): 816–818.

40. Lillias Underwood, *Fifteen Years among the Topknots* (Seoul: Royal Asiatic Society, Korea Branch, 1987), 173.

41. Paik, *History of Protestant Missions in Korea,* 204–205.

42. Paik, *History of Protestant Missions in Korea,* 291–292.

43. Paik, *History of Protestant Missions in Korea,* 292–296.

44. Arthur Brown, *Report of a Visitation of the Korea Mission of the Presbyterian Board of Foreign Missions* (New York: Board of Foreign Missions of the Presbyterian Church, 1902), 13, 15.

45. The missionaries' influence was not only rooted in their control over conversion and baptism. As will be examined in later chapters, the social institutions that missionaries constructed were expensive to build and maintain. Koreans were ill-equipped, at least until the 1920s, to operate these institutions. For an example of the money and networks involved in building Severance Hospital, see Yunjae Park, "Between Mission and Medicine: The Early History of Severance Hospital," in *Encountering Modernity: Christianity in East Asia and Asian America,* ed. Albert L. Park and David K. Yoo (Honolulu: University of Hawai'i Press, 2014), 140–161. For a more general history of modern medicine in Korea, see Pak Yun-jae (Park Yunjae), *Han'guk kŭndae ŭihak ŭi kiwŏn* (Seoul: Hyean, 2005).

46. For an examination of the Great Revival, see Pak Yong-gyu, *P'yŏngyang tae puhŭng undong* (Seoul: Saengmyŏng ŭi Malssŭmsa, 2000). For an examination of the Great Revival through primary sources, see Sung Deuk Oak, ed., *Primary Sources of the Korean Great Revival, 1903–1908* (Seoul: Changnohoe Sinhak Taehakkyo, 2007).

47. Graham Lee, "How the Spirit Came to Pyeng Yang," *KMF* (March 1907).

48. As Hong Chae-bŏm has noted, in general the field is divided on several issues concerning how to interpret the significance of this event: (1) the role of the political situation in the Great Revival, (2) how to understand the emotional outbursts displayed during the Great Revival, and (3) how the Great Revival affected church growth. For more information on these debates, see Hong Chaebŏm, "Han'guk kaesin'gyo ŭi 1907 nyŏn P'yŏngyang tae puhŭng undong e taehan haesŏk tŭl ŭi pigyo yŏn'gu," *Chonggyo yŏn'gu* (2006): 233–259.

49. Ok Sŏng-dŭk, "P'yŏngyang tae puhŭng undong kwa Kil Sŏn-ju yŏngsŏng ŭi togyojŏk yŏnghyang," *Han'guk kidokkyo wa yŏn'gu* 25 (September 2006): 57–95.

50. J. Z. Moore, "The Great Revival Year," *KMF* (August 1907): 118.

Chapter 4: Christian Oasis

1. Kim Yŏng-sam, *Widaehan Han'guk in* (Seoul: T'aeguk Ch'ulp'ansa, 1979), 27.

2. One feature of Korean society was what is called the *pon'gwan* system. In addition to being marked by a surname, lineages also were distinguished by a *pon'gwan,* which referred to the ancestral clan-seat of the family. Thus, here Kwangsan refers to the *pon'gwan* of the Kim clan living in Sorae.

3. *HKY I,* 242–247.

4. Kim, *Widaehan Han'guk in,* 27.

5. Ha Wŏn-ho, *Han'guk kŭndae kyŏngje sa yŏn'gu* (Seoul: Sŏsinwŏn 1997).

6. While most of them only passed through the village, some stayed for an extended period of time. For example, James Scarth Gale spent three months in 1889 studying the language and teaching the gospel. He was followed by Malcolm Fenwick, who arrived as an independent missionary the subsequent year.

7. In 1905, Horace G. Underwood took his family to spend the first of what would be many summer vacations at a secluded beach located on the coast of Hwanghae Province, near Sorae village. Underwood first visited this beach in 1888 during one of his early itineration trips and was at the time taken with the white sand, peaceful bay, and overall beauty of the surroundings. His 1905 journey with his family was part of a greater plan to see this beach become a summer resort for missionaries stationed in Korea, and soon others followed. The number of Westerners choosing to vacation at what would become known as Sorae Beach had grown to such an extent that the missionaries established the "Sorai [Sorae] Beach Company," with an honorary mayor to oversee the administration of the community. In their annual reports, missionaries described the joys of spending time with their friends, family, and colleagues swimming in the ocean, playing volleyball on the beach, or even yachting in the harbor. Evenings were often spent at worship services intended to reenergize missionaries to engage in the spread of the gospel and their spiritual responsibilities. For more on Sorae Beach, see Donald Clark, *Living Dangerously in Korea* (Norwalk, CT: EastBridge, 2003), 79–84.

8. Lillias Underwood, *Fifteen Years among the Topknots* (Boston: American Tract Society, 1904), 190.

9. Elizabeth McCully, *A Corn of Wheat* (Toronto: Westminster, 1903), 252–254.

10. Horace G. Underwood, "Evangelistic Report, 1897," KLC—BFMPCUSA, Roll 180, PHS.

11. Horace G. Underwood, "Evangelistic Report for the Year Ending Sept. 15, 1899 of Work Under H. G. Underwood, of Seoul to the Presbyterian Mission," KLC—BFMPCUSA, Roll 181, PHS.

12. Horace G. Underwood, "Evangelistic Report for Year Ending July 31, 1900," KLC—BFMPCUSA, Roll 181, PHS.

13. *Kŭrisŭdo sinmun*, April 1, 1897.

14. Horace G. Underwood, "Korea: Evangelistic Work for Year Ending September 30, 1898," KLC—BFMPCUSA, Roll 181, PHS.

15. Horace G. Underwood, "Evangelistic Report for Year Ending July 31, 1899," KLC—BFMPCUSA, Roll 181, PHS.

16. Sorae had more than three times the total number of church members than Ŭllyul, in 1899. Despite this numerical advantage, Ŭllyul possessed more financial resources because of the wealth of its members. See Horace G. Underwood, "Evangelistic Report for Year Ending July 31, 1899."

17. William Baird, "Evangelistic Report Pyeng Yang, 1898," KLC—BFMP-CUSA, Roll 180, PHS.

18. William Swallen, "Pyeng Yang Station Report, 1899," KLC—BFMP-CUSA, Roll 181, PHS.

19. Underwood, "Evangelistic Report for the Year Ending Sept. 15, 1899."

20. McCully, *A Corn of Wheat,* 281.

21. Hyaeweol Choi, *Gender and Mission Encounters in Korea* (Berkeley: University of California Press, 2009), 155–157.

22. Maria Kim's relatives also gained prominence. For example, her aunt, Kim P'il-rye (1891–1983), eventually left Sorae and became active in Seoul as a founding member of the YWCA. Another uncle, Kim P'il-sun, was a member of the first class of Severance Medical School graduates.

23. *Kŭrisŭdo sinmun,* October 1897.

24. Pak Ch'an-sik, "Hanmal ch'ŏnju kyohoe wa hyangch'on sahoe" (PhD diss., Sŏgang University, 1996), 131.

25. O Yŏng-sŏp, *Han'guk kŭn-hyŏndae sa rŭl sunoŭn inmul tŭl I* (Seoul: Kyŏngin Munhwasa, 2007), 233–238.

26. Yun Sŏn-ja, "'Han-Il hapbyŏng' chŏnhu Hwanghae-do ch'ŏnju kyohoe wa Pillem sinbu," *Han'guk kŭndae sa yŏn'gu* 4 (1996): 107–131.

27. Yumi Moon, *Populist Collaborators* (Ithaca, NY: Cornell University Press, 2013), 50–58.

28. *KSTN* 25, 270–271.

29. *KSTN* 25, 360.

30. In the case of Alexis Hwang Sa-yŏng, in 1801 he was caught attempting to smuggle a "silk letter" to the bishop of Beijing detailing the anti-Catholic persecutions and requesting foreign military intervention. Donald Baker has emphasized that Hwang exists as a problematic figure in Korean history because of his actions. Was he a devout Catholic seeking religious freedom, or was he a traitor? I suggest that Hwang's actions and the difficulties over how to historically assess his significance indicates the tensions produced by the ambiguity of competing communal identities of religious actors. See Donald Baker and Franklin Rausch, *Catholics and Anti-Catholicism in Chosŏn Korea* (Honolulu: University of Hawai'i Press, 2017), 102–104.

31. *KSTN* 25, 654.

32. The council was not simply composed of pro-Japanese officials. The composition of the Deliberative Council was complex. Some supported Japanese-style reforms. Others supported American-style reforms. Still others supported reforms with a Confucian basis. Finally, some opposed reforms. See Yu Yŏng-ik, "Kabo kyŏngjang," in *Han'guksa 40: Ch'ŏng-Il chŏnjaeng kwa kabo kaehyŏk*, ed. Kuksa P'yŏnch'an Wiwŏnhoe (Seoul: Kuksa P'yŏnch'an Wiwŏnhoe, 2003). Lew has published widely in English and is well known by his chosen Romanization "Young Ick Lew." Here Lew is his family name and Young Ick is his given name.

33. Kyung Moon Hwang, *Rationalizing Korea* (Berkeley: University of California Press, 2016), 146–167.

34. For a summary in English of the complex system of ownership and administration of *yŏktunt'o*, see Moon, *Populist Collaborators,* 167–170.

35. Pak Ch'an-sik has written extensively on the history of Catholic-related "church cases" *(kyoan)* in Korea during the late nineteenth century. On the one hand, he supports the conventional wisdom that many in Hwanghae converted to take advantage of the power offered by extraterritoriality and resist local officials. On the other hand, viewed on the whole, his work serves as a reminder of the importance of paying attention to regional variation in conversion patterns and the relationships that existed between missionaries, Korean Catholic leaders, and local officials. For his discussion of how the Hwanghae Church Cases reflects competing interests in the region, see Pak Ch'an-sik, "Hanmal ch'ŏnjugyohoe wa hyangch'on sahoe," 127–148.

36. One issue when examining the Hwanghae Church Cases is the reliance on Yi Ŭng-ik's report. Scholars have suggested that Yi was aware of the court's close relationship with the Protestant missionary community and was predisposed to viewing Catholics in a negative light. Considering the number of reports submitted by the governors of Hwanghae during the late 1890s, cited in this chapter, officials seemed to harbor a distrust of Korean Catholics. Whether this was rooted in a longer history of official disdain for this religion—dating back to the number of anti-Catholic persecutions during the century—or for more contemporary reasons, such as Catholic abuses of power, is an area for more investigation. I have examined Yi's report and official complaints against Catholicism aware of biases held by Korean officials for this branch of Christianity more generally.

37. *Korea Review,* November 1901.

38. *KSTN* 26, 240–241, 255, 259–260.

39. *KSTN* 25, 642–643, 645–646.

40. *KHOM* 11, 212–214.

41. *KSTN* 25, 271–272.

42. Horace G. Underwood, "Evangelistic Report for the years 1896–1897," KLC—BFMPCUSA, Roll 180, PHS.

43. Mary Barrett to F. F. Ellinwood, December 28, 1901, KLC—BFMPCUSA, Roll 280, PHS.

44. *Hwangsŏng sinmun,* March 16, 1903.

45. *KSTN* 26, 648–650.

46. *KSTN* 26, 672.

47. *KSTN* 26, 686.

48. *KSTN* 26, 643–648. In this, as in other cases, it is likely that the patrolmen and Korean Protestant witnesses exaggerated the number of Catholics who gathered. However, more important than the exact number was the fact that Catholics appeared in large groups.

49. Pak Chi-t'ae, ed., *Taehan chegukki chŏngch'aek sa charyojip* 7 (Seoul: Sŏnin Munhwasa, 1999), 41–47.

50. *KSTN* 26, 657–664.

51. *KSTN* 26, 683–684.

52. *KSTN* 26, 245.

53. *KSTN* 26, 251, 254.

54. As one illustration, Sung Deuk Oak has observed that in the aftermath of the Tonghak Uprising, Christians in the northwestern provinces began raising the flag of St. George's Cross. William MacKenzie first instituted this practice in 1894, while he was staying at Sorae. Upon hearing rumors that Tonghak forces intended to wipe out the Christians in the village, MacKenzie raised the flag to demonstrate that they were not afraid and would not run away. After Sorae survived the Tonghak Uprising without incident, raising a flag with St. George's Cross became popular. According to Sung Deuk Oak, the flag came to represent the power of the "great Westerner" and the protection provided to those who gathered under it. Yet while Christians living in Hwanghae may have raised the flag of St. George's Cross, it did not protect them from oppression, as demonstrated in this chapter. Sung Deuk Oak, *The Making of Korean Christianity* (Waco, TX: Baylor University Press, 2015), 13–16.

55. W. L. Swallen to F. F. Ellinwood, May 12, 1899; Graham Lee, "Station Letter: Pyeng Yang," August 23, 1899; Bertha Hunt, "Personal Report of Bertha F. Hunt," 1900; W. L. Swallen, "Pyeng Yang Station, Annual Report for 1899–1900," 1900; William Hunt to F. F. Ellinwood, March 5, 1900; Samuel A. Moffett to F. F. Ellinwood, January 25, 1900; Hunter Wells to F. F. Ellinwood, December 7, 1900, KLC—BFMPCUSA, Roll 179, PHS.

56. Horace N. Allen to Samuel A. Moffett, October 29, 1902, KLC—BFMPCUSA, Roll 280, PHS.

Chapter 5: Redefining Relations

1. Yun Kyŏng-no, *Han'guk kŭndae sa ŭi kidokkyo sajŏk ihae* (Seoul: Yŏkminsa, 2003), 29–30, 56–58; No Ch'i-jun, *Ilche ha Han'guk kidokkyo minjok undong yŏn'gu* (Seoul: Han'guk Kidokkyo Yŏksa Yŏn'guso, 1993), 50–52; Jai-keun Choi, *The Korean Church under Japanese Colonialism* (Seoul: Jimoondang, 2007), 22–23.

2. Joseph Esherick, *The Origins of the Boxer Uprising* (Berkeley: University of California Press, 1987), 1–37, 68–95.

3. James Hevia, *English Lessons* (Durham, NC: Duke University Press, 2003), 236–240.

4. "Missionaries in China," *New York Times,* February 24, 1901.

5. John W. Foster, "The Mission Question in China," *Gospel in All Lands* 22, no. 9 (September 1901): 410–412; Llewellyn James Davies, "The Church and Chinese Indemnities," *Missionary Review of the World* 24, no. 9 (September 1901): 672–676; J. L. Whiting, "Missions in China: Shall We Advance or Retire," *Missionary Review of the World* 24, no. 12 (December 1901): 905–909.

6. "Chyangnohoe kong ŭi hoe ilgŭi," *Kŭrisŭdo sinmun,* October 3, 1901.

7. Yun, *Han'guk kŭndae sa ŭi kidokkyo,* 56–58.

8. Arthur Brown, *Report of a Visitation of the Korea Mission of the Presbyterian Board of Foreign Missions* (New York: Board of Foreign Missions of the Presbyterian Church, 1902), 6.

9. Alfred Sharrocks to Arthur Brown, March 19, 1904; Carl Kearns to Arthur Brown, April 4, 1904; Helen Kirkwood to Arthur Brown, April 12, 1904, KLC—BFMPCUSA, Roll 280, PHS.

10. Carl E. Kearns to Arthur Brown, April 4, 1904, KLC—BFMPCUSA, Roll 280, PHS.

11. Samuel A. Moffett to Horace N. Allen, August 15, 1904, KLC—BFMPCUSA, Roll 281, PHS.

12. Hunter Wells to Arthur Brown, November 7, 1905, KLC—BFMPCUSA, Roll 281, PHS.

13. William Baird to Arthur Brown, October 14, 1905, KLC—BFMPCUSA, Roll 281, PHS.

14. Alexander Pieters to Arthur Brown, December 10, 1905, KLC—BFMPCUSA, Roll 281, PHS.

15. James E. Adams to Arthur Brown, October 6, 1905, KLC—BFMPCUSA, Roll 281, PHS.

16. Carl E. Kearns to Horace N. Allen, March 12, 1905, KLC—BFMPCUSA, Roll 281, PHS.

17. Horace N. Allen to Carl Kearns, April 12, 1905, KLC—BFMPCUSA, Roll 281, PHS. See also Carl Kearns to Arthur Brown, November 15, 1905, KLC—BFMPCUSA, Roll 281, PHS.

18. Carl E. Kearns to Arthur Brown, July 5, 1905, KLC—BFMPCUSA, Roll 281, PHS. In a similar account, William Baird reported that Japanese soldiers had burned houses in one village because of its refusal to hand over a chicken. See William Baird to Arthur Brown, March 14, 1906, KLC—BFMPCUSA, Roll 281, PHS.

19. Hallim Taehakkyo Asea Munhwa Yŏn'guso, ed., *Chu-Han Miguk kongsagwan, yŏngsagwan kirok 20* (Seoul: Hallim Taehakkyo Ch'ulp'anbu, 2000–2001), 199–201.

20. William Baird to Arthur Brown, March 14, 1906; Horace G. Underwood to Halsey, March 13, 1906, KLC—BFMPCUSA, Reel 281, PHS.

21. In March 1912, Arthur Brown wrote the US State Department inquiring whether US citizens enjoyed the right of extraterritoriality in Korea. Brown had asked this question to see whether schools operated by the missionaries needed to abide by the GGK's 1911 ordinances on education. Brown received a reply stating that the US government recognized Japanese jurisdiction in Korea. In other words, US citizens in Korea fell under the jurisdictional control of the Japanese colonial government. See Huntington Wilson to Arthur J. Brown, March 27, 1912, RG 140.12.1.

22. Joseph Henning, *Outposts of Civilization* (New York: New York University Press, 2000), 114–136.

23. George T. Ladd, *In Korea with Marquis Ito* (London: Longmans, Green, 1908), 5, 6, 21, 162–163.

24. Many missionaries stationed in Korea were upset over George Ladd's portrayal of their work in the country. For one response, see Charles Allen Clark to Arthur Brown, February 5, 1908, KLC—BFMPCUSA, Roll 281, PHS.

25. Ladd, *In Korea with Marquis Ito,* 166–167.

26. For example, the *Seoul Press* provided summaries of the daily proceedings of the World's Student Christian Federation meeting held in Tokyo in 1907. Gotō Shinpei, who at the time was in charge of the South Manchuria Railway Co. and an important political figure, addressed the delegates, stating that he felt an affinity with them in the common cause of promoting peace and harmony. See "World's Student Christian Federation—Conference Meetings," *Seoul Press,* April 9, 1907; and "World's Christian Student Conference—Baron Goto's Address," *Seoul Press,* April 14, 1907.

27. "Excitement at Pyongyang," *Seoul Press,* April 12, 1907.

28. "Pyong-yang, I," *Seoul Press,* April 13, 1907.

29. "Pyong-yang (II)," *Seoul Press,* April 14, 1907.

30. "Pyong-yang (III)," *Seoul Press,* April 16, 1907.

31. An Chung-gŭn assassinated Itō Hirobumi in October 1909. For more on how the Catholic missionaries responded to An's actions, see Franklin Rausch, "The Bishop's Dilemma: Gustave Mutel and the Catholic Church in Korea, 1890–1910," *Journal of Korean Religions* 4, no. 1 (April 2013): 43–69.

32. "Must Work in Harmony," *Seoul Press*, November 11, 1909. Emphasis added.

33. Yun Kyŏng-no, *105 in sagŏn kwa sinminhoe yŏn'gu* (Seoul: Ilchisa, 1990); Kenneth Wells, *New God, New Nation* (Honolulu: University of Hawai'i Press, 1990), 73–79.

34. "Extract from letter to Speer from G. W. Fulton, Japan, 1911," Missionary Research Library Series 8: Korea, Korea Conspiracy Case Records, Box 1, Folder 1, Burke Library Archive at Union Theological Seminary, Columbia University, New York. Hereafter, this record will appear as MRL 8 followed by the box number, folder number, and BLA.

35. "Syen Chyun Station, 1911–12," August 1912, Record Group 140, Box 6, Folder 45, Presbyterian Historical Society, Philadelphia. Hereafter, this record will appear as RG 140, followed by the box number, folder number, and PHS.

36. Samuel Moffett et. al, "Statement Concerning Conspiracy Case," February 1912, MRL 8, Box 1, Folder 1, BLA.

37. "Editorial," *Seoul Press,* August 28, 1912. This editorial was responding specifically to a letter that the missionaries had sent to the Continuation Committee of the Edinburgh World Missionary Conference. The missionaries accused colonial officials of abuses in Korea and asserted that the various donations the GGK provided to Christian organizations were in fact bribes for control

of these institutions. See *Keijō nippo*, September 6, 1912. For the response of Philip Gillet, head of the YMCA in Korea, to the Korean Conspiracy Trial and observations of colonial rule, see "Correspondence of Philip L. Gilett, New York, 1912," MRL 8, Box 1, Folder 1, BLA.

38. "Christians Incapable of Crime," *Seoul Press,* August 29, 1912; "Alleged Opposition to Christian Movement in Chosen," *Seoul Press,* August 30, 1912; "Alleged Attempt to Japanise Christian Movement in Chosen," *Seoul Press,* August 31, 1912.

39. "The Korean People as a Whole Resent Japanese Authority," *Seoul Press,* September 4, 1912.

40. "What Should Be the Proper Attitude of Missionaries toward the Unjust Acts of Government Officials," MRL 8, Box 1, Folder 1, BLA.

41. Paul S. Cha, "Establishing the Rules of Engagement," *International Journal of Korean History* 17, no. 1 (February 2012): 67–107.

42. Arthur Brown to Viscount Chinda, May 28, 1912, RG 140.16.10, PHS.

43. "Editorial," *KMF* 5, no. 1 (January 1909): 2.

44. "Shiritsu gakkō kisoku ju kaisei" [Revised regulations on private school education], *Chōsen sōtokufu kanpō,* March 24, 1915.

45. Komatsu Midori, "Separation of Education and Religion," *Seoul Press,* April 3, 1915.

46. The passage of a set of regulations on religious propagation four months after the revised private school directives only heightened the missionaries' fears. Kyung Moon Hwang has examined how the new propagation law fit into the colonial government's broader policies on religion. See Kyung Moon Hwang, *Rationalizing Korea* (Berkeley: University of California Press, 2016), 156–163. On the regulations, see "Fukyō kisoku" [Regulations on propagation], *Chōsen sōtokufu kanpō,* August 16, 1915.

47. James E. Adams to H. W. Guthrie, August 17, 1915, RG 140.12.4, PHS.

48. Yi Sŏng-chŏn, *Miguk sŏn'gyo sa wa Han'guk kŭndae kyoyuk* (Seoul: Han'guk Kidokkyo Yŏn'guso, 2007), 100–112.

49. Arthur J. Brown to Komatsu Midori, June 16, 1915, RG 140.12.3, PHS.

50. Komatsu Midori to Arthur Brown, November 4, 1915, RG 140.12.3, PHS.

51. "Extract of Letter from Robert Speer to Arthur Brown," September 20, 1915, RG 140.12.3, PHS.

52. Arthur J. Brown, "Memorandum on the Separation of Education and Religion in Chosen," December 21, 1915, RG 140.12.3, PHS.

53. Arthur Brown to Chosen Mission, January 27, 1916, RG 140.12.7, PHS.

54. Franklin Rausch, "Truth Unacknowledged," in *Religion, Culture, and the Public Sphere in China and Japan*, ed. Albert Welter and Jeffrey Newmark (Singapore: Palgrave Macmillan, 2017), 219.

55. Horace G. Underwood to Arthur Brown, January 16, 1906, KLC—BFMPCUSA, Roll 281, PHS.

56. William Baird to Arthur Brown, September 15, 1905, KLC—BFMP-CUSA, Roll 281, PHS.

57. Horace G. Underwood, "'Constitution of the Educational Foundation Committee,' The Minutes of the Korea Mission, PCUSA, 1911," in *Ŏndŏudŭ charyojip IV*, ed. Yi Manyŏl and Sung Deuk Oak (Seoul: Yŏnse Taehakkyo Ch'ulp'anbu, 2009), 547–548. Hereafter, this sourcebook will appear as *HGU* plus volume number.

58. For more on the growth of Protestant Christianity, broken down according to denominations, in Korea during the early period, see Alfred Wasson, *Church Growth in Korea* (New York: International Missionary Council, 1934); and Roy E. Shearer, *Wildfire: Church Growth in Korea* (Grand Rapids, MI: Eerdmans, 1966).

59. Major cities, such as Seoul and P'yŏngyang, were open to all mission societies. Methodists, thus, worked in P'yŏngyang, though the province fell within the territory overseen by the Northern Presbyterian Mission.

60. William Baird to Arthur Brown, September 15, 1905.

61. In the end, Seoul became the location of Chōsen Christian College. However, the Presbyterian mission societies also funded and administered Union Christian College, which was located in P'yŏngyang.

62. The Presbyterians who advocated having a united Christian college in P'yŏngyang admitted that Seoul was more centrally located. They also acknowledged the historical, social, and political importance of Seoul. But they countered that the center of Protestantism's strength on the peninsula was P'yŏngyang. See W. A. Venable to Egbert W. Smith, February 26, 1913, RG 140.11.26, PHS.

63. Much like the earlier conflicts between Horace Allen, John Heron, and Horace Underwood, the conflict over Chōsen Christian College devolved into petty character attacks. For instance, Underwood complained to Arthur Brown that "some of the younger missionaries were told that it was the policy of the Underwoods to be awfully nice to the young missionaries so as to win them over to their schemes." See Horace G. Underwood to Arthur Brown, April 7, 1914, in *HGU* V, 380.

64. "Fourth Annual Meeting of the Federal Council of Protestant Evangelical Missions," September 1915, Institute for the Study of Korean Church History, Seoul, Republic of Korea.

65. Frank M. Brockman to John Mott, September 6, 1915, RG 140.12.4, PHS.

66. "Fifth Annual Meeting of the Federal Council of Protestant Evangelical Missions in Korea," August 1916, Institute for the Study of Korean Church History, Seoul, Republic of Korea.

67. "Fifth Annual Meeting."

68. "Extract of letter of John F. Genso to Dr. Brown dated July 10th, 1918," RG 140.12.9, PHS.

69. Arthur Brown to the Chosen Committee and the Executive Council, December 26, 1917, RG 140.12.19, PHS.

70. "Extract from letter of Mr. R. O. Reiner to Dr. Brown July 11, 1917," RG 140.12.9, PHS.

71. The Executive Committee of Korea approved this brief in November 1917. See James E. Adams, "A Brief on the Subject of the Desirability of an Adjustment between Home Base and Field as Relates to Field Administration," RG 140.11.37, PHS.

72. "Memorandum on Actions of the Chosen Mission and Its Executive Committee Regarding Readjustment of the Powers of the Board and the Mission," RG 140.11.38, PHS. Arthur Brown wrote most of this memorandum at the order of the BFMPCUSA.

73. The scholarly work on the March First Movement has been voluminous. Many early studies on the March First Movement examined the class background of the participants and the implications of this background for the development of Korean nationalism. Representative studies include An Pyŏng-jik, "3.1 undong e ch'amgahan sahoe kyech'ŭng kwa kŭ sasang," *Yŏksa hakbo* 41 (Autumn 1969): 20–51; and Pak Ch'an-sŭng, "3.1 undong ŭi sasangjŏk kiban," in *3.1 minjok haebang undong yŏn'gu* (Seoul: Ch'ŏngnyŏnsa, 1989). For studies emphasizing the activities of Christians, see Chung-shin Park, *Protestantism and Politics in Korea* (Seattle: University of Washington Press, 2003), 117–138; and Yi Man-yŏl, "Hanmal kidokkyo in ŭi minjok ŭisik hyŏngsŏng kwajŏng," *Han'guk saron* 1 (May 1973): 335–405. More recent works have examined the politics of historical memory and how different eras have remembered the March First Movement. See Ch'oe Pyŏng-t'aek, "Haebang hu yŏksa kyokwasŏ ŭi 3.1 undong kwallyŏn sŏsul kyŏnghyang," *Yŏksa wa hyŏnsil* 74 (December 2009): 265–297; and Ryu Si-hyŏn, "1920 nyŏndae samil undong e kwanhan kiŏk—sigan, changso kŭligo 'minjok/minjung,'" *Yŏksa wa hyŏnsil* 74 (December 2009): 176–202.

74. Commission on Relations with the Orient of the Federal Council of the Churches of Christ in America, ed., *The Korean Situation* (New York: Commission on Relations with the Orient of the Federal Council of the Churches of Christ in America, 1919), 5–7.

75. "Syen Chun Station Report, 1918–1919," RG 140.6.46, PHS.

76. Prime Minister Hara Takashi, in particular, led the call for reforms of colonial rule. One motivating factor for Hara was his belief that these harsh policies hindered the "assimilation" of Koreans. See Mark E. Caprio, *Japanese Assimilation Policies in Colonial Korea, 1910–1945* (Seattle: University of Washington Press, 2009), 123–124.

77. "Tenth Annual Meeting of the Federal Council of Protestant Evangelical Missions in Korea," 1921, Institute for the Study of Korean Church History, Seoul, Republic of Korea.

Chapter 6: Ecclesiastical Extraterritoriality

1. W. M. Clark, "The Council of Churches and Missions in Korea: Its Tendencies and Future Development," *KMF* 21, no. 7 (July 1926).

2. Charles A. Clark, "The Korean Presbyterian Church and the Missionaries," *KMF* 17, no. 9 (September 1922): 191–194.

3. Kenneth Saunders, "The Passing of Paternalism in Missions," *Journal of Religion* 2, no. 5 (September 1922): 471.

4. W. L. Swallen, "Problems Relating to Helpers and Pastors," *KMF* 10, no. 6 (June 1915): 163.

5. R. E. Winn, "The Relation of the Missionary to Organized Churches," *KMF* 13, no. 4 (April 1918): 91.

6. I came across this term when reading documents concerning a series of meetings Protestant missionaries held in the United States from 1942 to 1945. These meetings concerned the mission societies' potential return to Korea after World War II. See "Chosen Mission Conference on Post-War Work: Proceedings," March 12, 1943, RG 140.16.28, PHS.

7. Dong Wang, *China's Unequal Treaties* (Plymouth: Lexington, 2008), 9–27.

8. Dae Young Ryu, "Treaties, Extraterritorial Rights, and American Protestant Missions in Late Joseon Korea," *Korea Journal* 43, no. 1 (Spring 2003): 175–190.

9. As another important point, though Koreans may have had theoretical control over matters related to church administration, most Korean helpers, elders, and pastors passed through the missionaries' system of education—from primary schools to their seminary. In this manner, the missionaries indirectly, and subtly, had an influence at General Assembly meetings that went beyond simply their numbers.

10. During the 1930s, there was at least one instance when the General Assembly of the Korean Presbyterian Church ordered a Northern Presbyterian missionary, William Kerr, to appear and answer questions regarding charges that he adhered to "modernist" teachings. According to Charles Clark, this missionary "stood on his rights as a missionary and defied their right to question him." See Charles Allen Clark to Cleland McAfee, March 15, 1935, RG 140.11.3, PHS.

11. Clark, "The Korean Presbyterian Church and the Missionaries," 193.

12. "Editorial: Korean Missionaries," *CR* 49, no. 2 (February 1918): 74.

13. The Korean Presbyterian Church would continue supporting this work in Shandong throughout much of the colonial period. See *HKY II,* 137.

14. "Editorial, Korean Missionaries," 74.

15. "Missionary News: The Korean Mission at Laiyang Shantung," *CR* 49, no. 2 (February 1918): 134–135.

16. Missionaries in China and Chinese church leaders stipulated that all members of churches overseen by Korean missionaries would belong to the Chinese Presbyterian Church. In 1913, the General Assembly of the Korean Presbyterian Church stated that it did not seek to establish a separate church in China but instead that converts would belong to a Chinese presbytery. It is important to realize that this was a condition that missionaries in China and the Chinese

Presbyterian Church placed on their Korean colleagues as a prerequisite to gaining access to the China field. See "Yesugyo changnohoe Chosŏn ch'onghoe che 2 hoe hoerok," 1913. See also *HKY II*, 134.

17. Clark, "The Korean Presbyterian Church and the Missionaries." The issue of holding membership and voting rights in more than one presbytery was more controversial than Charles Clark admitted in this article. For example, the Southern Presbyterians debated this issue for three years in the lead-up to the establishment of the Korean Presbyterian Church in 1907. See George Paik, *History of Protestant Missions in Korea, 1832–1910* (P'yŏngyang: Union Christian College Press, 1929), 293–294.

18. J. S. Ryang, "The Aims of Methodist Union in Korea," *KMF* 22, no. 9 (September 1927).

19. J. S. Ryang, "Greetings from the Korean Methodist Church and the Report for 1931," Series: IMC Archives, Asia-Korea, 26.5.112, Folder 12, World Council of Churches Archives, Geneva, Switzerland. Hereafter this series will appear as Series: IMC-Korea followed by box number, folder number, and WCC.

20. "Relationship of the Korean Methodist Church," *KMF* 26, no. 1 (January 1931). Emphasis added.

21. Ryang, "Greetings from the Korean Methodist Church and the Report for 1931."

22. Clark, "The Korean Presbyterian Church and the Missionaries."

23. Mattie Noble, *The Journals of Mattie Wilcox Noble, 1892–1934,* ed., Han'guk kidokkyo yŏksa yŏn'guso (Seoul: Han'guk kidokkyo yŏksa yŏn'guso, 2003), 167–168. This source is a typescript volume of the personal journals, or rather diaries, of Mattie Noble.

24. Noble, *The Journals of Mattie Wilcox Noble,* 167–168.

25. Noble, *The Journals of Mattie Wilcox Noble,* 171–172. According to Noble, the three who refused to return went to the Presbyterians.

26. Noble, *The Journals of Mattie Wilcox Noble,* 173.

27. Noble, *The Journals of Mattie Wilcox Noble,* 169.

28. Just over a month after writing in relief of Yi's support of the missionaries, Mattie Noble lamented that Yi had "back-slid." On August 24, she reported how Yi had "gone astray" and was led by "the evil one." Events such as this fueled the missionaries' fears that even leaders like Yi could one day go from being relied on to protect the church to suddenly damaging the church by returning to their former lifestyle. See Noble, *The Journals of Mattie Wilcox Noble,* 175.

29. For an examination of Lewis Tate's pioneering work in spreading Protestantism in North Chŏlla Province and his work with Ch'oe Chung-jin, see Ryu Tae-yŏng, "Miguk nam changnohoe sŏn'gyosa T'eit'ŭ (Lewis Boyd Tate) kajok ŭi Han'guk sŏn'gyo," *Han'guk kidokkyo wa yŏksa* 37 (September 2012): 5–35.

30. The independent Korean presbytery established in 1907 governed the Korean Presbyterian Church, which consisted of all the Presbyterian churches in Korea. The intention was that the Korean Presbyterian Church would eventually

consist of multiple presbyteries, organized largely along regional lines, as the number of ordained pastors and churches grew. From 1907 to 1911, Korean Presbyterian churches were overseen by sub-presbyteries *(taelihoe)*. These sub-presbyteries served as provisional presbyteries. In 1911, the Chŏlla Presbytery was established. In 1917, reflecting the continued growth of Presbyterianism in the region, the presbytery of Chŏlla Province was divided, with the establishment of North Chŏlla Presbytery and South Chŏlla Presbytery.

31. Han In-su, *Honam kyohe hyŏngsŏng inmul* 3 (Seoul: Kyŏnggŏn, 2010), 293–294.

32. Taehan Yesugyo Changnohoe, Chŏnbuk Nohoe, ed., *Chŏnbuk nohoe hoeŭi rok I* (Kunsan, South Korea: Taehan Yesugyo Changnohoe Nohoe rok Palgan Wiwŏnhoe, 2000), 88–98.

33. Annabel Major Nisbet, *Day In and Day Out in Korea* (Richmond, VA: Presbyterian Committee of Publication, 1920), 84.

34. Emily Anderson, *Christianity and Imperialism in Modern Japan: Empire for God* (London: Bloomsbury Academic, 2014), 131; Motokazu Matsutani, "Church over Nation: Christian Missionaries and Korean Christians in Colonial Korea," (PhD diss., Harvard University, 2012), 234–248.

35. Nisbet, *Day In and Day Out in Korea,* 84.

36. Han, *Honam kyohe hyŏngsŏng inmul,* 296.

37. "Minutes of the Thirteenth Annual Meeting of the Southern Presbyterian Mission in Korea, September 1904," RG 444, Box 1, Folder 3, PHS. Hereafter this series will appear as RG 444, followed by box number, folder number, and PHS.

38. This early foray into missions differs from the General Assembly's later efforts in Shandong in that the former remained within the territorial boundaries of the Korean nation and the latter crossed into a foreign land.

39. "1907 Minutes of the Fifteenth Annual Meeting of the Council of Presbyterian Missions in Korea and the First Annual Meeting of the Presbytery of the Presbyterian Church in Korea," KLC—BFMPCUSA, Roll 282, PHS.

40. "Minutes of the Seventeenth Annual Meeting of the Southern Presbyterian Mission in Korea, 1908," RG 444.1.6, PHS.

41. In 1907, the sub-presbytery of North Chŏlla passed a provision to provide assistance to theological students. In 1908, Ch'oe received a sum of $50. At the time, theological training lasted three months per year.

42. For example, Kim Chang-ho in Pongsan, Hwanghae Province, attempted to create a Korean church (Chosŏn kidok kyohoe). He would eventually publish *Chosŏn kidok kyohoe yŏksa,* distinguishing between "Korean" Christianity and the Christianity imported by missionaries.

43. *HKY II*, 194–195.

44. Albert Park, *Building a Heaven on Earth* (Honolulu: University of Hawai'i Press, 2015), 121–122.

45. Chŏng T'ae-sik and Mun Chang-su, "Taegu 3.1 manse undong kwa Yi Man-jip ŭi kyohoe chach'i sŏnŏn sagŏn e taehan sahoe ch'ŏlhakchŏk koch'al," *Ch'ŏlhak non ch'ong* 36, no. 2 (2004): 275–302.

46. Clara Hedberg Bruen, ed., *40 Years in Korea* (Seoul: Han'guk Kidokkyo Yŏksa Yŏn'guso, 1998), 292. Clara Bruen compiled her and her husband's letters, reports, and diaries. She published these documents under the title *40 Years in Korea.*

47. Chŏng and Mun, "Taegu 3.1 manse undong kwa Yi Man-jip ŭi kyohoe chach'i sŏnŏn sagŏn e taehan sahoe ch'ŏlhakchŏk koch'al," 292.

48. Chŏng and Mun, "Taegu 3.1 manse undong kwa Yi Man-jip ŭi kyohoe chach'i sŏnŏn sagŏn e taehan sahoe ch'ŏlhakchŏk koch'al," 293.

49. *HKY II,* 195.

50. Bruen, *40 Years in Korea,* 295.

51. Walter Erdman, "Taiku—Monthly Station Letter," December 28, 1908, KLC—BFMPCUSA, Roll 281, PHS; Bruen, *40 Years in Korea,* 145.

52. Charles A. Clark to Arthur Brown, February 5, 1924, RG 140.11.2, PHS. This letter to Brown included a translation of the Japanese court's decision on the first Taegu lawsuit.

53. Charles Allen Clark to Arthur J. Brown, July 9, 1923, RG 140.11.2, PHS.

54. Cleland B. McAfee to Norman Whittermore, June 23, 1925, RG 140.11.2, PHS.

55. Herbert E. Blair to Arthur J. Brown, April 1, 1925, RG 140.11.2, PHS. Blair followed up this letter with another report to Brown that the governor of North Kyŏngsang Province had decided not to challenge the missionaries' legal claim to the land. However, the issue of ownership still remained a point of concern. See Herbert E. Blair to Arthur J. Brown, May 16, 1925, RG 140.11.2, PHS.

56. Herbert E. Blair, "Taigyu Church Litigation," 1931, RG 140.11.2, PHS.

57. Chŏng and Mun, "Taegu 3.1 manse undong kwa Yi Man-jip ŭi kyohoe chach'i sŏnŏn sagŏn e taehan sahoe ch'ŏlhakchŏk koch'al," 275–302.

58. William B. Hunt, "Personal Report of Wm. B Hunt for 1920–1921," RG 140.8.17, PHS.

59. *HKY II*, 218–219.

60. Kim Sang-t'ae, "[Kihwaek] Han-Mi chisik'in ŭi sangho insik' Ilche ha kaesin'gyo chisik in ŭi Miguik insik—Sin Hŭng-u wa chŏkgŭk sinang tan ŭl chungsim ŭro," *Yŏksa wa hyŏnsil* 58 (December 2012): 104–109.

Chapter 7: Ties Severed

1. In their letters and reports, the missionaries in Korea used the term "State Shinto" and contrasted it to "Religious Shinto."

2. For critical reflection and overviews on the scholarly examination of State Shinto, see Susumu Shimazono and Regan E. Murphy, "State Shinto in the Lives of People," *Japanese Journal of Religious Studies* 36, no. 1 (2009): 93–124; and Michiaki Okyuama, "'State Shinto' in Recent Japanese Scholarship," *Monumenta Nipponica* 66, no. 1 (2011): 123–145.

3. Helen Hardacre, *Shintō and the State, 1868–1988* (Princeton, NJ: Princeton University Press, 1989).

4. Bob Tadashi Wakabayashi, *Anti-Foreignism and Western Learning in Early Modern Japan: The New Theses of 1825* (Cambridge, MA: Council on East Asian Studies, Harvard University, 1986), 3–16; Trent Maxey, *The "Greatest Problem"* (Cambridge, MA: Harvard University Asia Center, 2014), 18–24.

5. Trent Maxey examines five "separations," as the Japanese governments created and continuously redefined the category of "religion" from the start of the Meiji government to 1900. See Maxey, *The "Greatest Problem."*

6. Trent E. Maxey, "Finding Religion in Japan's Empire," in *Belief and Practice in Imperial Japan and Colonial Korea,* ed. Emily Anderson (Singapore: Palgrave Macmillan, 2017), 1–18; Taehoon Kim, "The Place of 'Religion' in Colonial Korea around 1910," *Journal of Korean Religions* 2, no. 2 (October 2011): 25–46.

7. For a concise overview of the theological divisions between Protestant denominations and the challenges that "modernism" injected into Korean Protestant communities during the 1920s and 1930s, see Ryu Tae-yŏng, *Han kwŏn ŭro ingnŭn Han'guk kidokkyo ŭi yŏksa* (Seoul: Han'guk Kidokyyo Yŏksa Yŏn'guso, 2018), 200–220.

8. *HKY II,* 157–158. Of note, another major issue of contention was whether women could be ordained as pastors.

9. "Taehan yesugyo changnohoe ch'onghoe che 23 hoe hoerok," 1934, 59.

10. James G. Holdcroft to All Presbyterian and United Church of Canada Mission Stations, November 27, 1934, RG 140.11.3, PHS.

11. James G. Holdcroft to Cleland B. McAfee, March 22, 1935, RG 140.11.3, PHS.

12. Offering an alternative explanation for this conflict was James G. Holdcroft. He viewed the efforts of the Kyŏngsŏng presbytery to lead a schism as being linked to modernism and the Positivist Faith League (Chŏkkŭk sinang tang), which he stressed the Japanese colonial government suspected possessed a "'communistic' flavor." In this assessment, Holdcroft failed to recognize, or did not acknowledge, the fascist origins of the Positivist Faith League. Rather, he implied that those who held to a modernist platform or emphasized social programs were closely aligned with communism. See Holdcroft to McAfee, March 22, 1935.

13. For an exploration of the issue of regional discrimination, see Sun Joo Kim, *Marginality and Subversion in Korea* (Seattle: University of Washington Press, 2007), 35–65; and O Su-ch'ang, *Chosŏn hugi P'yŏngan-do sahoe palchŏn yŏn'gu* (Seoul: Ilchogak, 2002).

14. *HKY II,* 162–163.

15. T. Stanley Soltau to George T. Scott, November 23, 1936, RG 140.11.3, PHS.

16. Bradley J. Longfield, *The Presbyterian Controversy* (New York: Oxford University Press, 1991), 9–27; D. G. Hart, *Defending the Faith* (Phillipsburg, NJ: P&R, 1994).

17. In reporting on the potential schism led by the Kyŏngsŏng presbytery, the missionaries in Korea specifically discussed John Gresham Machen, the Independent Board for Foreign Presbyterian Missions, and the limits of the General Assembly's constitutional powers.

18. Cleland B. McAfee to James G. Holdcroft, December 21, 1934, RG 140.11.3, PHS.

19. Mark Caprio has reminded us that a discourse on the assimilation of Korea and an emphasis on the supposed racial and cultural similarities between Koreans and Japanese predated colonization of the peninsula and underwent shifts after the annexation of Korea in 1910. On the early formulation of assimilation policies in colonial Korea, see Mark E. Caprio, *Japanese Assimilation Policies in Colonial Korea, 1910–1945* (Seattle: University of Washington Press, 2009), chap. 3.

20. Caprio, *Japanese Assimilation Policies in Colonial Korea,* 141–142.

21. Caprio, *Japanese Assimilation Policies in Colonial Korea,* 147.

22. The issue of shrine obeisance in Korea, during the 1930s, has been well researched by scholars of Korean Christianity. For an in-depth English-language examination of Shinto obeisance in Korea, see Sung-gun Kim, "Korean Christianity and the Shinto Shrine Issue in the War Period, 1931–1945," (PhD diss., University of Hull, 1989). For a shorter English-language treatment of this issue, see James H. Grayson, "Christianity and State Shinto in Colonial Korea," *Diskus: The Journal of the British Association for the Study of Religions* 1, no. 2 (1993): 13–30, http://basr.ac.uk/diskus_old/diskus1-6/GRAYSON.TXT. For a comparative examination of Shinto in Korea and Japan, see Kyutae Park, "Religion, National Identity, and Shinto," *Review of Korean Studies* 3, no. 1 (June 2000): 76–92. For a comprehensive volume canvasing major interpretations of the Shinto obeisance issue, see Kim Sŭng-t'ae, ed., *Han'guk kidokkyo wa sinsa ch'ambae munje* (Seoul: Han'guk Kidokkyo Yŏksa Yŏn'guso, 1991); and Kim Sŭng-t'ae, *Singmin kwŏllyŏk kwa chonggyo* (Seoul: Han'guk Kidokkyo Yŏksa Yŏn'guso, 2012). Han'guk Kidokkyo Yŏksa Yŏn'guso has also published a three-volume sourcebook on Shinto shrine obeisance. See Kim Sŭng-t'ae, ed., *Sinsa ch'ambae munje charyojip* (Seoul: Han'guk Kidokkyo Yŏksa Yŏn'guso, 2014).

23. Kim Sŭng-t'ae, *Hanmal-Ilche kangjŏm ki sŏn'gyosa yŏn'gu* (Seoul: Han'guk Kidokkyo Yŏksa Yŏn'guso, 2006), 224–266; An Chong-ch'ŏl, *Miguk sŏn'gyosa wa Han-Mi kwangye* (Seoul: Han'guk Kidokkyo Yŏksa Yŏn'guso, 2010), 47–60.

24. Yi Man-yŏl, ed., *Sinsa ch'ambae munje Yŏngmun charyojip* I (Seoul: Han'guk Kidokkyo Yŏksa Yŏn'guso, 2003), 54–58.

25. For the Northern Presbyterian missionaries' assessment of the situation, see "Notes on the Shrine Problem," RG 140.12.14, PHS. For a broader analytical assessment of the situation from the perspective of diplomatic relations, see An, *Miguk sŏn'gyosa wa Han-Mi kwangye,* 48–51.

26. James G. Holdcroft to C. B. McAfee, July 4, 1935, RG 140.12.14, PHS.

27. According to James G. Holdcroft, some within the mission wanted a stronger statement rejecting any form of compromise and clearly rejecting any order to attend shrine ceremonies. See "Statement Concerning our Attitude Toward Patriotic Ceremonies," July 1935; and Holdcroft to McAfee, July 4, 1935, RG 140.12.14, PHS.

28. The Executive Committee of the Northern Presbyterians met with Watanabe Toyohiko, the head of the GGK's Educational Department, to discuss the command to bow at shrines. Of the issues discussed, the Executive Committee asked Watanabe whether there were "spirits" at the shrine ceremonies. James Holdcroft reported that while Watanabe's response gave the "impression that he thought not," he did not make a clear, definitive statement that "there were not." This type of ambiguous response given by Watanabe was a continuous source of frustration and anxiety for missionaries. James G. Holdcroft to C. B. McAfee, October 7, 1935, RG 140.12.14, PHS.

29. "Executive Committee Resolution Concerning Government Order to Attend Ceremonies at the Chosen Shrine, October 15th and 16th," October 5, 1935, RG 140.12.14, PHS.

30. James G. Holdcroft to Cleland B. McAfee, October 22, 1935, November 18, 1935, RG 140.12.14, PHS.

31. George McCune and the other principals had prior knowledge that an order for the principals to bow at shrines would be made. The previous day, the principals of the primary schools met with the governor. At the end of the meeting, Japanese officials ordered the principals to travel to the shrine to bow. Principals of Christian primary schools "slipped out" and avoided going to the shrine. For this reason, according to McCune, when the middle school principals met the following day, the governor decided to start the meeting by conducting shrine ceremonies. George S. McCune to C. B. McAfee, November 25, 1935, RG 140.12.14, PHS.

32. James G. Holdcroft to C. B. McAfee, July 4, 1935, and October 7, 1935, RG 140.12.14, PHS.

33. Though they initially refused to attend shrine ceremonies in P'yŏngyang, the Seventh Day Adventists eventually complied.

34. James G. Holdcroft to Cleland B. McAfee, December 18, 1935, RG 140.12.14, PHS.

35. "Copy of Letter from George S. McCune to N. Yasutake," December 13, 1935, RG 140.12.14, PHS.

36. "Copy of Letter from George S. McCune to N. Yasutake," December 19, 1935, RG 140.12.14, PHS.

37. Watanabe Toyohiko, "A WARNING, to Dr. G. S. McCune, President of the Union Christian College of Korea from the Government General of Korea by Educational Director Hon. Watanabe," December 31, 1935, Series: IMC-Korea, 26.16.08, Folder 5, WCC.

38. "Copy of Letter from George S. McCune to N. Yasutake," January 18, 1936, Series: IMC-Korea, 26.16.08, Folder 5, WCC.

39. The Executive Committee's request for the Home Board to issue a "strong opinion" did not directly state what that opinion should be. However, urging the Home Board to make clear its stance, the committee emphasized that the "majority of spiritually minded Korean Christians" and "many missionaries"

believed that the ceremonies contravened "Christian conscience." "Notes on the Shrine Problem," October 6, 1935, RG 140.12.14, PHS.

40. James G. Holdcroft to C. B. McAfee and Members of the Board, March 1, 1936, RG 140.12.17, PHS.

41. Son Chŏng-mok, "Chosŏn ch'ongdokbu ŭi sinsa pogŭb sinsa ch'ambae kangyo chŏngch'aek yŏn'gu," in *Han'guk kidokkyo wa sinsa ch'ambae munje*, ed. Kim Sŭng-t'ae (Seoul: Han'guk Kidokkyo Yŏksa Yŏn'guso, 1991), 260.

42. The Executive Committee attempted to include schools in Taegu and Seoul, but both the Taegu and Seoul stations protested and insisted that closure of their institutions be discussed at the next annual meeting.

43. Board of Missions, M.E. Church, South, "The Shrine Question," May 3, 1937, Series: IMC-Korea, 26.5.113, Folder 11, WCC.

44. James G. Holdcroft to Cleland B. McAfee, December 18, 1935, RG 140.12.14, PHS.

45. A cynical reading of James Holdcroft's claim would be that he chose to emphasize the opposition of Korean Christian leaders of the northwestern provinces of Korea. He had earlier admitted that one challenge that confronted the Executive Committee in responding to the shrine issue was a lack of uniformity within the Korean Christian community in regards to State Shinto. On his claim that Korean Christians were staunch in opposition to shrine ceremonies, see James G. Holdcroft to Cleland B. McAfee, February 7, 1936, RG 140.12.17, PHS. On his earlier statement that Korean Christians were not uniform in their response, see Holdcroft to McAfee, October 7, 1935.

46. For instance, in one of the Presbyterian churches of P'yŏngyang, a number of teachers, who were members of the church leadership, attended shrine ceremonies. The pastor of the church was sympathetic to their plight. In turn, the deacons and church members protested, and the pastor had to withdraw from his position. See Charles T. Leber and Joseph L. Dodds, "Confidential Report of the Board's Second Commission to Chosen," April 12, 1937, RG 140.12.19.

47. James G. Holdcroft wrote that "it may be that we [Northern Presbyterians] are called upon instead to fight a battle for real religious liberty for the whole Japanese Empire." See James G. Holdcroft to Cleland B. McAfee, February 7, 1936, RG 140.12.17, PHS.

48. The collection and submission of these petitions were organized by missionaries stationed in Seoul. These petitions were the same in terms of form and content. For these petitions, see RG 140.12.23, PHS.

49. C. Darby Fulton to Executive Committee of Foreign Missions, April 6, 1937, Series: IMC-Korea, 26.16.08, Folder 6, WCC.

50. R. O. Reiner, "Personal Annual Report, Mr. and Mrs. R. O. Reiner, 1937–1938," RG 140.9.24, PHS.

51. Samuel A. Moffett to Cleland McAfee, February 23, 1936; James G. Holdcroft to Cleland McAfee, March 1, 1936, RG 140.12.17, PHS.

52. "Board Actions Regarding Withdrawal from General Education in Chosen—Board Action of February 21, 1938," RG 140.12.13, PHS.

53. An, *Miguk sŏn'gyosa wa Han-Mi kwangye,* 117–121.

54. For a detailed explanation of these efforts, see Kim, *Singmin kwŏllyŏk kwa chonggyo,* 87–97.

55. Charles T. Leber to Furloughed Missionaries from Chosen, October 19, 1937, RG 140.12.20, PHS.

56. Harold Henderson to J. L. Hooper, July 14, 1938, RG 140.12.25, PHS.

57. Harold Henderson, "Keisung Academy Annual Report, 1937–1938," RG 140.7.55, PHS.

58. Herbert E. Blair, "Report: Taiku Boys Academy, 1923–1924," RG 140.7.41, PHS; "Report of Sin Myung Girls Academy, Taiku, Chosen, 1938," RG 140.12.55, PHS. The colonial government set a high bar to receive designation. For example, schools had to upgrade their facilities and ensure that the quality of education they provided would be on par with that of government schools. Upgrading facilities was extremely expensive. Moreover, schools were evaluated on the basis of the performance of their students at annual exams. Harold Henderson and other school principals repeatedly complained of their failed efforts to receive designation in their annual reports during the 1920s.

59. Harold Henderson, "Personal Annual Report, 1938–1939," RG 140.10.1, PHS; Henderson, "3rd Annual Report, 1938–1939—Keisung Academy Changes Hands," RG 140.7.56, PHS.

60. Horace H. Underwood to Charles T. Leber, July 6, 1937, RG 140.12.20, PHS; Harry Rhodes to Charles T. Leber, November 3, 1937, RG 140.12.21, PHS.

61. Though control transferred to the Koreans, ownership of property and land did not automatically transfer. The Home Board ordered that property be sold to Koreans. This order added to the Executive Committee's anger over the apparent compromise on the issue of bowing at Shinto ceremonies.

62. Harry Rhodes to Charles T. Leber, November 3, 1937, and December 6, 1937, RG 140.12.21, PHS; Henry W. Lampe to Charles T. Leber, December 3, 1937, RG 140.12.21, PHS.

63. Harry Rhodes to Charles T. Leber, December 6, 1937, RG 140.12.21, PHS.

64. Henry Lampe to Charles T. Leber, December 3, 1937, RG 140.12.21, PHS. Importantly, some missionaries viewed the transfer of these institutions with suspicion. In much the same way that some missionaries believed that colonial officials had coerced the Korean Presbyterian General Assembly to officially declare that bowing at shrines was merely a patriotic act, in 1938, so too did many believe that colonial officials had coerced local presbyteries to exercise their "right" to take over schools.

65. The efforts of the Seoul station to have John D. Wells Boy's School transfer to Korean leadership produced perhaps the most anger within the Northern Presbyterian Mission. After years of not meeting, the Board of Control for the school was reconstituted in late 1937 on the pretext of implementing the plan

to withdraw from secular education. But, in January 1938, the Board of Control appointed two additional "founders," one of whom was Korean. Though the Executive Committee of the Northern Presbyterian Mission protested that proper procedure had not been observed, the colonial government approved the appointment. In writing to the Executive Committee, the new Korean founder asserted his right of control and bluntly stated: "I may suggest to you that the only proper way of disposing the school property is to hand it over to me." See Choi Tai Yeng to James G. Holdcroft, May 17, 1938, RG 140.12.24, PHS.

66. Harold Henderson to J. L. Hooper, July 14, 1938, RG 140.12.25, PHS.

67. Kim Sŭng-t'ae has argued that the colonial government had desired for missionaries to devolve into infighting. While the GGK may have been pleased with this turn of events, I suggest that it would have preferred if the Northern Presbyterians had uniformly accepted its position that State Shinto was a nonreligious affair. Such a declaration would have been an acknowledgment of Japanese authority and right to rule in Korea. Kim, *Singmin kwŏllyŏk kwa chonggyo,* 79.

68. Ch'a Chong-sun has noted the differences within the Presbyterian Church in Korea along geographical lines. His primary focus was between the Northern and Southern Presbyterian divide. However, a similar conflict existed within the Northern Presbyterian Mission. See Ch'a Chong-sun, "Honam kwa sŏbuk chiyŏk kaesin'gyo t'ŭksŏng pigyo yŏn'gu," *Han'guk kyohoe sa hakhoe chi* 15 (2004): 233–250.

69. As one missionary put it, "The Board does not presume to control the conscience of the Korean Church, nor to criticize it for any action. The question is for our conscience, and whether we can approve such a surrender of property entrusted to us by our Church." See C. R. Erdman to Herrick Cheesman, January 9, 1939, RG 140.12.29, PHS.

70. James G. Holdcroft to Charles T. Leber, April 8, 1938, RG 140.12.25, PHS.

71. Blanche Winn to the Board of Foreign Missions, April 28, 1936, RG 140.12.16, PHS.

72. Cleland McAfee urged James G. Holdcroft to avoid confusing "conscience" with "moral judgment." McAfee wrote: "That we must not compromise our Christian loyalty to the one true God is doubtless a dictate of conscience and about it we should not and do not differ. But whether a given action is such a compromise will always be a matter of moral judgment rather than of conscience." See Cleland McAfee to James G. Holdcroft, April 5, 1936, RG 140.12.18, PHS.

73. Kim Sŭng-t'ae has noted that missionaries were not uniform in their response to the order to bow at shrines. In regards to the Northern Presbyterians, he argues that McCune, for example, opposed shrines as a form of idolatry. In contrast, Horace H. Underwood believed that even if there were religious elements, since the Japanese colonial government was insistent that it was a merely a patriotic ceremony, missionaries should acquiesce for the sake of saving Christian education in Korea. Offering a similar line of reasoning is Jong-chol An,

who has argued that Underwood advocated a "conditional acceptance" of Shinto ceremonies. Students would attend and bow at ceremonies that colonial officials officiated. Students were not actively participating but rather bowing as a show of courtesy. This argument, however, minimizes Underwood's own carefully reasoned arguments regarding bowing at shrines. At the heart of Underwood's argument were the dual issues of personal conscience and whether Koreans had the right to make their own evaluations. Underwood was not simply rationalizing accommodations or searching for loopholes. See Kim Sŭng-t'ae, "1930 nyŏndae kidokkyogye hakkyo ŭi sinsa ch'ambae sogo," in *Han'guk kidokkyo wa sinsa ch'ambae munje,* ed. Kim Sŭng-t'ae (Seoul: Han'guk Kidokkyo Yŏksa Yŏn'guso, 1991), 372–375; and Jong Chol An, "No Distinction between Sacred and Secular: Horace H. Underwood and Korean-American Relations, 1934–1948," *Seoul Journal of Korean Studies* 23, no. 2 (December 2010): 232–233.

74. Horace H. Underwood to W. L. Swallen, January 10, 1936, RG 140.12.16, PHS.

75. For a detailed examination of the Home Board's relationship with its workers in Korea, see An, *Miguk sŏn'gyosa wa Han-Mi kwangye,* 164–170.

76. "Board Actions Regarding Withdrawal from General Education in Chosen—Board Action of September 21st, 1936," RG 140.12.13, PHS.

77. Board Actions Regarding Withdrawal from General Education in Chosen—Board Action February 15, 1937," RG 140.12.13, PHS.

78. Leber and Dodds, "Confidential Report."

79. T. Stanley Soltau to George T. Scott, February 25, 1937, RG 140.12.20, PHS.

80. In April 1937, Stanley Soltau reported to the Home Board that Korean leaders in P'yŏngyang were celebrating as if the transfer of the schools was all but a done deal—one merely requiring the BFMPCUSA to put a rubber stamp on the proposals that had been submitted to the Home Board. Given that in his previous letters in January and February Soltau had emphasized the numerous threats the missions had received from Koreans in regards to the potential closure of schools, Soltau and the Executive Committee were likely concerned about what would happen if the Home Board rejected the proposals for transfer. See T. Stanley Soltau to Charles Leber, April 10, 1937, RG 140.12.21, PHS. See also T. Stanley Soltau to George T. Scott, January 22, 1937, February 5, 1937, February 16, 1937, and February 25, 1937, RG 140.12.20, PHS.

81. The Home Board was responding to a series of proposals made by the Executive Committee in June 1938. The Executive Committee felt that the Home Board had undermined its authority by its September directives. See "Executive Committee Minutes," June 20, 1938, RG 140.12.25; and "Board Action of September 19, 1938," RG 140.12.13, PHS.

82. John F. Genso to C. R. Erdman, November 3, 1938, RG 140.12.26, PHS.

83. Charles Allen Clark to Dr. Hooper, Erdman, and Scott, November 12, 1938, RG 140.12.26, PHS.

84. Marion Dodge to the Presbyterian Board of Foreign Mission, May 22, 1938, RG 140.12.28, PHS. This was one of many letters from concerned American Presbyterians writing the Home Board to protest any compromise with orders to participate in Shinto shrine ceremonies. To see other letters, see RG 140.12.28, PHS.

85. "Copy of letter from the Executive Committee of Chosen Mission to Dr. Hooper, Dated—Dec. 10, 1938," RG 140.12.26, PHS.

86. In particular, the Executive Committee argued pedantically that the Home Board must have been unaware that Chungsin Women's Academy was wholly under the control of the Northern Presbyterian Mission and thus could be closed without any interference from outside forces. See "Copy of letter from the Executive Committee of Chosen Mission to Dr. Hooper"; "C. 686, Reply to Board Letter No. 823"; and "Mission Action November 25–29, 1938," RG 140.12.30, PHS.

87. William Chisholm to Friends, April 11, 1940, RG 140.12.33, PHS.

88. W. L. Swallen to Cleland McAfee, May 1, 1936, RG 140.12.15, PHS.

89. Caprio, *Japanese Assimilation Policies in Colonial Korea,* 147.

90. "A Warning Sent to All Korean Churches by the Moderator of the Korean Presbyterian General Assembly, December 1939," RG 140.12.29, PHS. Translation into English of Korean original.

91. Many Presbyterian missionaries argued that the General Assembly had made its decision under duress. This was one reason why they opposed this decision. Likewise, those Presbyterian missionaries who called for a strong stand against bowing at Shinto shrines pointed to the repressive tactics colonial officials used. For example, they argued that those presbyteries that sought to receive control over secular educational institutions from the Northern Presbyterians only did so because of colonial pressure.

92. Seunghak Cho to Charles T. Leber, November 7, 1938, RG 140.12.26, PHS.

93. A. G. Fletcher to Charles T. Leber, March 18, 1938, RG 140.12.29, PHS.

94. Richard H. Baird, "Personal Report, Richard H. and Golden S. Baird, 1938–1939," RG 140.10.3, PHS.

95. E. H. Miller, "Annual Report to Mission & Board, E. H. Miller, April 1941," RG 140.10.7, PHS.

96. Baird, "Personal Report."

97. Charles Allen Clark, "Personal Report of Mr. and Mrs. C. A. Clark for the Year ending June 1 1940," RG 140.10.5, PHS.

98. D. B. Avison, "These Later Days. Annual Report, 1939–1940," RG 140.10.5, PHS.

Conclusion

1. A. Karl Reischauer, "Religious Liberty in Japan," September 30, 1942, Series: IMC-Korea, 26.16.08, Folder 4, WCC.

2. William P. Parker to Fellow Workers and Friends of the PYFS, March 5, 1936, Series: IMC-Korea, 26.16.08, Folder 5, WCC.

3. "Some Observations Concerning the Problem of Christianity and the State in Japan with Special Reference to the Problems of Christian Education," Summer 1936, Series: IMC-Korea, 26.16.08, Folder 4, WCC.

4. Ryu Tae-yŏng, "Sinsa ch'ambae kwallyŏn sosup'a ŭigyŏn—Herŏldŭ Hendŏsŭn (Harold H. Henderson) ŭi sarye," *Han'guk Kidokkyo Yŏksa* 39 (September 2013): 145–180.

5. The argument that the Korean Presbyterian Church should possess the right to decide how to respond to the issue of Shinto shrine ceremonies influenced the final decision of the BFMPCUSA. Writing to the Executive Committee of the Northern Presbyterian Mission in Korea, J. L. Hooper explained that the Home Board's basic policy was "to recognize the full rights and autonomy of the Presbyterian Church in Chosen [Korea] under all circumstances." See J. L. Hooper to the Chosen Mission, November 18, 1940, RG 140.12.33, PHS.

6. Importantly, even those missionaries opposed to bowing at shrines were not immune to colonial pressure. D. B. Avison, for one, reported to his father: "We talk glibly of our disappointment that Koreans are not willing to go to jail even for conscience sake, yet we missionaries—to avoid jail or expulsion or perhaps the loss of our land—will carry on and go to the shrine for three or four years to save ourselves from any such troubles." See "Excerpt from letter by Dr. DB Avison to Dr. OR Avison," November 14, 1937, RG 140.12.22, PHS.

7. "Chosen Mission Conference on Post-War Work: Proceedings," March 12, 1943, RG 140.16.28, PHS.

8. "Chosen Mission Conference on Post-War Work: Proceedings."

9. J. L. Hooper, "Chosen (Korea)," RG 140.16.29, PHS.

10. Monica Kim, *The Interrogation Rooms of the Korean War* (Princeton, NJ: Princeton University Press, 2019), 12–18, 33–78.

11. Edward Adams, "Report on Korea," January 15, 1946, RG 140.30.29, PHS.

12. Rowland Cross, "Minutes of Korea Committee of FMC," March 4, 1949, Board of Missions Administrative Fields Series of the Board of Missions of the Methodist Church, 1912–1955, Microfilm, Roll 88, General Commission on Archives and History, United Methodist Church, Madison, New Jersey.

13. Elizabeth Underwood, "Contested Heritage: The 'Yanghwajin Controversy' and Korean Protestantism," *Journal of Korean Religions* 4, no. 1 (April 2013): 172.

14. Underwood, "Contested Heritage," 173–174.

15. "'When they returned to Jerusalem' / The Week of the 2nd Anniversary," July 8, 2008, http://100church.org. This sermon was based on Acts 8:14–25. In this sermon, Yi used "candlesticks" as a metaphor to describe the passing on of the responsibility for preaching to the Gentiles from Peter and John to Paul.

16. "'When they returned to Jerusalem' / The Week of the 2nd Anniversary."

17. Not all denominations in South Korea are supportive of the HAMC's claim. Thus, it is important to note that the controversy over Yanghwajin cannot be cast simply as a conflict between Korean and foreign Christians.

18. Underwood, "Contested Heritage," 182–183.

19. "100th Anniversary Memorial Church's Position on the Responsibility for the Management of Yanghwajin Foreign Missionary Cemetery Park," http://100church.org/ie/include/yang_p1_eng.php.

20. "The Truth about Yanghwajin Foreign Missionary Cemetery," September 15, 2014, http://www.100thcouncil.com/down/Truth%20about%20Yanghwajin.pdf.

21. The HAMC has maintained that it does not represent any single denomination and has resisted attempts by other denominations to either mediate on behalf of Seoul Union Church or assert a rival claim over the administration of the cemetery.

22. "Sirijŭ 48—Han'guk in poda Han'guk ŭl tŏ saranghan Hŏlbŏtŭ Sŏn'gyosa," January 17, 2005, http://www.missionnews.coo.kr/news/read.php?idxno=5060&rsec=99.

Bibliography

Archives

Burke Library Archives, New York, NY
Presbyterian Historical Society, Philadelphia, PA
United Methodist Archives and History Center, Drew University, Madison, NJ
World Council of Churches, Geneva, Switzerland

Collections

Annual Report of the Board of Foreign Missions of the Methodist Episcopal Church: Korea Mission, 1884–1943. Comp. and ed. Han'guk Kidokkyo Yŏksa Yŏn'guso. Seoul: Han'guk Kidokkyo Yŏksa Yŏn'guso, 2001.

Chōsen sōtokufu kanpō [Official gazette of the Government-General of Korea]. Reprint. 142 vols. Seoul: Asea Munhwasa, 1985.

Chosŏn wangjo sillok [Veritable records of the Chosŏn dynasty]. 48 vols. Seoul: Kuksa P'yŏnch'an Wiwŏhoe, 1955–1958.

Chu-Han Miguk kongsagwan, yŏngsagwan kirok [Despatches from US ministers to Korea]. 20 vols. Comp. and ed. Hallim Taehakkyo and Asea Munhwa Yŏn'guso. Seoul: Hallim Taehakkyo Ch'ulp'anbu, 2000–2001.

Kaksa tŭngnok [Copies of administrative bureaus records]. 82 vols. Comp. and ed. Kuksa P'yŏnch'an Wiwŏnhoe. Kwach'ŏn: Kuksa P'yŏnch'an Wiwŏnhoe, 1995.

Ku Han'guk oegyo munsŏ [Diplomatic documents of the late Chosŏn dynasty]. 22 vols. Comp. and ed. Koryŏ Taehakkyo, Asea Munje Yŏn'guso, and Ku Han'guk Woegyo Munsŏ P'yŏnch'an Wiwŏnhoe. Seoul: Koryŏ Taehakkyo Ch'ulp'anbu, 1965–1973.

Ŏndŏudŭ charyojip [Underwood sourcebook]. 5 vols. Comp. and ed. Yi Man-yŏl and Sung Deuk Oak. Seoul: Yŏnse Taehakkyo Ch'ulp'anbu, 2009.

Personal Reports of the Southern Presbyterian Missionaries in Korea. 19 vols. Comp. and ed. Han'guk Kyohoesa Munhŏn Yŏn'guwŏn. Seoul: Han'guk Kyohoesa Munhŏn Yŏn'guwŏn, 1993.

Sŏul kyogu yŏnbo (1878–1903) [Annual report of the Seoul diocese]. Comp. and ed. Han'guk kyohoesa yŏn'guso. Seoul: Ch'ŏnjugyo Myŏngdong Kyohoe, 1984.

Taehan yesugyo changno hoeŭirok [Records of the meeting of the General Assembly of the Korean Presbyterian Church]. 7 vols. Comp. and ed. Taehan Yesugyo Changnohoe Ch'onghoe. Seoul: Taehan Yesugyo Changnohoe Ch'onghoe, 1980.

Diaries and Journals

40 Years in Korea. Comp. and ed. Clara Hedberg Bruen. Seoul: Han'guk Kidokkyo Yŏksa Yŏn'guso, 1998.

Noble, Mattie. *The Journals of Mattie Wilcox Noble, 1892–1934*. Comp. and ed. Han'guk Kidokkyo Yŏksa Yŏn'guso. Seoul: Han'guk Kidokkyo Yŏksa Yŏn'guso, 2003.

Journals and Newspapers (English)

Chinese Recorder
Christianity Today
Gospel in All Lands
Korea Mission Field
Korea Review
Korean Repository
Missionary Review of the World
New York Times
Seoul Press

Journals and Newspapers (Korean)

Hansŏng sunbo
Hwangsŏng sinmun
Kŭrisŭdo sinmun

Books and Articles in Korean

An Chong-ch'ŏl (An Jong Chol). "Chung-Il chŏnjaeng palbal chŏnhu sinsa ch'ambae munje wa P'yŏngyang ŭi kidokkyo kye chungdŭng hakkyo ŭi tonghyang" [The Shinto shrine issue and the P'yŏngyang mission school's response around the outbreak of the second Sino-Japanese war]. *Han'guk munhwa* 48 (December 2009): 93–116.

———. *Miguk sŏn'gyosa wa Han-Mi kwangye* [American missionaries and Korea-US relations]. Seoul: Han'guk Kidokkyo Yŏksa Yŏn'guso, 2010.

An Pyŏng-jik. "3.1 undong e ch'amgahan sahoe kyech'ŭng kwa kŭ sasang" [Social-class status of participants in the March First Movement and their philosophy]. *Yŏksa hakbo* 41 (Autumn 1969): 20–51.

Ch'a Chong-sun. "Honam kwa sŏbuk chiyŏk kaesin'gyo t'ŭksŏng pigyo yŏn'gu" [A comparative study of the special characteristics of Protestantism in the Honam and the northwest regions]. *Han'guk kyohoe sa hakhoe chi* 15 (2004): 233–250.

Chang Kyu-sik. *Ilche ha Han'guk kidokkyo minjok ŭi yŏn'gu* [A study on Korean Christian nationalism under Japanese colonialism]. Seoul: Hyean, 2001.

Ch'oe Pyŏng-t'aek. "Haebang hu yŏksa kyogwasŏ ŭi 3.1 undong kwallyŏn sŏsul kyŏnghyang" [Trends in how history textbooks portray the March First Movement in the postliberation period]. *Yŏksa wa hyŏnsil* 74 (December 2009): 265–297.

Chŏng T'ae-sik and Mun Chang-su. "Taegu 3.1 manse undong kwa Yi Man-jip ŭi kyohoe chach'i sŏnŏn sagŏn e taehan sahoe ch'ŏlhakchŏk koch'al" [A social-philosophical examination of the March First Movement in Taegu and Yi Man-jip's declaration of church independence]. *Ch'ŏlhak nonch'ong* 36, no. 2 (2004): 275–302.

Ha Wŏn-ho. *Han'guk kŭndae kyŏngje sa yŏn'gu* [A study in modern Korean economic history]. Seoul: Sŏsinwŏn, 1997.

Han In-su. *Honam kyohoe hyŏngsŏng inmul* 3 [Founders of the Honam church, vol. 3]. Seoul: Kyŏnggŏn, 2010.

Han'guk Kidokkyo Yŏksa Yŏn'guso, ed. *Han'guk kidokkyo ŭi yŏksa II* [A history of Korean Christianity, vol. 2]. Seoul: Han'guk Kidokkyo Yŏksa Yŏn'guso, 1990.

Han'guk Kyohoe sa Yŏn'guso, ed. *Sŏul kyogu nyŏnbo I (1878–1903)* [Annual report of the Seoul Diocese, vol. 1]. Seoul: Ch'ŏnjugyo Myŏngdong Kyohoe, 1984.

Hong Chae-bŏm. "Han'guk kaesin'gyo ŭi 1907 nyŏn P'yŏngyang tae puhŭng undong e taehan haesŏk tŭl ŭi pigyo yŏn'gu" [A comparative study of the interpretations of Korean Protestantism's P'yŏngyang Great Revival of 1907]. *Chonggyo yŏn'gu* (2006): 233–259.

Kang Man-gil. *Chosŏn hugi sangŏp chabon ŭi paldal* [Development of commercial capital during the late Chosŏn period]. Seoul: Koryŏ Taehakkyo Munkwa Taehak, 1970.

Kim Sang-t'ae. "[Kihwaek] Han-Mi chisik in ŭi sangho insik Ilche ha kaesin'gyo chisik in ŭi Miguk insik—Sin Hŭng-u wa chŏkgŭk sinang tan ŭl chungsim ŭro" [(Special section) The mutual perceptions of US and Korean intellectuals exhibited by the intellectuals of the Protestant church during the Japanese occupation period—examination of the actions of Hugh Cynn and the Positive Religion Band]. *Yŏksa wa hyŏnsil* 58 (December 2012): 95–118.

Kim Sŭng-t'ae, ed. *Han'guk kidokkyo wa sinsa ch'ambae munje* [The problem of Shinto shrine obeisance and Korean Christianity]. Seoul: Han'guk Kidokkyo Yŏksa Yŏn'guso, 1991.

———. *Hanmal-Ilche kangjŏm ki sŏn'gyosa yŏn'gu* [A study on missionaries during the Hanmal and colonial occupation period]. Seoul: Han'guk Kidokkyo Yŏksa Yŏn'guso, 2006.

———. *Singmin kwŏllyŏk kwa chonggyo* [Colonial authority and religion]. Seoul: Han'guk Kidokkyo Yŏksa Yŏn'guso, 2012.

———, ed. *Sinsa ch'ambae munje charyojip* [Sourcebook on the problem of Shinto shrine obeisance]. Seoul: Han'guk Kidokkyo Yŏksa Yŏn'guso, 2014.

Kim To-hyŏng (Do-hyung). *Taehan cheguk ki ŭi chŏngch'i sasang yŏn'gu* [A study on the political thought of the Taehan Empire]. Seoul: Chisik sanŏpsa, 1994.

Kim Yŏng-sam. *Widaehan Han'guk in: Kim Maria* [Great Korean figures: Kim Maria]. Seoul: T'aeguk Ch'ulp'ansa, 1979.

Kim Yong-sŏp. *Chosŏn hugi nonghak ŭi paldal* [Advances in agriculture during the late Chosŏn period]. Seoul: Han'guk Munhwa Yŏn'guso, 1970.

Min Kyŏng-bae. *Han'guk ŭi kidokkyohoe sa* [A history of the Korean Christian church]. Seoul: Taehan Kidokkyo Sŏhoe, 1972.

No Ch'i-jun. *Ilche ha Han'guk kidokkyo minjok undong yŏn'gu* [A study on the Korean Christian nationalist movement under Japanese colonialism]. Seoul: Han'guk Kidokkyo Yŏksa Yŏn'guso, 1993.

O Su-ch'ang. *Chosŏn hugi P'yŏngan-do sahoe palchŏn yŏn'gu* [A study on social development of P'yŏngan Province during the late Chosŏn period]. Seoul: Ilchogak, 2002.

O Yŏng-sŏp. *Han'guk kŭn-hyŏndae sa rŭl sunoŭn inmul tŭl I* [Major figures of modern and contemporary Korean history, vol. 1]. Seoul: Kyŏngin Munhwasa, 2007.

Ok Sŏng-dŭk (Oak Sung Deuk). *Ch'ŏt sagŏn ŭro pon ch'odae Han'guk kyohoe sa* [A history of the early Korean church as seen through first events]. Seoul: Chitda, 2016.

———. "P'yŏngyang tae puhŭng undong kwa Kil Sŏn-ju yŏngsŏng ŭi togyojŏk yŏnghyang" [The P'yŏngyang Great Revival and the influence of Kil Sŏnju's daoist spirituality]. *Han'guk kidokkyo wa yŏn'gu* 25 (September 2006): 57–95.

Pak Ch'an-sik. "Hanmal ch'ŏnju kyohoe wa hyangch'on sahoe" [Village society and the Catholic Church during the Hanmal period]. PhD diss., Sŏgang University, 1996.

Pak Ch'an-sŭng. "3.1 undong ŭi sasangjŏk kiban" [Intellectual origins of the March First Movement]. In *3.1 minjok haebang undong yŏn'gu*, ed. Han'guk Yŏksa Yŏn'guhoe Yŏksa Munje Yŏn'guso. Seoul: Ch'ŏngnyŏnsa, 1989.

Pak Chi-t'ae, ed. *Taehan cheguk ki chŏngchaek sa charyojip* 7 [Sourcebook on the history of policies of the Taehan Empire, vol. 7]. Seoul: Sŏnin Munhwasa, 1999.

Pak Yong-gyu. "Han'guk kyohoe sŏn'gyo chŏngch'aek ŭrosŏ ŭi Nebiusŭ pangbŏp" [Nevius method as the missionary policy of the Korean church]. *Sinhak chinam* (Fall 2002): 57–83.

———. *P'yŏngyang tae puhŭng undong* [P'yŏngyang Great Revival movement]. Seoul: Saengmyŏng ŭi Malssŭmsa, 2000.

Pak Yun-jae (Park Yunjae). *Han'guk kŭndae ŭihak ŭi kiwŏn* [Origins of the modern Korean medicine]. Seoul: Hyean, 2005.

Ryu Si-hyŏn. "1920 nyŏndae samil undong e kwanhan kiŏk—sigan, changso kŭrigo 'minjok/minjung'" [Time, place, and "*minjok/minjung*"—remembrance of the 1920s March First Movement]. *Yŏksa wa hyŏnsil* 74 (December 2009): 176–202.

Ryu Tae-yŏng (Ryu Dae Young). "Miguk nam changnohoe sŏn'gyosa T'eit'ŭ (Lewis Boyd Tate) kajok ŭi Han'guk sŏn'gyo" [Missionary activities of the Southern Presbyterian missionary Lewis Boyd Tate's family], *Han'guk kidokkyo wa yŏksa* 37 (September 2012): 5–35.

———. "Sinsa ch'ambae kwallyŏn sosup'a ŭigyŏn—Helŏldŭ Hendŏsŭn (Harold H. Henderson) ŭi sarye" [The "minority" opinion of the Shinto shrine controversy: The case of Harold H. Henderson]. *Han'guk kidokkyo yŏksa* 39 (September 2013): 145–180.

Sin Kwang-ch'ŏl. *Ch'ŏnjugyo wa kaesin'gyo: Mannam kwa kaltŭng ŭi yŏksa* [Catholicism and Protestantism: history of meeting and conflict]. Seoul: Han'guk Kidokkyo Yŏksa Yŏn'guso, 1998.

Sin Tong-wŏn. *Han'guk kŭndae pogŏn ŭiryo sa* [A history of health and medicine in modern Korea]. Seoul: Hanul, 1997.

Sin Yong-ha. *Tongnip hyŏphoe wa kaehwa undong* [The Independence Club and the enlightenment movement]. Seoul: Sejong Taewang Kinyŏm Saŏphoe, 1976.

Sŏ Kwang-sŏn. *Han'guk kidokkyo ŭi sae insik* [A new understanding of Korean Christianity]. Seoul: Taehan Kidokkyo Ch'ulp'ansa, 1985.

Son Chŏng-mok. "Chosŏn ch'ongdokbu ŭi sinsa pogŭb sinsa ch'ambae kangyo chŏngch'aek yŏn'gu" [A study on the Government-General's policies on spreading Shinto shrines and forcing Shinto shrine attendance]. In *Han'guk kidokkyo wa sinsa ch'ambae munje*, ed. Kim Sŭng-t'ae. Seoul: Han'guk Kidokkyo Yŏksa Yŏn'guso, 1991.

Song Kil-sŏp. *Han'guk sinhak sasang sa* [A history of Korean theological thought]. Seoul: Taehan Kidokkyo Ch'ulp'ansa, 1987.

Wang Hyŏn-chong. *Han'guk kŭndae kukka ŭi hyŏngsŏng kwa Kabo kaehyŏk* [Kabo reforms and formation of a modern Korean state]. Seoul: Yŏksa Pip'yŏngsa, 2002.

Yi Ki-baek. *Kuksa sillon* [A new history of Korea]. Seoul: T'aesŏngsa, 1961.

Yi Man-yŏl. "Hanmal kidokkyo in ŭi minjok ŭisik hyŏngsŏng kwajŏng" [Process of formation of the national consciousness of Christians during the Hanmal period]. *Han'guk saron* 1 (May 1973): 335–405.

———. "Ilche kwanhakcha tŭl ŭi singmin sagwan" [Colonial historical viewpoint of Japanese colonial official scholars]. In *Han'guk ŭi yŏksa insik II*, ed. Yi U-sŏng and Kang Man-gil. Seoul: Ch'angjak kwa Pip'yŏngsa, 1993.

———, ed. *Sinsa ch'ambae munje yŏngmun charyojip* I [English-language sourcebook on Shinto shrine obeisance]. Seoul: Han'guk Kidokkyo Yŏksa Yŏn'guso, 2003.

———. "Sŏ Sang-ryun ŭi haengjŏk e kwanhan myŏk kaji munje" [Several problems regarding the activities of Sŏ Sang-ryun]. *Han'guk kidokkyo sa yŏn'gu* 19 (April 1988).

Yi Sŏng-chŏn, *Miguk sŏn'gyosa wa Han'guk kŭndae kyoyuk* [Missionaries and modern Korean education]. Trans. Sŏ Chŏng-min and Kamiyama Minako. Seoul: Han'guk Kidokkyo Yŏn'guso, 2007.

Yi, T'ae-jin. *Kojong sidae ŭi chae chomyŏng* [A revision of the Kojong period]. Seoul: T'aehaksa, 2000.

Yi Tŏk-chu. *T'och'akhwa wa minjok undong yŏn'gu* [Inculturation and the nationalist movement]. Seoul: Han'guk Kidokkyo Yŏn'guso, 2018.

Yi Wŏn-sun. "Kyohoe sajŏk, kyohoe munhwajae pojŏn ŭi ch'am ttŭk ŭl saenggak hamyŏ" [Considering the importance of preserving historical church artifacts and cultural assets]. *Kyohoesa yŏn'gu* 20 (2003): 9–18.

Yu Yŏng-ik (Lew Young Ick). "Kabo kyŏngjang" [Kabo reforms]. In *Han'guksa 40: Ch'ŏng-Il chŏnjaeng kwa Kabo kaehyŏk*, ed. Kuksa P'yŏnch'an Wiwŏnhoe. Seoul: Kuksa P'yŏnch'an Wiwŏnhoe, 2003.

Yun Kyŏng-no. *105 in sagŏn kwa sinminhoe yŏn'gu* [A study on the 105 case and the New People's Society]. Seoul: Ilchisa, 1990.

———. *Han'guk kŭndae sa ŭi kidokkyo sajŏk ihae* [A Protestant historical understanding of modern Korean history]. Seoul: Yŏkminsa, 2003.

Yun Sŏn-ja. "'Han-Il hapbyŏng' chŏnhu Hwanghae-do ch'ŏnju kyohoe wa Pillem sinbu" [The Catholic Church in Hwanghae and Priest Wilhelm before and after the establishment of the Japanese protectorate in Korea]. *Han'guk kŭndae sa yŏn'gu* 4 (1996): 107–131.

Books and Articles in English

An, Jong Chol (Chong-ch'ŏl). "No Distinction between Sacred and Secular: Horace H. Underwood and Korean-American Relations, 1934–1948." *Seoul Journal of Korean Studies* 23, no. 2 (December 2010): 225–246.

Anderson, Benedict. *Imagined Communities: Reflections on the Origin and Spread of Nationalism*. Rev. ed. London: Verso, 2006.

Anderson, Emily, ed. *Belief and Practice in Imperial Japan and Colonial Korea*. Singapore: Palgrave Macmillan, 2017.

———. *Christianity and Imperialism in Modern Japan: Empire for God*. London: Bloomsbury Academic, 2014.

Assad, Talal. *Formations of the Secular: Christianity, Islam, Modernity*. Stanford, CA: Stanford University Press, 2003.

———. *Genealogies of Religion: Discipline and Reasons of Power in Christianity and Islam*. Baltimore, MD: Johns Hopkins University Press, 1993.

Baker, Donald, and Franklin Rausch. *Catholics and Anti-Catholicism in Chosŏn Korea*. Honolulu: University of Hawai'i Press, 2017.

Beaver, R. Pierce. *Ecumenical Beginnings in Protestant World Mission: A History of Comity*. New York: Thomas Nelson & Sons, 1962.

Blair, William N. *Gold in Korea*. 2nd ed. Topeka, KS: H. M. Ives and Sons, 1947.

Brown, Arthur. *The Foreign Mission: An Incarnation of a World Movement*. New York: Fleming H. Revell Co., 1907.

———. *Report of a Visitation of the Korea Mission of the Presbyterian Board of Foreign Missions*. New York: Board of Foreign Missions of the Presbyterian Church, 1902.

Caprio, Mark E. *Japanese Assimilation Policies in Colonial Korea, 1910–1945*. Seattle: University of Washington Press, 2009.

Cha, Paul S. "Establishing the Rules of Engagement: American Protestant Missionaries, the U.S. Legation, and the Chosŏn State." *International Journal of Korean History* 17, no. 1 (Spring 2012): 67–107.

———. "Unequal Partners, Contested Relations: Protestant Missionaries and Korean Christians, 1884–1907." *Journal of Korean Studies* 17, no. 1 (Spring 2012): 5–37.

Chang, Uk Byun. "Comity Agreements between Missions in Koreas from 1884 to 1910: The Ambiguities of Ecumenicity and Denominationalism." PhD diss., Princeton Theological Seminary, 2003.

Choi, Hyaeweol. *Gender and Mission Encounters in Korea: New Women, Old Ways*. Berkeley: University of California Press, 2009.

———. "The Missionary Home as a Pulpit: Domestic Paradoxes in Early Twentieth-Century Korea." In *Diving Domesticities: Christian Paradoxes in Asia and the Pacific*, ed. Hyaeweol Choi and Margaret Jolly, 29–55. Canberra: Australian National University Press, 2014.

Choi, Jai-keun. *The Korean Church under Japanese Colonialism*. Seoul: Jimoondang, 2007.

Chung, David. *Syncretism: The Religious Context of Christian Beginnings in Korea*. Albany: State University of New York Press, 2001.

Clark, Charles Allen. *The Korean Church and the Nevius Method*. New York: Fleming H. Revell Co., 1930.

Clark, Donald. *Living Dangerously in Korea: The Western Experience, 1900–1950*. Norwalk, CT: EastBridge, 2003.

Comaroff, Jean, and John Comaroff. *Of Revelation and Revolution: Christianity, Colonialism, and Consciousness in South Africa*. Chicago: University of Chicago Press, 1991.

Commission on Relations with the Orient of the Federal Council of the Churches of Christ in America, ed. *The Korean Situation: Authentic Accounts of Recent Events by Eye Witnesses*. New York: Commission on Relations with the Orient of the Federal Council of the Churches of Christ in America, 1919.

Davies, Daniel M. "Henry G. Appenzeller: Pioneer Missionary and Reformer in Korea." *Methodist History* 30, no. 4 (July 1992): 195–205.

Duara, Prasenjit. *Rescuing History from the Nation: Questioning Narratives of Modern China*. Chicago: University of Chicago Press, 1996.

Dunch, Ryan. "Beyond Cultural Imperialism: Cultural Theory, Christian Missions, and Global Modernity." *History and Theory* 41, no. 3 (October 2002): 301–325.

———. *Fuzhou Protestants and the Making of Modern China, 1857–1927*. New Haven, CT: Yale University Press, 2001.

Em, Henry H. *The Great Enterprise: Sovereignty and Historiography in Modern Korea*. Durham, NC: Duke University Press, 2013.

Emirbayer, Mustafa, and Ann Mische. "What Is Agency?" *American Journal of Sociology* 103, no. 4 (January 1998): 962–1023.

Esherick, Joseph. *The Origins of the Boxer Uprising*. Berkeley: University of California Press, 1987.

Fairbank, John K. *The Missionary Enterprise in China and America*. Cambridge, MA: Harvard University Press, 1974.

Foucault, Michel. *Discipline and Punish: The Birth of the Prison*. 2nd ed. Trans. Alan Sheridan. New York: Vintage, 1995.

———. *Security, Territory, Population*. Ed. Arnold I. Davidson. Trans. Graham Burchell. New York: Palgrave Macmillan, 2007.

Freston, Paul. *Evangelicals and Politics in Asia, Africa, and Latin America*. Cambridge: Cambridge University Press, 2001.

Frykenberg, Robert Eric. *Christianity in India: From Beginnings to the Present*. New York: Oxford University Press, 2010.

Gellner, Ernest. *Nations and Nationalism*. 2nd ed. Ithaca, NY: Cornell University Press, 2008.

Grayson, James H. "Christianity and State Shinto in Colonial Korea: A Clash of Nationalisms and Religious Beliefs." *Diskus: The Journal of the British Association for the Study of Religions* 1, no. 2 (1993): 13–30.

Hall, Andrew. "Japan's Education Policies in Korea in the 1910s: 'Thankful and Obedient.'" *Journal of Korean Studies* 25, no. 1 (March 2020): 115–145.

Hall, Rosetta Sherwood. *The Life of Rev. William James Hall, M.D.: Medical Missionary to the Slums of New York, Pioneer Missionary to Pyong Yang*. New York: Press of Eaton and Mains, 1897.

Hamburger, Philip. *Separation of Church and State*. Cambridge, MA: Harvard University Press, 2004.

Han, Ju Hui Judy. "Urban Megachurches and Contentious Religious Politics in Seoul." In *Handbook of Religion and the Asian City: Aspiration and Urbanization in the Twenty-First Century*, ed. Peter van der Veer, 133–151. Oakland: University of California Press, 2015.

Handy, Robert. *A Christian America: Protestant Hopes and Historical Realities*. New York: Oxford University Press, 1971.

Hardacre, Helen. *Shintō and the State, 1868–1988*. Princeton, NJ: Princeton University Press, 1989.

Harrington, Fred. *God, Mammon, and the Japanese: Dr. Horace N. Allen and Korean-American Relations, 1884–1905*. Madison: University of Wisconsin Press, 1944.

Hart, D. G. *Defending the Faith: J. Gresham Machen and the Crisis of Conservative Protestantism in Modern America*. Phillipsburg, NJ: P&R, 1994.

Hastings, Adrian. *The Construction of Nationhood: Ethnicity, Religion, and Nationalism*. Cambridge: Cambridge University Press, 1997.

Henning, Joseph M. *Outposts of Civilization: Race, Religion, and the Formative Years of American-Japanese Relations*. New York: New York University Press, 2000.

Hevia, James. *English Lessons: The Pedagogy of Imperialism in Nineteenth-Century China*. Durham, NC: Duke University Press, 2003.

Hobsbawm, Eric J. *Nations and Nationalism since 1780: Programme, Myth, and Reality*. Cambridge: Cambridge University Press, 1990.

Hollinger, David. *Protestants Abroad: How Missionaries Tried to Change the World but Changed America*. Princeton, NJ: Princeton University Press, 2017.

Hong, Kyong-man. "Formation of Korean Protestantism and Its Political Nature." *Korea Journal* 23, no. 12 (December 1983): 18–29.

Hunt, Everett N. *Protestant Pioneers in Korea*. Maryknoll, NY: Orbis, 1990.

Hunter, Jane. *The Gospel of Gentility: American Women Missionaries in Turn-of-the-Century China*. New Haven, CT: Yale University Press, 1989.

Huntley, Martha. *Caring, Growing, Changing: A History of the Protestant Mission in Korea*. New York: Friendship, 1984.

Hutchinson, William. *Errand to the World: American Protestant Thought and Foreign Missions*. Chicago: University of Chicago Press, 1987.

Hwang, Kyung Moon. *Rationalizing Korea: The Rise of the Modern State, 1894–1945*. Berkeley: University of California Press, 2016.

Kang, Wi Jo. *Christ and Caesar in Modern Korea*. Albany: State University of New York Press, 1997.

Kawase, Takaya. "State Shinto Policy in Colonial Korea." In *Belief and Practice in Imperial Japan and Colonial Korea*, ed. Emily Anderson, 19–37. Singapore: Palgrave Macmillan, 2017.

Kim, Do-hyung [To-hyŏng]. "Introduction: The Nature of Reform in the Taehan Empire." In *Reform and Modernity in the Taehan Empire*, ed. Dong-no Kim, John B. Duncan, and Do-hyung Kim Seoul: Jimoondang, 2006.

Kim, Esther Ahn. *If I Perish*. Chicago: Moody Bible Institute, 1977.

Kim, Henry Hyunsuk. "Horace N. Allen: Missions, Expansionism, Structural Holes, and Social Capital." *Journal for the Sociological Integration of Religion and Society* 3, no. 1 (2013): 1–21.

Kim, Ku. *Paekpŏm ilchi: The Autobiography of Kim Ku*. Trans. Jongsoo Lee. New York: University Press of America, 2000.

Kim, Monica. *The Interrogation Rooms of the Korean War: The Untold History*. Princeton, NJ: Princeton University Press, 2019.

Kim, Sonja. "The Search for Health: Translating *Wisaeng* and Medicine during the Taehan Empire." In *Reform and Modernity in the Taehan Empire*, ed.

Kim Dong-no, John B. Duncan, and Do-hyung Kim, 299–341. Seoul: Jimoondang, 2006.

Kim, Sun Joo. *Marginality and Subversion in Korea: The Hong Kyŏngnae Rebellion of 1812*. Seattle: University of Washington Press, 2007.

Kim, Sung-gun. "Korean Christianity and the Shinto Shrine Issue in the War Period, 1931–1945." PhD diss., University of Hull, 1989.

Kim, Taehoon. "The Place of 'Religion' in Colonial Korea around 1910: The Imperial History of 'Religion.'" *Journal of Korean Religions* 2, no. 2 (October 2011): 25–46.

Kingsolver, Barbara. *The Poisonwood Bible: A Novel*. New York: HarperCollins, 1998.

Ladd, George T. *In Korea with Marquis Ito*. London: Longmans, Green, 1908.

Lee, Chengpang, and Suh Myung-sahm. "State Building and Religion: Explaining the Diverged Path of Religious Change in Taiwan and South Korea, 1950–1980." *American Journal of Sociology* 123, no. 2 (September 2017): 465–509.

Lee, Namhee. *Making of the Minjung: Democracy and the Politics of Representation in South Korea*. Ithaca, NY: Cornell University Press, 2007.

Lee, Timothy S. "A Political Factor in the Rise of Protestantism in Korea: Protestantism and the 1919 March First Movement." *Church History* 69, no. 1 (March 2000): 116–142.

———. "What Should Christians Do about a Shaman-Progenitor? Evangelicals and Ethnic Nationalism in South Korea." *Church History* 78, no. 1 (March 2009): 66–98.

Liu, Lydia. *The Clash of Empires: The Invention of China in Modern World Making*. Cambridge, MA: Harvard University Press, 2004.

Longfield, Bradley J. *The Presbyterian Controversy: Fundamentalists, Modernists, and Moderates*. New York: Oxford University Press, 1991.

Lutz, Gregory. *Opening China: Karl F. A. Gutzlaff and Sino-Western Relations, 1827–1852*. Grand Rapids, MI: William B. Eerdmans, 2008.

Matsutani, Motokazu. "Church over Nation: Christian Missionaries and Korean Christians in Colonial Korea." PhD diss., Harvard University, 2012.

Maxey, Trent E. "Finding Religion in Japan's Empire." In *Belief and Practice in Imperial Japan and Colonial Korea*, ed. Emily Anderson, 1–18. Singapore: Palgrave Macmillan, 2017.

———. *The "Greatest Problem": Religion and State Formation in Meiji Japan*. Cambridge, MA: Harvard University Asia Center, 2014.

McConnell, Michael. "Believers as Equal Citizens." In *Obligations of Citizenship and Demands of Faith*, ed. Nancy Rosenblum, 90–110. Princeton, NJ: Princeton University Press, 2000.

McCully, Elizabeth. *A Corn of Wheat*. Toronto: Westminster, 1903.

McLeod, Hugh. "Christianity and Nationalism in Nineteenth-Century Europe." *International Journal for the Study of the Christian Church* 15, no. 1 (April 2015): 7–22.

Moon, Yumi. *Populist Collaborators: The Ilchinhoe and the Japanese Colonization of Korea, 1896–1910.* Ithaca, NY: Cornell University Press, 2013.

Nakai, Kate Wildman. "Chinese Ritual and Native Identity in Tokugawa Confucianism." In *Rethinking Confucianism*, ed. Benjamin A. Elman, John B. Duncan, and Herman Ooms, 258–291. Los Angeles: UCLA Asian Pacific Monograph Series, 2002.

Nisbet, Annabel Major. *Day In and Day Out in Korea.* Richmond, VA: Presbyterian Committee of Publication, 1920.

Noble, Mattie. *The Journals of Mattie Wilcox Noble, 1892–1934.* Ed. Han'guk Kidokkyo Yŏksa Yŏn'guso. Seoul: Han'guk Kidokkyo Yŏksa Yŏn'guso, 2003.

Oak, Sung Deuk (Ok Sŏng-dŭk). *The Making of Korean Christianity: Protestant Encounters with Korean Religions, 1876–1915.* Waco, TX: Baylor University Press, 2015.

———, ed. *Primary Sources of the Korean Great Revival, 1903–1908.* Seoul: Changnohoe Sinhak Taehakkyo, 2007.

Okyuama, Michiaki. "'State Shinto' in Recent Japanese Scholarship." *Monumenta Nipponica* 66, no. 1 (2011): 123–145.

Paik, George. *History of Protestant Missions in Korea, 1832–1910.* P'yŏngyang: Union Christian College Press, 1929.

Palais, James B. *Politics and Policy in Traditional Korea.* Cambridge, MA: Harvard University Press, 1975.

Park, Albert. *Building a Heaven on Earth: Religion, Activism, and Protest in Japanese Occupied Korea.* Honolulu: University of Hawai'i Press, 2015.

Park, Chung-shin. *Protestantism and Politics in Korea.* Seattle: University of Washington Press, 2003.

Park, Kyutae. "Religion, National Identity, and Shinto: A Comparative Study of State Shinto in Japan and Colonial Korea." *Review of Korean Studies* 3, no. 1 (June 2000): 76–92.

Park, Yunjae (Pak Yun-jae). "Between Mission and Medicine: The Early History of Severance Hospital." In *Encountering Modernity: Christianity in East Asia and Asian America*, ed. Albert L. Park and David K. Yoo, 140–161. Honolulu: University of Hawai'i Press, 2014.

PCUSA, ed. *Manual of the Board of Foreign Missions of the Presbyterian Church in the U.S.A.: For the Use of Missionaries and Missionary Candidates.* New York: [s.n.], 1889.

Rausch, Franklin. "The Bishop's Dilemma: Gustave Mutel and the Catholic Church in Korea, 1890–1910." *Journal of Korean Religions* 4, no. 1 (April 2013): 43–69.

———. "Like Birds and Beasts: Justifying Violence against Catholics in Late Chosŏn Korea." *Acta Koreana* 15, no. 1 (June 2012): 43–71.

———. "Truths Unacknowledged: The Public Sphere and Japan's Colonial Project in Korea." In *Religion, Culture, and the Public Sphere in China and*

Japan, ed. Albert Welter and Jeffrey Newmark, 205–231. Singapore: Palgrave Macmillan, 2017.

———. "Wicked Officials and Virtuous Martyrs: An Analysis of the Martyr Biographies in Alexius Hwang Sayŏng's *Silk Letter*." *Kyohoesa yŏn'gu* 32 (July 2009): 5–30.

Rhodes, Harry, and Archibald Campbell, eds. *History of the Korea Mission, Presbyterian Church in the U.S.A.* Vol. 2: 1935–1959. Commission on the Ecumenical Mission and Relations, United Presbyterian Church in the U.S.A., 1965.

Robert, Dana L. *Christian Mission: How Christianity Became a World Religion.* Malden, MA: Wiley-Blackwell, 2009.

Robinson, Michael. *Cultural Nationalism in Colonial Korea, 1920–1925.* Seattle: University of Washington Press, 2015.

Ryu, Dae Young (Ryu Tae-yŏng). "American Protestant Missionaries in Korea, 1882–1910: A Critical Study of Missionaries and Their Involvement in Korean-American Relations and Korean Politics." PhD diss., Vanderbilt University, 1998.

———. "The Origin and Characteristics of Evangelical Protestantism in Korea at the Turn of the Twentieth Century." *Church History* 77, no. 2 (June 2008): 371–398.

———. "Treaties, Extraterritorial Rights, and American Protestant Missions in Late Joseon Korea." *Korea Journal* 43, no. 1 (Spring 2003): 174–203.

———. "Understanding Early American Missionaries in Korea (1884–1910): Capitalist Middle-Class Values and the Weber Thesis." *Archives de sciences sociales des religions* 46, no. 113 (January–March 2001): 93–117.

Sanneh, Lamin. *Translating the Message: The Missionary Impact on Culture.* Maryknoll, NY: Orbis, 2009.

Saunders, Kenneth. "The Passing of Paternalism in Missions." *Journal of Religion* 2, no. 5 (September 1922): 466–475.

Schlesinger, Arthur, Jr. "The Missionary Enterprise and Theories of Imperialism." In *The Missionary Enterprise in China and America*, ed. John K. Fairbank, 336–373. Cambridge, MA: Harvard University Press, 1974.

Schmid, Andre. *Korea between Empires, 1895–1919.* New York: Columbia University Press, 2002.

Sehat, David. *The Myth of American Religious Freedom.* New York: Oxford University Press, 2010.

Sewell, William, Jr. *Logics of History: Social Theory and Social Transformation.* Chicago: University of Chicago Press, 2005.

Shearer, Roy E. *Wildfire: Church Growth in Korea.* Grand Rapids, MI: W. B. Eerdmans, 1966.

Shimazono, Susumu, and Regan E. Murphy. "State Shinto in the Lives of People." *Japanese Journal of Religious Studies* 36, no. 1 (2009): 93–124.

Speer, Robert E. *Christianity and the Nations*. New York: Fleming H. Revell, Co., 1910.

———. *Report on the Mission in Korea of the Presbyterian Board of Foreign Missions*. New York: The Board of Foreign Missions of the Presbyterian Church in the U.S.A., 1897.

Spence, Jonathan. *To Change China*. New York: Penguin, 2002.

Stanley, Brian. *The Bible and the Flag: Protestant Mission and British Imperialism in the Nineteenth and Twentieth Centuries*. Nottingham: SPCK, 1990.

———. *The World Missionary Conference, Edinburgh 1910*. Grand Rapids, MI: W. B. Eerdmans, 2009.

Tsurumi, E. Patricia. "Colonial Education in Korea and Taiwan." In *The Japanese Colonial Empire, 1895–1945,* ed. Ramon H. Meyers and Mark R. Peattie, 275–311. Princeton, NJ: Princeton University Press, 1984.

Uchida, Jun. *Brokers of Empire: Japanese Settler Colonialism in Korea, 1876–1945*. Cambridge, MA: Harvard University Asia Center, 2011.

Underwood, Elizabeth. "Contested Heritage: The 'Yanghwajin Controversy' and Korean Protestantism." *Journal of Korean Religions* 4, no. 1 (April 2013): 169–188.

Underwood, Lillias. *Fifteen Years among the Topknots*. Seoul: Royal Asiatic Society, Korea Branch, 1987.

———. *Underwood of Korea*. Seoul: Yonsei University Press, 1983.

Viswanathan, Gauri. *Outside the Fold: Conversion, Modernity, and Belief*. Princeton, NJ: Princeton University Press, 1998.

Wakabayashi, Bob Tadashi. *Anti-Foreignism and Western Learning in Early Modern Japan: The New Theses of 1825*. Cambridge, MA: Council on East Asian Studies, Harvard University, 1986.

Walls, Andrew F. *The Cross-Cultural Process in Christian History*. Maryknoll, NY: Orbis, 2002.

Wang, Dong. *China's Unequal Treaties: Narrating National History*. Plymouth: Lexington Books, 2008.

Wasson, Alfred. *Church Growth in Korea*. Concord, NH: International Missionary Council, 1934.

Wells, Kenneth. *New God, New Nation: Protestants and Self-Reconstruction Nationalism in Korea, 1896–1937*. Honolulu: University of Hawai'i Press, 1990.

Weston, William. *Presbyterian Pluralism: Competition in a Protestant House*. Knoxville: University of Tennessee Press, 1997.

Wong, R. Bin. *China Transformed: Historical Change and the Limits of European Experience*. Ithaca, NY: Cornell University Press, 1997.

———. "Citizenship in Chinese History." In *Extending Citizenship, Reconfiguring States*, ed. Michael Hanagan and Charles Tilly. Oxford: Rowman & Littlefield, 1999.

Index

About the Author

Paul S. Cha is assistant professor of Korean Studies at the University of Hong Kong.